Language
and **Literacy**
3-7

Jeni Riley

Language
and Literacy
3–7

Creative Approaches to Teaching

SAGE Publications
London • Thousand Oaks • New Delhi

First published 2006

SAGE Publications Ltd
1 Oliver's Yard
55 City Road
London EC1Y 1SP

SAGE Publications Inc.
2455 Teller Road
Thousand Oaks, California 91320

SAGE Publications India Pvt Ltd
B-42, Panchsheel Enclave
Post Box 4109
New Delhi 110 017

British Library Cataloguing in Publication data

A catalogue record for this book is available
from the British Library

ISBN-10 1-4129-1985-1   ISBN-13 978-1-4129-1985-2
ISBN-10 1-4129-1986-X   ISBN-13 978-1-4129-1986-9 (pbk)

Library of Congress Control Number 2006903704

Typeset by C&M Digitals (P) Ltd., Chennai, India
Printed and bound in Great Britain by The Athenaeum Press, Gateshead, Tyne & Wear
Printed on paper from sustainable resources

Contents

This book is dedicated to James Read our very own
15 month old, whose language learning is evidence
of the genius he truly is.

Acknowledgements

An African proverb says that it takes a village to educate a child. It is also true of big projects, such as writing a book, particularly one which draws both on complex theory and informed practice.

Many people have enabled this book to be what it has become. I would like to express my gratitude to those mentioned here for their generosity of spirit and the gift of their time in an increasingly frenetic world.

Professor Morag Stuart, Professor Rhona Stainthorp, Professor Roger Beard and Angela Hobsbaum have listened to my articulation of thoughts on the latest research evidence on literacy development and learning and its relationship with successful practice in early years settings and classrooms and have made suggestions.

Subject specialists have read individual chapters and offered invaluable advice: Sue Collins on the example of a science project in Chapter 7: Dr Liz Brooker on Chapter 10, which is about bilingual learners; Gill Brackenbury and Dr Sue Burroughs-Lange on Chapter 12, about children who learn literacy slowly; and Sarah Martyn on Chapter 11, about literacy learning and ICT.

I am indebted to two former co-authors and friends. David Reedy has kindly allowed me to develop ideas from our jointly authored book *Developing Writing for Different Purposes:Teaching Young Children* about Genre for Chapter 8, and Andrew Burrell has advised on Chapters 7 and 8 and provided me with recent examples of children's work.

Classroom practitioners too have made their valued contributions. Anoula Redstone and Jenny Pearce, from Dropmore Infants School, Burnham, offered me children's work and Sue Peacock, from Thornhill Primary School, the most gifted reception teacher I have ever met, provided me with inspirational ideas for practice.

My thanks go also to Marianne Lagrange, Education Publisher at Paul Chapman Publishing/SAGE for commissioning this my fourth book with her publishing house and for her encouragement.

And last, but very far from least, I am deeply grateful to two pillars of strength: Roy Prentice for his meticulous proofreading and James O'Toole for his technological expertise and help with formatting.

Jeni Riley
School of Early Childhood and Primary Education
Institute of Education, University of London
March 2006

Foreword

Jeni Riley has written a balanced, scholarly and accessible introduction to the study of young children's language and literacy. She combines a great deal of sound, practical advice with reference to many of the researchers and theorists who have influenced the field in recent years. Her concern is to explain, illustrate and support the kinds of practice in schools and homes on which children's literate lives can be based. The book is distinguished by its sensitivity to children's needs and its awareness of the needs of the teachers and carers who are responsible for children's language and literacy development.

Roger Beard
Professor of Primary Education
Institute of Education
University of London

Introduction

The limits of my language mean the limits of my world.

(Ludwig Wittgenstein).

The pinnacle of young children's educational development is the acquisition of literacy. Literacy is the ticket of entry into our society, it is the currency by which social and economic positions are waged, and it is the central purpose of early schooling. In some sense, we send children to school at the age of about five so that they will learn to read. Future academic success depends on how well they master that skill, and academic success in our part of the world determines much about children's futures.

(Bialystok, 2001: 152)

It is universally recognized that a highly literate population is essential for an advanced society and that this is important for both humanitarian and economic reasons. At an individual level, literacy determines quality of life, personal growth and a self-image, and the ability to function in an ever-changing and increasingly technological world. Being literate allows access to knowledge, offers the ability to make choices and to achieve self-fulfilment. At a national level, the smooth functioning and economic prosperity of our society depends upon a well-educated, flexible and highly skilled workforce.

Literacy is fundamental to success in formal education, central to learning and the development of thinking. The link between academic success and high levels of literacy occurs, first, through allowing access to the curriculum and, secondly, by enabling the individual to achieve educationally and to complete and be successful at school (McGaw et al., 1989).

The need for higher levels of literacy

Schools, are exhorted continually to strive to improve literacy standards and, with increasingly advanced levels of literacy required by society, more is ever demanded of them. Reading and writing have become even more crucial with the increased use of information and communications technology, albeit that the production and form of texts are changing with the use of fax, e-mail, text messaging on mobile phones and use of the Internet.

Early years education and improvement in standards of literacy

Access to a high-quality education in the early years is key to the success of the educational system. Also, there is a body of research evidence that suggests that the foundations of literacy are laid in the first two years of schooling. I have argued elsewhere, that a positive early start to school benefits pupils for the whole of their school career (Riley, 1996). Nearly 20 years ago, Australian research indicated, that efforts to correct literacy difficulties after the third grade are largely unsuccessful. Kennedy et al. (1986) suggest that children who fail to make progress in literacy during the first 2 years of school rarely catch up with their peers and are at risk of becoming low achievers, become alienated with school and drop out at the earliest opportunity.

Conversely, there is also empirical evidence that it *is* possible for all, except a *very* small percentage of children, to be successfully taught to read and write (Piluski, 1994). This encouraging evidence comes from the evaluations of the effectiveness of whole-school programmes such as 'Success for all' (Slavin et al., 1996) and the literacy intervention programme, 'Reading Recovery' (Hurry, 1995).

The National Literacy Strategy and the raising of standards

It would appear that the introduction in England of the National Literacy Strategy (NLS) in 1998 (DfEE, 1998) has had a positive effect on the literacy levels of 11-year-olds, according to international comparisons (PIRLS, 2004). This improvement would seem to have been brought about through the guidance of the *National Literacy Strategy Framework for Teaching* (DfEE, 1998) which offers continuity and progression of content clearly laid out from the Reception year through to Year 6 in primary schools. The recently published *Independent Review of the Teaching of Reading* (Rose Report – DfES, 2006) states:

> Despite improvements made overall, there are particularly urgent concerns nationally about the comparatively weak performance of the 15% of children who do not reach the target level for their age in reading by the end of Key Stage 1 (7 years of age), and the 16% of children who do not reach it by the end of Key Stage 2 – around 85,000 and 95,000 children respectively. There are concerns, too, about the generally weaker performance of boys compared with girls. (2006: 13)

The proposed solution advanced in this report, and which supports the underlying principle of this book, is that 'high-quality first teaching' lies at the heart of continued improvements. The fundamental issues which Rose affirms are:

- the importance of developing speaking and listening
- that letter/sound relationships need to be taught systematically through adherence to one synthetic phonics scheme
- the effective monitoring of progress, all of which should take place within a lively, meaningful and rich language and literacy curriculum.

In addition, the enhancement of the professional practice of early years practitioners and teachers is an important recommendation of the Rose Report (DfES, 2006). The drive to implement the NLS has striven to buttress the subject knowledge of teachers regarding the teaching of English, the structures of language and the cognitive processes involved in becoming literate. However the picture has not been totally positive. The guidance has at times been conflicting for those practitioners working in the Foundation Stage (particularly as the *Curriculum Guidance for the Foundation Stage* – DfEE/QCA, 2000 – did not articulate coherently with that for the Reception Year guidance in the NLS Framework for Teaching). The result of this is that confusion has arisen regarding the transition from the Foundation Stage (FS) to Key stage 1 (KS1). It would appear that this discontinuity has largely been remedied with the introduction of two consultation documents: the Early Years Foundation Stage (DfES, 2006) and the Primary National Stategy: Framework for teaching literacy (DfES, 2006).

Why this book?

Given the robust research findings which increasingly point to the importance of the early years of education (Sylva et al., 2004), it seemed necessary to write a book which would inform, support and, hopefully, inspire practitioners. It is my belief that early years professionals will benefit from being aware of the current state of thinking about the ways infants and young children learn to speak, and later learn to read and write. So the intention of this title is to translate understandings gained from the extensive body of research evidence into informed, creative and lively practice for early years settings in the Foundation Stage (for England and Wales) and primary classrooms in Key Stage 1.

Language and Literacy 3–7: Creative Approaches to Teaching is eclectic in that it draws upon a range of disciplines: linguistic, socio-linguistic, psychological and from English education. In addition, it is informed by government guidelines and documents in order to offer practitioners and teachers the type of broad, balanced picture of the development of language and literacy which underpins effective, developmentally appropriate practice.

Where are we now on the swing of the pendulum?

Fashions and thinking change about the 'what' and the 'how' of the teaching and learning of the curriculum. Language and literacy in the early years of education are no exception and are perhaps even more susceptible to these swings of the pendulum than other subjects. Practitioners, at the beginning of the introduction of the NLS in 1998, were advised to teach directly and explicitly large groups of Reception children, sitting cross-legged on the carpet for up to 20 minutes at a time, to identify letters of the alphabet, and the sounds they represent, most frequently through the vehicle of an enlarged text. Two years later this seemed to change with the publication of the *Curriculum Guidance for the Foundation Stage* (*CGFS*) (DfEE/QCA, 2000). What is most valuable for 3-, 4- and 5-year-olds to learn? The research evidence is clear, if children are to learn to read successfully they need to develop proficiency in the sub-skills of reading, namely, phonological awareness leading to phonemic awareness. To identify letters of the alphabet and how these letters relate to the sounds of spoken language (that is, phonics), children need a wide vocabulary and they need to understand that reading is purposeful. In other words they realize that comprehension is essential and the centre of the whole activity. If we are clear about the 'What', the most controversial issue is 'How' children learn these concepts and skills most successfully.

I have recently become more sharply aware of the key issues within this debate. I am trying to learn Greek, and this is the closest I can be to a 5-year-old on the path to literacy. In order to speak Greek, it is essential to learn to read and write it, as this also powerfully assists the speaking and listening. What follows is my own experience of learning a language with a different alphabet system.

Lessons learned for literacy teaching from struggling to learn Greek

As an experienced and literate language user no progress was made at all until I was able to access the written forms. The spoken language I heard remained simply a stream of sound, indistinguishable and completely unmemorable. Over several years of holidays, the most I had managed was the odd word and phrase ... mainly socially essential words such as 'Good Day', 'please' and 'thank you'.

Learning the Greek alphabet was a huge challenge; taxing my memory and deeply unsatisfying despite the mature appreciation of the necessity of getting to grips with it. I found a confusing similarity of many of the symbols, issues of orientation being crucial: as with the English letters u/n/m/ ... and p/b/d/g/q ... in Greek there are five different symbols/graphemes representing the phoneme *i* – but happily no instance of the same grapheme representing different phonemes in different situations as in English – but there are different versions of a grapheme for different places in words still to trip one up. There were new and very alien symbols to learn – irritatingly and completely unrelated differences between lower and upper case letters in many instances.

Most memorable to me are the letters linked to personally salient words, such as my own name and my husband's, where we live; common day-to-day items constantly seen and used, for example, P the Greek symbol R for Roy, the pi symbol Π for Prentice, ϕ is F for fish, the combination which makes the B sound in our village's name; and the very distinctive letters, for example the shape of the letter Ω which is used by a wristwatch company, Omega, as a logo.

Learning the letters of the alphabet was achieved by means of several multi – sensory methods, recalling and covering, writing them to learn the unfamiliar shapes kinaesthetically, and through a matching game of cards made with both upper and lower case letters, their names and sounds ... played daily and with someone (and an extremely patient someone!) more knowledgeable to check my accuracy. Practice made fluent/flexible use, leading to confidence.

Automaticity allowed painful, slow blending of the symbols in order to sound out a word, this was helped if it is a word seen and heard frequently such as the name (Σ Á M Á P I Á) of the bottled water used daily, or similarity with a well-known word in English – this became more possible as fluency was gained – but the big issue became then one of accessing the meaning, that is, reading is not just decoding a word, the word has to be in one's lexicon through one's world knowledge.

The Rose Report (DfES, 2006) highlights precisely these aspects of reading. The research evidence which underpins the report's recommendations for teaching early reading is to be found in its 'Appendix 1: the searchlights model – the case for change' by Professors Morag Stuart and Rhona Stainthorp, where they provide an account of the 'simple view of reading' as proposed by Gough and Tunmer (1986). They write:

12. Two components of reading identified in the simple of view of reading first put forward by Gough and Tunmer (1986) are 'decoding' and 'comprehension': according to these authors, 'reading is the product of decoding and comprehension'. We would not want to suggest accepting this statement as a complete description or explanation of reading; rather we want to advocate the good sense of considering reading in terms of two components.

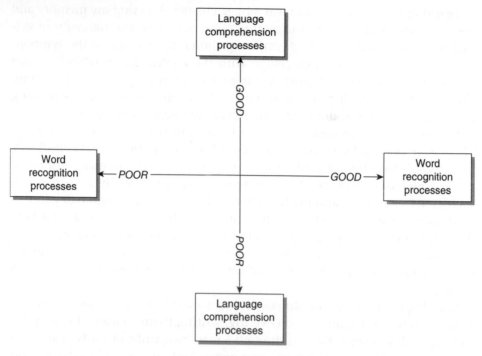

Figure I.1   *The simple view of reading*

13. However, it is important to be clear as to the meaning the authors ascribe to the terms used in this statement, so that we can understand what each component comprises. Gough and Tunmer make clear that by 'decoding' they mean the ability to recognise words presented singly out of context, with the ability to apply phonic rules a crucial contributory factor to the development of this context-free word recognition ability.

14. They also make clear that by 'comprehension' they mean not reading comprehension but *linguistic* comprehension, which they define as 'the process by which, given lexical (that is word) information, sentences and discourse are interpreted'. A common set of linguistic processes is held to underlie comprehension of both oral and written language. (DfES, 2006: 76)

It needs to be added that by 'comprehension' Gough and Tunmer do not mean formal question and answer exercises!

Stuart and Stainthorp provide figures representing the 'simple view of reading' which show distinctly the two crucial dimensions of reading (Figure I.1) and how individual children may vary along either dimension independently (Figure I.2). The authors assert that teachers need to be clear in which of the four quadrants in these figures a child can be placed, in terms of developing skill and competence in both dimensions of performance, as neither are sufficient alone. This professional understanding will then inform teaching precisely.

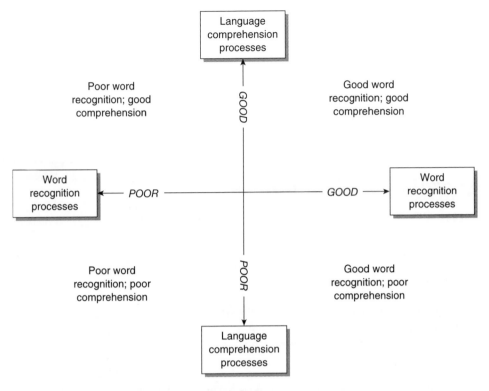

Figure I.2 *Different patterns of Performance*

The fundamental thrust of both the Rose Report and its 'Appendix 1' are in harmony with the principles of this book. I aim to offer in *Language and Literacy 3–7: Creative Approaches to Teaching* detailed explanation on how to support young children become fluent, successful and motivated readers and writers by 7 years of age at the end of Key Stage 1.

The book takes the stance that the teaching of reading is complementary to and dovetailed with that of writing: and, crucially, literacy is seen as integral and interdependent with speaking and listening. The inter- and intra-related nature of oracy and literacy is acknowledged throughout the book as a whole, and is reflected in the order of the chapters.

My sincere hope is that practitioners and teachers will find my book an insightful and inspiring read as they face the complex and demanding, but joyful, challenge of enabling young children to achieve the life-enhancing capacity to be literate.

Jeni Riley
Institute of Education, University of London
March 2006

Chapter 1

Learning to Communicate and to Think

Language is the most powerful tool in the development of any human being. It is undeniably the greatest asset we possess. A good grasp of language is synonymous with a sound ability to think. In other words language and thought are inseparable.

(Vygotsky, 1986: 120)

The pattern is familiar: cries evolve to babbles, babbles are shaped into words, and words are joined into sentences. This sequence describes the path taken by all children as the language they hear around them is examined, internalized, and eventually developed into native-speaker competence.

(Bialystok, 2001: 21)

Introduction

For the most part, we take our own language powers for granted. We treat the ability to speak, to listen and understand, to read and write as instinctive. Yet we use language in increasingly complex ways. We employ new technologies to communicate more variously and flexibly. New words find their way into our vast vocabularies in order to express fresh and subtle nuances as situations demand. But amid this complexity and change, we all appreciate that the purpose of the phenomenon of language is, put at its most crude, the human race needs to communicate to survive.

Early communication

There cannot be an adult anywhere who has been around babies and infants and who is not amazed by their capacity to communicate without misunderstanding and ambiguity. This command of communication develops seemingly with ease for the vast majority of children. At 10 months, babies point to a beaker of juice with tension in gesture and cry, leaving adults in no doubt of their desires. Toddlers hold up their arms and refuse to take a single step, ensuring a lift to car or buggy. Only a few months later, the child is able to communicate needs and concerns through body language and intonation, which is followed by single words and action, then by speech alone. Chomsky (1957) referred to language being a window on the mind and that by studying the way that children become users of spoken language we are provided with an insight into the way that the minds of these young learners work. We can observe how they order words into sentences, how they over-generalize grammatical rules and then dismantle their own hypotheses in order to use the correct forms. Not only are we offered a glimpse of the formidable intellectual mechanism that is at work, but we become aware of the interests of the child as it impacts on her growing understanding of the world. A language system is being constructed with an ability to reason and to think alongside it. While recent research shows there is a wide variability in both the rate and achievement for children learning language (Fenson et al., 1994) the process has an indisputable consistency.

The stages of language development

Children are propelled into the ability to speak through the twin processes of their own drive to communicate and the desire of adults to enable the child to occupy a full place in their world of shared meanings. It would appear, that adults are motivated to talk to babies but, similarly, the infants are programmed to respond with their own communicative skills and, according to Chomsky (1957), they possess an innate ability to process the language they hear around them.

Communication begins with the building of a relationship between a mother (and it is most frequently the mother) and her newborn infant from the first few hours of life, and this bonding stems from and signifies mutual enjoyment of one another. The establishment of this relationship is shown when babies as young as 1 week old prefer to gaze at a human face, rather than other objects, however interesting, patterned or mobile (Trevarthen, 1975, cited in Harris, 1992). Researchers are in agreement that babies at 5 or 6 weeks old are able to engage in mutually satisfying and conversational-type activities. This prototype of conversation is demonstrated by a variety of turn-taking activities, such as mouth-opening, tongue-poking, eye gazing and vocalizing, all of which occur, most commonly, at care-giving and changing times. These behaviours soon become ritualized. These activities are crucial as precursors to speech as they reinforce the supportive roles that speaker and listener need to adopt in order to maintain communication. Also, as Whitehead suggests, these activities are 'something to do with the complex business of getting two minds in contact, because the exchange of meanings and language is at the centre of human communication' (1997: 4).

The interactive behaviours become more elaborate and prolonged, the smiling, cooing, chuckling and pointing develop into games of peekaboo, throwing and retrieving of objects, and hide, find and show. Playful actions and sounds, often repeated, maintain pleasurable response and prepare the way for a genuine conversation.

Early speech – the first word

The articulation of the first word is not a clear-cut event. The sounds made by the infant initially are playful and random; also the baby's phonological (sound-making) production mechanism is immature. This makes word iden-tification difficult. Whitehead suggests that for an utterance to be considered a 'word' it needs to be:

-   produced and used spontaneously by the child;
-   identified by the caregiver who is the authority on what the child says (Nelson, 1973); and that
-   it occurs more than once in the same context or activity (Harris, 1992). (Cited by Whitehead, 1997: 5)

The first word is considered to be a developmental milestone and with some babies can be detected as early as 9 months old (Halliday, 1975), but it is likely to be observed around the first birthday. The initial utterance offers an insight into the child and her life situation. The name of a pet, a food, a drink, a com-fort blanket or toy reflect the main preoccupations of these young minds, sometimes, even before the time-honoured 'Mum-mum-aa' and 'Dad-dadaaa'. The richness of the meaning embedded in single-word utterances is described as a semantic field by linguists, and is specific to both context and each indi-vidual child.

Case Study 1.1

My own daughter at 15 months, when living on a military base, cried 'Dadaaa' to every blushing teenage cadet in uniform she glimpsed from her pram. Her response (and one that is classified by psychologists as 'over-extension'!) to all males in uniform was habit-ual and of abiding fascination. Another 14-month-old child has the sole working vocab-ulary of 'I'm gorgeous!' and 'tractor'. The phrase he repeats parrot-fashion to attract the amusement of adults but the noun denotes a current obsession. 'No' and (rather less use-fully to the child!) 'Yes' are the early words that are understood universally and carry unambiguous meaning.

Learning and Teaching Suggestions

Learning to speak develops initially from the need to express a deeply personal concern or pre-occupation. Compare your recollections with a colleague. What is your experience of children learning to speak? Can you recall their first words? What categories did these words come in?

The 'two-word' stage

Children experiment with speech as they approach 2 years of age and in so doing they become more inventive and adventurous in the use of language. Combinations of words are attempted and, if they are rewarded by the intended results, the structures are used again and again, and perfected. The two-word stage relies on intonation to achieve full linguistic clarity, so for example, 'Daddy house' can mean 'This is Daddy's house' or 'Daddy is in the house' but said with a rising intonation might mean 'Is Daddy in the house?'

Case Study 1.2

My grandson, Benjamin, at 19 months demanded 'Choclate! fetch it! – shall us?' The first three words were spoken with firm, clear expectation and then the softer, wheedling 'shall us?' applied persuasive pressure. The ability to exert authority is not curtailed by a limited command of speech structures; at this age, determination and shrewd judgement of people wins over linguistic expertise. A few months after the incident above, during an exhausting (for me!) afternoon baby-sitting, Benjamin, now about 2 years old, noticed his father's juggling balls (forbidden to him!) safely stored on a high shelf. 'I juggle now,' he stated with a firm resolve. Demonstrating a clear case of premature senility, I reached down the box of balls. The ensuing damage caused by balls hurled enthusiastically into the air got us both into a great deal of trouble!

This stage of language development, involving the combination of two or three words, is governed by the rules of grammar. The ability to combine words in this way in order to express meaning denotes an appreciation of syntactical structure that has intrigued and excited linguists for years. The rules that children generate for themselves may not be conventional, nor are they those that they have heard used by anyone previously, but there is an applied logic and a system and the product is, indisputably, functional.

Developing speech

Through the pre-school years children are exposed to many language-enriching experiences. Spoken language is developed through being surrounded by conversations, through the multiple interactions that occur with different people, through watching and listening to television and videos, through chanting rhymes and poems. Alongside this, children experience the speech-enhancing effect of written language. Children are exposed to and are encouraged to interact with books, through hearing stories, looking at and talking about the illustrations, enjoying magazines, using video box labels, receiving birthday greetings and postcards. They observe adults e-mailing and text messaging, writing notes, shopping lists and letters.

By the age of 4 most children have acquired at least 1,600 words and can understand many more (Crystal, 1987). The physiological mechanisms of the use of mouth, tongue, lips and hard palate to produce speech are now well developed and enunciation is more intelligible and clearer. The powerful intellectual capacity to exploit the rules of language that have been worked out on their own, not merely to repeat language, is demonstrated by children's overgeneralization of past tenses as in 'goed' and 'see-ed', the logical regularization of plurals with 'mouses' and 'foots' and the transformation of nouns into verbs such as 'boxing' an object. These creative inventions remind us that language acquisition is a process far beyond simple imitation. Children powerfully construct language in order to communicate, to get things done, to learn and to comment on the world; in short, to share meaning.

Classifications of language functions

The development of spoken language, we have seen, is dependent upon the opportunity and the need to communicate. Gradually the use of language broadens through greater linguistic expertise and advancing conceptual and social maturity. Halliday developed a classification system of the different functions of language. Using only three examples from his system, the following shows well how children use language in increasingly complex ways. First, children see the need to employ an instrumental function of language, that is, the use of speech in order 'to get things done' (Halliday, 1975). Later the functions become refined into both regulatory, which is controlling of the behaviour of others, and interactional, which is concerned with the establishment and then the maintenance of relationships with others. This reflects the growing complexity of the individual's social interactions through childhood. Early years educators need to be aware of the different dimensions of function and use of oral language in order to be able to determine the level of a child's growing control.

Wilkinson suggests another classification of language which compares interestingly to that of Halliday. This is based on questions surrounding three basic activities: 'Who am I?', 'Who are you?' and 'Who or what is it, was it, will it be?'

Who am I?	1. Establishing and maintaining self
	2. Language for analysing self
	3. Language for expressing self (for celebrating or despairing)
Who are you?	4. Establishing and maintaining relationships
	5. Co-operating
	6. Empathising, understanding the other
	7. Role playing, mimicry
	8. Guiding, directing the other
Who/what is	9. Giving information
he/she/it?	10. Recalling past events
	11. Describing past events (present)
	12. Predicting future events
	statement of intention
	statement of hypothesis
	what might happen
	13. Analysing, classifying
	14. Explaining, giving reasons for
	15. Exploring asking questions etc
	16. Reflecting on own/others' thoughts and feelings. (Wilkinson, 1982: 56)

Children gradually learn to express their needs, thoughts and feelings more precisely and with greater articulation, and in turn, so their ideas expand with the ability to talk. Using language more precisely enables them to generalize, to categorize, to manipulate ideas and to explore notions of cause and effect. Opportunities to use spoken language in a variety of ways and for many different purposes are part of the provision in nursery and reception classrooms so that pupils fully develop their ability not only to use language richly but also to use it as a tool with which to question, reason, hypothesize, wonder and think.

Some theories of language acquistion

The individual's innately human ability to use language and to think has its seeds, as we have discussed in the previous section, in first learning how to communicate. The many theories explaining the development of the ability to communicate personal meaning differ and are complex.

This work has to a great extent been undertaken by psychologists (who are interested in issues of learning and cognitive processes) and linguists (who are concerned with language and speech) who have investigated jointly the journey from the newborn baby's first cry through to competent language use in order to give us a psycholinguistic explanation. 'Psycholinguists are interested in the underlying knowledge and abilities people must have in order to use language and to learn to use language in childhood' (Slobin, 1979: 2, cited in Whitehead, 2004: 49). These studies have shed considerable light on the development of communication and language as a system and not merely the production of sounds and individual words linked together.

A linguistic theory

The most daring theory, which revolutionized the way educators viewed language acquisition was Noam Chomsky's (1957) suggestion that human beings are equipped with a Language Acquisition Device (LAD) which particularly predisposes them to be receptive to the learning of and using language for a myriad of purposes. This Language Acquisition Device has a grammatical orientation which preprogrammes us to understand our individual human languages in a way that no other mammal can achieve. This theory informs us of the system aspect of language construction and, as Chomsky claimed, explains the over-generalization of the rules for plurals and tenses which we have noted earlier when 2–5-year-olds talk about 'mens' and 'sleeped'. Although this theory has been debated since the 1950s, it does offer some explanation for the production of speech structures, which indisputably cannot have been just copied from other language users.

Psychological theories

Different branches of psychology have attempted to explain what fuels this 'explosion' of language.

Behaviourists

Behaviourists have suggested that babies are reinforced into making approximate sounds for early words by their parents who, in enthusiastic delight, reward the early attempts of 'bye bye' and 'woof woof'. There is an explanation of language acquisition which derives from the Behaviourist school but, as many of us have personally experienced, it can only be a part of the story. Children constantly surprise and delight us with their creative turn of phrase, for example, the favourite game of a 3-year-old nephew, was 'making magician spolls' and a 4-year-old complained to me that he had 'gone grumbling down' a slope and badly grazed his knees.

Nativist approaches

Nativist approaches build on seventeenth- and eighteenth-Century views of biological development and Chomsky's notion of the preprogrammed and sensitized human being making linguistic capital of what the environment has to offer. Pinker (1994) talks of the 'language instinct' and elaborated further in 2002 on the astonishing capacity of the young mind to extract vital ingredients from the conversations taking place around it in order to make sense of the world and to respond to it.

Cognitive approaches

Cognitive approaches differ from Chomsky and Pinker's views of the development of linguistically specific abilities but view language learning as an activity subsumed within a much more general view of learning which has its roots in motivation, intentions and support from more experienced others. Language development as seen from this perspective is a part (or feature) of general cognitive development. Piaget suggested that the child explores the world, initially through sensori-motor activity and then language builds on these 'schemas' or primitive thought networks. And Vygotsky (1986) believed that language development is interactional; it builds on mental structures but as it does so it also enhances their development. In support of this theory, the empirical work of Gopnik and Meltzoff (1986) found a relationship between the appearance of certain phrases such as 'All gone!' and the child's acquisition of the concept of object permanence.

Social-interactionists

Social-interactionists moved these ideas on further still to acknowledge the crucial role of experienced language users in the development of spoken language. Language is a vehicle for getting things done, making relationships and enabling one to be a member of a social group. It is essentially functional as Halliday and Wilkinson have shown us. Bruner (1983) introduced us to the notion of the adult intuitively 'scaffolding' the child's innate language learning abilities through mutually enjoyable interaction and with specific linguistic support. In this way, children are initiated into the world as social beings by parents and care-givers.

Language acquisition is, then, both a cognitive and linguistic achievement. If, as educators, we acknowledge a broad, rich view of how we learn to communicate and that becoming able to speak is integral with a capacity to learn generally, we are offered more to consider when thinking about provision in early years settings and classrooms. The two most influential theorists who propose the importance of the interpersonal, the cultural and social factors in all human learning are Bruner and Vygotsky. Let us clarify briefly the contributions of these two pivotal educational thinkers.

Bruner, like Piaget before him, viewed cognitive development in the first 18 months of life as having, initially, an active, physical basis. 'Enactive' or action-based thinking is replaced by 'iconic' thinking or thinking through internalized images or 'pictures in the head' stimulated by experiences or encounters in the child's own context. However, between 2 and 3 years of age, intellectual progress is accelerated by the development of language as it enables the individual to think symbolically. Language, suggests Bruner, has a reorganizing and restructuring function on the mind; in fact, as Whitehead (2004: 74) puts it, the outcome is 'a transformation of the child's thinking and behaviour'. Whitehead continues:

The transforming power of language as a tool for thinking is one of the two distinctive aspects of Bruner's view of language and thought. The other is the immense significance of the human social and cultural environments into which children are born. The activities of older people who care for children, participate in language-like games and real conversations with them, and organize small and manageable chunks of social and cultural experience for them to engage with, actually create a scaffold for easy access to the language and culture of the community. These may be complex ideas but they are also describable in terms of everyday metaphor: infants, and small children are apprentices to life, language and learning. (2004: 74)

Access to the systems of symbols of a specific culture is the greatest advantage human beings have to support, enhance and develop their thinking. In infancy, learning a spoken language is the first and the most naturally accessible of these symbol systems, a little later children will meet symbols related to written language in books, stories and labels, the numerals related to the mathematical system, semiotics, graphics, and art and design. Being able to think symbolically frees the individual from the immediate, the here and the now. Children are able to express themselves as well as having recourse to physical action, they can plan for the future, remember the past and, most powerfully of all, imagine.

Vygotsky contributed to the debate regarding thought and language. After studying the attempts to teach apes to speak, he believed that in humans thought and speech develop separately but at about the age of 2 years they fuse to become a different and more advanced mental function, namely, verbal thinking. This is characterized by what Vygotsky termed egocentric speech, a kind of personal, sub-vocalizing speech which directs and organizes action and is a precursor of an inner speech or advanced mental process so valuable to all human beings.

Case Study 1.3

William, my grandson, at 3 years old had a passion for jigsaw puzzles, and while doing them he tutored himself aloud ... 'does dis go here? Does dis go here? ... nooooooo ... does dis go here? YES ... **hurraaay**'.

The developmental sequence is that, first, social speech occurs, then egocentric speech which later becomes internal or inner speech, and this develops finally into verbal thought. Vygotsky believed that the origin of all thinking is primarily social and that higher cognitive activity such as thinking symbolically through words and concepts has at its heart social relationships and processes. As cultures advance, more and more refined symbol systems are invented as tools for thought; these in turn enable thinking to develop and to become more complex. The impact of written language on the development of thought will be discussed in greater detail later, when we consider literacy.

The complementary idea, that there are multimodal ways of responding to experience, is Vygotsky's suggestion that symbolic systems aid thinking. He suggests that we can only have access to another's thought processes via a symbolic system of one kind or another. We are able to share another's view of the world through conversation, through their writing, their paintings, films or sculpture. So in this sense mental activity is mediated through symbolic systems which are culturally acknowledged, agreed and valued, and are constantly evolving, albeit that different cultures privilege certain symbolic systems in preference to others.

Young children gain access first to ideas, stories and culturally appropriate ways of behaving through the symbolic system of spoken language. Conversely, as practitioners, we acquire insights into children's thinking through their body language, gestures, talk, drawings and models.

Supporting pre-school language development

The first section of this chapter has briefly charted the young child's acquisition of speech from early infancy through to the end of the Foundation Stage and has offered explanations for language development. Research evidence suggests that there is a wide variation in the spoken language of children when they arrive at school. Now, we will consider what factors in the home environment encourage the development of spoken language.

The Bristol Study, despite being 20 years old, provides substantial empirical evidence into this aspect of child development. This research project (Wells, 1987) studied the language development of 128 children from the age of 13 months through to starting mainstream school. The research evidence from this project is a rich source of information about the differing domestic situations, the material circumstances and the variety and type of adult support of the children involved, and comparing it with their differing levels of linguistic competence. Wells and his colleagues provide informed speculation about the relationship between the progress of the children, their circumstances and their experiences.

Immense variation in the rate at which children acquire spoken language was found. As the researchers worked from the mass of audiotape transcripts, they attempted to explain the reasons for this. Adults, it would appear are intuitively very good at enabling infants to crack the code system of speech. Parents take their babies' pre-vocalizations seriously and input meaning; they support interaction with sustained eye-gaze, encouragement and evident enjoyment. Mothers speak to their children in a manner described by psychologists as 'motherese', which is highly facilitative to the development of speech. This is a form of talking that is raised in pitch and is simple and repetitive. The child's utterance is frequently expanded upon for the purpose of clarification and this also provides supportive tutoring. So, for example, if the child says, 'Dan sock!'

the response might be 'Yes, you're right that is Dan's sock, he must have put on his red ones this morning'.

All the evidence is that children learn language best not through intentional drills and instruction, but when parents and practitioners attend to, and are interested in, what children say and mean, and engage them in real conversations. Children's language skills need personal interaction in order to develop. If children learn through being taught to speak, rather like a parrot, it has implications for the way in which the adults closest to them, should interact with them. Wells is clear from the evidence of his study that this is not so. In fact, he gives examples where it is plainly counter-productive and discouraging for the toddler when his mother, as in the instance below, deliberately sets out to teach didactically.

Case Study 1.4

Thomas (age 25 months) has seen a plate of biscuits (cookies) on the table. His first utterance consists of three words, but only the third is intelligible.

Thomas: *** biscuits.
Mother: Those were got specially 'cos we had visitors at the weekend. Who came to see Tommy? Who came in a car?
Thomas: See Grannie Irene uh car.
Mother: Grannie Irene's coming next weekend. But who came last weekend?
Thomas: Auntie Gail *in a train.*
Mother: *Auntie Gail's* coming. They're coming on the train, yes.
Thomas: Colin uh Anne *a train.*
Mother: Colin … Colin and Anne came in the car, didn't they??
Thomas: Colin uh Anne. Colin uh Anne.
Mother: Yes.
Thomas: Colin uh Anne. Colin uh Anne.
Mother: Colin and Anne came in the train.
Thomas: In uh train. Auntie train.
Mother: No, not Auntie train, darling. Auntie Gail and Grannie are coming on the train on Friday.
Thomas: Auntie Gail in uh train.
Mother: That's right. (Wells, 1987: 49)

Learning and Teaching Suggestions

What effect do you think this kind of experience of a conversation has on Thomas?

What is he really interested in?

What, then, does appear to be valuable for language development? If we take the stance that children are largely constructors of their own personal version of spoken language, perhaps, it might be argued that adults have little to contribute to the process. However, this is patently not true. In order to make progress, children need feedback about the effectiveness of their linguistic efforts, to talk to people and, through conversations, to test hypotheses about the way that language works, and to have the hypotheses confirmed. The extent to which children have this opportunity is important. Wells identified a clear and positive relationship between those children who were exposed to a large number of conversations and the rate at which they developed. So, the amount of experience of talk is important but there is more to it than that as Wells points out:

> What seems to be important is that, to be most helpful, the child's experience of conversation should be in a one-to-one situation in which the adult is talking about matters that are of interest and concern to the child, such as what he or she is doing, has done or plans to do, or about activities in which the child and adult engage together. (1987: 44)

The explanation of the value of the shared experience is that it maximizes the possibility of the meaning being appropriately interpreted by both participants and built upon further. The less experienced language user is supported through interest and the context, and in this way is motivated into sustaining the dialogue. The role of the more experienced speaker is crucial, Wells continues: 'This therefore places a very great responsibility on the adult to compensate for the child's limitations and to behave in ways that make it as easy as possible for the child to play his or her part as effectively as possible' (1987: 45). A parent or carer is well placed to do this at the earliest stages of spoken language development, as they have insight into a child's own context, model of the world and linguistic resources. This enables them to be skilful and co-operative listeners, and to make a rich interpretation of the child's utterances.

Case Study 1.5

An example of a parent doing exactly that follows:

In the first extract from the recordings of Mark, we see very clear examples of these strategies for sustaining and extending Mark's meanings:

Mark: [looking out of the window at the birds in the garden] Look at that jubs [birds] Mummy.
Mother: Mm.
Mark: Jubs.
Mother: [inviting Mark to extend his own meaning] What are they doing?
Mark: Jubs bread [Birds eating bread]

Mother: [extending Marks meaning]: Oh, look! They're eating the berries, aren't they?
Mark :   Yeh.
Mother: [extending and paraphrasing] That's their food. They have berries for dinner.
Mark: Oh. (Wells, 1987: 47)

Learning and Teaching Suggestions

Compare the above case study with the previous example of Thomas and his mother. What are the most obvious differences?

Why do you think that this conversational experience is so valuable for children?

The mother is adjusting her speech to take into account Mark's ability and is responding to him. The topic of conversation is one in which Mark is interested, as he initiated it. The adult provides information on the topic and extends his understanding of the world. Mark is acting as a full participant with acknowledgements of his mother's contributions. As Wells says, it is a collaborative enterprise in which they both are engaged. Adults do not need to be over-analytical concerning the linguistic complexity of how exactly they are operating but they do need to know that the value lies in the *way* they respond:

> All that is required is that they be responsive to the cues that children provide as to what they are able to understand. Rather than adults teaching children, therefore, it is children who teach adults how to talk in such a way as to make it easy for them to learn. (Wells, 1987: 48)

Children therefore play the major role in constructing their knowledge of oral language although they are greatly facilitated in this by adults. The children in the study who made less progress were not as frequently involved in one-to-one conversations or with adults who worked hard at trying to make mutual sense of a situation.

The teaching points that emerge for teachers, parents and carers from the findings of the Bristol Study are as follows:

> When the child appears to be trying to communicate, assume he or she has something important to say and treat the attempt accordingly.
>
> Because the child's utterances are often unclear or ambiguous, be sure you have understood the intended meaning before responding.

When you reply, take the child's meaning as the basis of what you say next – confirming the intention and extending the topic or inviting the child to do so for him or herself.

Select and phrase your contributions so that they are at or just beyond the child's ability to comprehend. (Wells, 1987: 50)

Summary

We have considered the way that language develops through the child striving to communicate and to make meaning has also been addressed. The development of speech is promoted most effectively by adults who are interested in having conversations with children. These adults 'tune in' to the children's early attempts to talk by encouraging and expanding their language structures. This approach can be adopted in early years settings and schools (despite the obvious drawback of one adult and many children) which offer meaningful, authentic opportunities for children to communicate orally and, when appropriate, in writing.

Further reading

Wells, C.G. (1987) *The Meaning Makers: Children Learning Language and Using Language to Learn*. London. Hodder and Stoughton.
Whitehead, M. (2004) *Language and Literacy in the Early Years*. 3rd edn. London. Paul Chapman Publishing/Sage.

Chapter **2**

Supporting Oracy in the Foundation Stage and Key Stage 1

Following Vygotsky (1962) I would emphasize the value of children's talk about events and ideas for their understanding of the world, and for their growing ability to articulate that understanding orally and in writing. Creating links between words and the world, and … between words and other words, is the heart of the educational process.

… All children must take an active part in negotiating meanings, and we teachers are responsible for creating conditions that make such negotiation possible. Younger students, especially those just entering school, deserve encouragement and time to expand and explain.

(Cazden, 1988: 13–14)

Introduction

The Rose Report on the teaching of early reading has reaffirmed the central place of oracy after a few years in the UK of relative neglect compared with the provision for literacy in the early years setting and KS 1 classroom:

> The indications are that far more attention needs to be given, right from the start, to promoting speaking and listening skills to make sure that children build a good stock of words, learn to listen attentively, and to speak clearly and confidently. … they are prime communication skills that are central to children's intellectual, social and emotional development. (DfES, 2006: 3)

Key principles underpinning effective communication with young learners

In Chapter 1, the intuitively powerful way that adults support the attempts of very young infants as they learn to communicate and to talk was discussed. Consideration will be given now to how and in what situations this is achieved most successfully. We will build upon the fundamental lessons learned in Chapter 1 with further research evidence in order to identify some key principles which will help to inform the planning and provision offered by early years practitioners in the FS and primary teachers in KS 1.

Research undertaken by Snow (1991) showed, after close analysis of transcriptions of audiotaped conversations between adults and very young children, the way that adults maximize the '**semantic contingency**' of their interactions when young children talk to them. Snow expands on Wells's hypotheses and describes how the more experienced language user continues the topic introduced by the child and facilitates linguistic progress in four important ways. Snow suggests that adults support the child by:

- expanding the topic introduced
- offering new information on the topic
- seeking clarification by asking the child questions if it's needed
- answering the child's questions.

In the previous chapter we see an example of this happening when Mark's mother joins in the observation of, and engages with, his fascination with the feeding birds. She supports his interest, expands on his knowledge about birds and models language structures which as yet he is unable to use. Both elements of scaffolding are carefully judged, they are neither excessively didactic nor do they provide more information than Mark wants or needs to know. Also, there is not too large a gap between the language used in her replies and his current level of language development. Conversely, Snow notes that where an adult introduces a new topic or switches from one topic to another it impacts negatively on the child's motivation to engage with the challenge and effort to communicate. Other examples of this type of intuitive linguistic tutoring occur when the semantic field is deliberately restricted by the adult in order to enhance success; this is the verbal equivalent of concentrating on one corner of a difficult jigsaw puzzle. Acceleration of language learning occurs also when adults 'up the ante' and refuse to accept babyish versions of words if the child can manage the conventional version.

> ### Key Term
>
> **Semantic contingency**: a conversation which maintains the topic of interest and focus

Language development and learning through conversations

Given that almost all children learn to speak largely through having many, many conversations with more experienced language users, it is worth us considering what makes a conversation successful.

The features of a conversation

- Two (or more) speakers co-operate.
- The speakers draw upon both their knowledge of the world and their ability to use language.
- Each speaker is supported by the listener through eye contact, attention and encouraging, affirming utterances of 'yes!', 'absolutely!', 'uh huh', and so on.
- A speaker ensures that the listener has understood and adapts the message accordingly.
- The co-constructed meaning is genuinely negotiated.
- There is interest and engagement from both parties.
- In the best of conversations the interaction occurs over a minimum of five exchanges from which both parties benefit, learn and gain enjoyment.

Clay (1998) corroborates with Wells's suggestion that children who are in the driving seat of conversations will profit the most.

When we speak we do not assume that the listener cannot think; we expect them to bring knowledge to bear on what we are talking about. Yet probably the most common error made by adults about the learning of young children is that we can bypass what the child is thinking and just push new knowledge into their heads by means of the things we do. However, any learning situation is like a conversation, for it requires the learner to bring what he or she already knows to bear on the problem to be explored. (Clay, 1998: 15)

Case Study 2.1

Two children are working in the water tray with some objects.

Boy 8 (4.1 years) who had been watching the various items floating on water, 'Look at the fir cone. There's bubbles of air coming out.'
Nursery Officer 1 'It's spinning round.'
(Demonstrating curiosity and desire to investigate further)
Boy 8 'That's cos it's got air in it.'
Nursery Officer 1 picked up the fir cone and shows the children how the scales go round in a spiral, turning the fir cone round and round with a winding action, 'When the air comes out in bubbles it makes the fir cone spin around'.
Girl 2E (4.9 years) uses a plastic tube to blow into the water. 'Look bubbles'.
Nursery Officer 1 'What are you putting in the water to make bubbles ... what is coming out of the tube?'
Girl 2E 'Air.' (Siraj-Blatchford et al., 2002: doc. 421)

Supporting language and thinking

Research findings – Researching Effective Pedagogy in the Early Years (REPEY) (Siraj-Blatchford et al., 2002) and Effective Provision of Pre-School Education (EPPE) (Sylva et al., 2004) – show the value of maximizing the conversational approach when working with young children, as Case Study 2.1 shows. The two related projects, EPPE which identified the features of the most effective early years settings and the REPEY project which explored the pedagogy within the those settings which might explain why they are effective. The REPEY research team go further than Clay's suggestion that thinking should not be 'bypassed', but assert that the interest of both parties has to be engaged for successful learning to occur. The term sustained shared thinking (SST) has been offered from this research project by the project team as a way of interacting with children that supports and challenges their thinking through conversations. Sustained, shared thinking involves:

- the adult being knowledgeable about children – that is, being aware of the children's interests and current level of understanding
- the adult capitalizing on opportunities to talk with a child developing an idea or skill.

This opportunity offers:

- appropriate contexts for interacting with children to challenge thinking and develop understanding.

The most effective interactions between adults and young children include the following adult behaviours:

- *sensitively* tuning in to what the child is doing or interested in by listening carefully and attending to body language
- *engaging* and demonstrating interest by paying full attention, smiling, nodding and maintaining eye contact
- *respecting* children's decisions and choices
- inviting children to elaborate – 'Oh really? Tell me how you are going to do it or why you like this … '
- *re-capitulating* – 'So it goes like this then … or you think that …'
- *offering* your own experience – 'Yes, I like sitting on a beanbag reading too especially when I am tired …'
- *clarifying* ideas – 'So you think that the truck won't go any faster even if it is going downhill?'
- *suggesting* – 'What about trying it this way up?'
- *reminding* – 'Don't forget you thought it might go just as slowly downhill.'
- *encouraging* further thinking – 'So if this doesn't work well with the wheels put on this way … what might happen if we try them another way?'

- *offering* an alternative viewpoint – 'I don't think the Bear in "We are going on a Bear Hunt!" wanted to hurt the children'
- *speculating* – 'What would have happened if the children had asked the Bear to come home and play with them?'
- *reciprocating* – 'Goodness you have worked hard in the sand ... you must be proud of that garden ... it is very decorative!'
- *asking* open questions – 'What will happen if ... ? Why have you made it like that? ... What are you going to do tomorrow?'
- *modelling* thinking – 'so ... to make our book ... we first have to get the card ... then decide on the colour and pattern for the cover ... and do we want to paint or colour the illustrations?'

The last example is the adult very explicitly modelling Vygotsky's notion of 'inner speech' (see Chapter 1) which guides thinking. Other opportunities to model the organizing role of language occur when working alongside children who may not yet have the vocabulary or language structures in place. For example, sitting by a child playing in the sandtray enjoying watching sand spill out of the cup and through a sieve and into the tray, the practitioner might comment on the way the sand flows, sprinkles and piles into a mound. Clearly contributions such as this have to be offered sensitively and with space and pause for the child to comment and take over if she/he wishes.

Supporting language development with small groups of children

All the evidence discussed so far suggests that children learn generally, and to use spoken language in particular, most effectively, by talking in one-to-one situations with empathetic and more experienced language users. Unfortunately in early years settings and classrooms, this is not always possible or achievable. Recent research (Riley, et al., 2004) undertaken in multicultural, reception classrooms situated in very deprived, inner-city areas has shown that with energy and careful, imaginative planning young children's language can be enhanced very successfully in class situations through the additional support of volunteers working with small groups of pupils.

The research project aimed to support language development through the use of volunteers implementing teacher-planned enrichment sessions. The study aimed to adopt the following features of classroom interaction as an integral part of the intervention by providing:

- opportunities for extended talk
- situations which require collaborative talk
- ground rules for task-orientated talk, for example, waiting and turn-taking
- support, guidance and encouragement, but not dominance, by the adult or teacher
- contexts which build on prior experience and enable new learning to occur.

In other words all the principles which support language learning that were discussed earlier in this chapter were built consciously into the intervention. The teachers spent study days with the researchers planning work around a theme for the volunteers to use with the groups of children. A typical activity is shown below.

Learning and Teaching Suggestions: The Car Park

Resources: car park playmat, five cars of different colours, trees and houses
Adult places the cars on the edge of the mat … children arrange the houses and trees to form a car park.
Aim: for the children to follow precise directional language instructions.
Language structures modelled by adult … First park the red car, second park the blue car … Park the green car between/next to/behind/in front of the blue car.
Vocabulary practised: First, second, third, fourth, fifth, *and* next to/between, beside, behind and in front.

Many of the reception pupils in the study had English as an additional language and, when assessed, appeared to find certain language structures more challenging than the monolingual children did. Additional opportunities to use these structures were incorporated into the volunteers' sessions in meaningful contexts. Examples of these are 'Wh... questions', understanding sentences with the main clause at the end and recalling sentences with two main ideas. The children were unfamiliar with some vocabulary. Typically words such as 'buttons', a 'band' meaning musicians, verbs such as 'cutting', 'sewing' and 'riding', and possessive pronouns such as 'his' and 'hers' were all a mystery. The project was successful in boosting children's spoken language development and had the added benefit of enhancing the teachers' and volunteers' understanding of how to support speaking and listening.

Suggestions to develop spoken language in the Foundation Stage

Spoken language develops most successfully when it is integrated and embedded in real situations, or in the ongoing topic work or current focus in the setting. Language is learned effectively, as we have discussed, within meaningful and genuine contexts. We learn language in an authentic and socially driven world because we have something important or interesting to say or we want or need to get something done. We talk when we have something to talk about.

Listening is the essential complementary skill to speaking, and in all group settings active listening needs to be encouraged and recognized as crucial to language development. Unlike most home environments, in early years settings there are many more children and fewer adults, and this alone leads children to acquire the necessary survival techniques that enable them to ignore most of the interaction that flows around them. Bringing to children's awareness when a situation requires their attention, and when they need to listen actively should be made explicit. Adults model positive listening skills by attending courteously to children when they speak, and by having real conversations together. In group situations, active listening is ensured by the adult waiting until everyone is paying attention and looking at them, using a quiet, natural voice, maintaining eye contact, keeping discussion and instructions short and relevant and not having long one-to-one interactions with a single child which excludes the others. When planning the provision it can be useful to keep the following in mind.

Examples of listening games and activities

Given the presence of continuous noise from traffic, televisions, radios, music in public spaces, and domestic equipment such as washing machines, games which help children to discriminate between background and foreground noise are well worth playing in the warm-up to physical education (PE) or in the playground at 'letting off steam' time.

- *Dodgem cars* – children run around in and between each other, using the space fully but wisely, avoiding colliding with each other, and as they do so they make the noise of a dodgem car. Complete silence and stillness is expected at an agreed signal such as clapping hands, banging a tambourine or ringing a bell. The same signal starts everyone off again.
- *Statues* is a similar game to the above except the background noise is generated by lively and strongly rhythmic music. At the agreed signal, possibly a whistle, the children immediately stop dancing around and stand in a statuesque shape. After a few seconds the sequence is repeated.
- *Listening walks* are a great favourite in all early years settings and classrooms. The children are taken for a walk in the local environment and asked to listen attentively for all the sounds that can be heard. A cassette recorder is an invaluable resource, as it will capture the experience to be relived on their return and allows the different sounds and noises to be identified and discussed. The number and type of environmental sounds that are hardly noticed and still less remarked upon always sparks surprise.
- *Listening tapes* are easily made by practitioners both at home and at school. Children greatly enjoy identifying common-place sounds such as a baby's cry, bathwater running, vegetables being chopped and then being fried, washing machines spinning, and so on.
- *Circle time* – this key activity offers much useful social learning and interaction as well as an exchange of information. Being able to listen to others when they have their turn to speak as well as taking the

opportunity to structure their own contribution clearly and appropriately is very valuable in nursery and reception classes and in Years 1 and 2. In the earliest years, care needs to be taken not to extend the session beyond the children's concentration span.

Specific vocabulary and language structures

The vocabulary and language structures should be emphasized in the planning documents linked to a current topic or story:

- *nouns* (the names of relevant objects, characters and relevant key players), for example, dinosaurs, firemen, nurses
- *verbs* (words which denote a state of being and action), for example, rush, look after, lumber
- *adjectives* (words which describe nouns), for example, brave, kind, enormous
- *adverbs* (words which add interest to or qualify verbs), for example, quickly, slowly
- *prepositions* (words used before a noun or pronoun to relate it to the other words in the sentence such as those which denote position), for example, up, down, through, under.
- *prepositions* (as above and which denote time and sequence), for example, when, later, soon
- *prepositions* (as above and which explain and reason), for example, if, so, then, because.

A display on an A5 sheet of paper or card as an aide-mémoire with the words and phrases to be emphasized during the course of the topic can ensure consistency when a large number of adults are working in a setting.

Examples of games

These games can be played with small groups of children in the nursery or those who need additional language practice in the reception year.

- *Naming objects:* 'I am putting in the basket … *a shell, a doll, a piece of Lego* …'. Who can remember what is in the basket? Who would like to put something in the basket? Nathan? Jo? What are you going to put in the basket? Child says 'I am putting in the basket … *an action man*'.
- *Kim's game*: Familiar objects are placed on a tray and shown briefly to the children then covered up. Who can remember what is on the tray? Pupils take it in turns to say what they saw, no repeats are allowed, the number and increasingly unusual nature of the objects can be built upon as the children become more practised.
- A *'feely bag'* is a time-honoured favourite in which objects chosen for their tactile qualities are placed in a bag and passed around the group of

children who in turn describe how they feel, using adjectives which are appropriate to each item … *rough, spiky, smooth, cold, heavy, with sharp edges or corners, hard, soft, fluffy, knobbly, rounded,* and so on.

Language in the environment

A well-ordered setting or classroom will have logical and systematically arranged resources and materials, and if these are clearly labelled also with the word and visual image, children have the opportunity to categorize objects every 'tidying up' time during a day. An approach which offers valuable learning for children encourages good habits, and preserves the sanity of the adults!

Practical and well-organized ways of working in early years settings such as the use of clear, consistent, well-written or computer-generated labels for displays, instructions and notices can be exploited as literacy learning opportunities as well, for example, 'Only four children can play in the home corner'.

Specific and focused language enrichment through stories

- *Positional prepositions* can be reinforced during PE and with picture books such as *Rosie's Walk* (Pat Hutchins) and *We're Going on a Bear Hunt* (Michael Rosen) when *under, over, through, behind, in front of* are contextually and delightfully exemplified.
- *Adjectives* denoting the qualities of creatures, such as *Toad* (Ruth Brown) which is a richly descriptive picture book accompanied by painterly and deliciously repulsive illustrations. *The Gruffalo* (Julia Donaldson) does a similar task, using patterned and rhyming language, satisfying if read aloud and invites children to join in, whilst offering opportunities for painting and drawing.

Supporting language development in Years 1 and 2

Emphasis on supporting language development will continue in KS 1. The conversational approach to teaching remains a useful tool in the teacher's repertoire. Research evidence demonstrates considerable variation between the way that language is used in the home and in the school setting. At home, children are very much more likely to initiate a conversation than at school (in some of Wells's, analyses the likelihood is as high as 70 per cent). He cites several depressing examples in which a teacher and a child appear to be talking completely at cross-purposes, with the result that both participants become frustrated and disinclined to repeat the experience, neither participant has enjoyed the experience and little learning is likely to have occurred. Even worse is the impression given by Rosie, in the most striking of the examples cited, to her teacher that she is linguistically incompetent: this contrasts poorly with her performance recorded at her home.

Case Study 2.2

Child:	Miss, I done it.
Teacher [to Rosie]:	Will you put it on top?
Child:	Miss, I done it, look.
	[Several seconds' pause]
Teacher:	[to Rosie, pointing with finger at card]: What are those things?
Child:	Miss, I done it.
	Miss, I done it.
	[Rosie drops something and then picks it up]
Teacher [to Rosie]:	What are those things?
Child:	Miss, *I done* it.
Teacher	[referring to skis in the picture]: *Do you know* what they are called?
	[Rosie shakes her head]
	What d'you think he uses them for? [Rosie looks at the card.
	The teacher turns to the other child's calendar] ...
Teacher:	[to Rosie, pointing at the skis on the card]: What's--------what are those?
	[Rosie looks blank]
	What do think he uses them for?
Rosie:	[rubbing one eye with the back of her hand] Go down. (Wells, 1983: 97]

Learning and Teaching Suggestions

Why do you think this conversational exchange is so unhelpful to Rosie?

What in your view might have made it more fruitful? How does this support Snow's notion of effective learning of language that occurs when adults maintain 'semantic contingency' and how much does it differ from the idea of sustained shared thinking of Siraj-Blatchford et al.?

Barriers to effective language learning in KS 1

The obvious and inescapable issue in KS 1 is the unrealistic expectation that one teacher can communicate effectively with 30 or more young children. However, this is not the only issue that militates against the most facilitative linguistic learning environment in the Key Stage 1 classroom.

It is a fact of life that teachers have parental pressures and diverse agendas with which to cope. They have prescribed curricula to cover with National Curriculum tasks and tests never far from their professional consciousness.

This situation ensures that the interactions that occur in classrooms usually have a predetermined goal, an idea or concept to be encountered or a skill to be acquired. This situation militates against the conversational approach, and in Wells's opinion, is counter-productive to genuinely valuable learning and can lead to the 'Guess what is in my head?' phenomenon, as the following case study demonstrates.

Case Study 2.3

The third extract once again comes from a session involving the whole class, following the reading of *Elmer the Elephant*. In the course of a discussion of some of the pictures, Stella volunteers a personal anecdote:

Teacher:	Can you see what that elephant's got on the end of his trunk?
Children:	(laugh)
Teacher:	What is it?
Children:	A blower?
Teacher:	A blower – a party blower. It is funny isn't it?
Stella:	My-my-my brother brought one home from a party.
Teacher:	Did he ? What does it do as well as blowing?
Stella :	Um.
First child:	(inaudible)
Teacher:	Sh! (signals she wants Stella to answer) What does it do?
Stella:	Mm!—the thing rolls out (makes an appropriate gesture).
Teacher:	Yes the thing rolls down and rolls up again doesn't it? But what does it do as well as unrolling and rolling up?
Stella:	Um.
Teacher:	Does it do anything else?
First child:	Squeaks.
Teacher:	Sh! (signals for Stella to answer) Does Adrian's squeak?— Adrian's blower squeak?
Stella :	(nods)
Teacher:	Does it? They usually squeak and they often have a little feather on it too, don't they? (intonation of finality)
Children:	Yes (chanted)
Teacher:	Well I think that's a lovely story. It's one of my favourites. (Wells, 1983: 139)

Learning and Teaching Suggestions

Was this a helpful exchange with this group of KS 1 pupils? What might the teacher have done to develop this discussion effectively?

This extract could be analysed productively to identify the types of questions most in evidence, namely, child-initiated, teacher-initiated, and **open** and **closed questions**. The children ask no questions at all and the teacher appears to use only one category, closed questions; those with one correct, predetermined answer. The most important point to make from this fairly typical example of group discussion from the Bristol Study is that although several sensible, logical answers may well have been accurate, frequently only one answer is acceptable to the teacher. Young children can be observed in their desperate search for clues, from the adult's facial expression and body language, which might hint at the 'correct' response before venturing a reply. Some will rarely volunteer a suggestion so disempoyered are they by this school 'game'. Wells makes a plea for teachers to adopt a flexible approach in their interactions with children so that if one of several answers is appropriate, alternative suggestions are accepted and developed. Doing this encourages pupils to continue to offer responses and so to participate in the collaborative act of meaning-making that is the nature of a genuine conversational exchange.

Key Terms

Closed questions: questions are said to be 'closed' when there is only one right answer. Closed questions tend to ask for information retrieval.

Open questions: questions are said to be 'open' when more than one answer, or one way of answering, is appropriate. Open questions tend genuinely to be seeking information. At best they prompt new thinking and reaffirm that alternatives coexist.

Spoken language will only flourish in an intellectually stimulating, activity-based, experience-rich learning environment. Conversation develops from the necessity to talk to 'get things done', to question, to establish issues of importance, to find out about things of interest, to express opinions and ideas. The language-rich classroom with purposeful talk, cannot be manufactured artificially; it arises from curiosity, intrigue and is highly specific and context embedded. Becoming a fluent speaker depends upon social interaction and this knowledge should influence the opportunities extended to children. The adults with whom children interact have great potential to enable them to operate within different registers and to experiment with language when talking with their peers. Teachers can probe and prompt pupils to learn to use language to convey meaning precisely, as they ask, for example, 'Why do you think the worm moves like that?' 'How would you describe the movement?'

Teachers of young pupils will be concerned with the way that activities are presented to their classes so that they offer a variety of learning approaches that have the potential to appeal to several types of cognitive style. Children will be encouraged to contribute to and function effectively in class discussion if treated courteously and appropriately with 'Thank you, Jane, that is a helpful suggestion, we could make a book about that ...' in the way that we have seen how the most facilitative parent or carer intuitively supports the pre-Foundation Stage child.

The value of oral narrative

Early years practitioners now are familiar with the value of sharing picture books and with reading stories to young children; the research evidence for this is clear-cut and proven. Early years professionals need to be aware also of the reasons why this is so powerful in the development of both spoken and written language. There is a need to appreciate fully why the ability to narrate orally or mentally is crucial for psychological health and cognitive development. It seems that along with hearing the oral art of storytelling and listening to stories read to them, children also need opportunities to narrate their own stories.

Key Terms

Narrative: is the recounting of an event and involves, most typically, people (or characters) and feelings.

Storying: is the activity of telling stories either to oneself (perhaps mentally) or to others.

So what is **narrative**? A narrative requires a retelling in a considered order or sequence of the events which builds, at best, an intrigue and mystery, but which essentially, engages interest. As Whitehead suggests:

Speculations about our very existence are linked with another very remarkable feature of narrative: the urge to evaluate or make judgements about persons and events. Narratives that are concerned with telling a sequence of events in time order can become very tedious; we are only prepared to tolerate a sequence of 'and then ... and then ... and then' for a limited time. We are really waiting for clues as to the teller's opinions, feelings and values. Indeed it seems that the urge to tell a tale is really directed towards explaining, gossiping and speculating about human behaviour and the chances of life. (2004: 112)

So the retelling, ordering and evaluating is a way that human beings use to try to make sense of their existence in the world, and as Whitehead adds 'narrative is a way of giving meaning and significance to the endless stream of sensations and events' (2004: 112). Through this personal activity of revisiting of events in our heads we re-present to ourselves why and how they happened, we relive joy and make pain bearable, this is described by some literary scholars as **storying**. Hardy (1977: 12) suggests that 'storying' is a primary act of mind, and is demonstrated in key cognitive activities such as remembering, planning and day-dreaming. This ability to reconstruct events for ourselves, sometimes making them more palatable (as after an argument!) enables us to cope with unpleasant situations and occurrences, and so restores self-esteem and a sense of well-being.

The creation and transmission of culture

Communities also participate in a sharing of their own collaborative stories, in a joint activity of 'storying', and so make meaning of their communal experience, in other words develop culture. Religious stories, explanations of creation, life and death, myths and legends, tales of battles, victories and disasters are the stuff of communal storying, begun in the oral tradition and passed down the generations and converted to history. Traditional storying or folk tales relay the hopes and fears, triumphs and failures of the commonplace and everyday as well as of heroes, victors, kings and queens to explain, console and to offer hope through life's confusions, difficulties and pain. Individuals draw upon this collective experience which influences their lives, helps them to form values and so shape their own personal stories.

Children narrate stories to themselves from about 2 years of age (Fox, 1993, cited in Whitehead, 2004). Scholars have described developmental patterns in the ability to narrate, of which adult–child talk consisting of reminiscing to create a kind of oral portrait of and for the child is a crucial part. Engel (1995) suggests that the stories we listen to and tell shape who we are. The literature read to and shared with infants and pre-school children not only influences their ideas of the world, but impacts also on the patterns and structures of their language. In stories, children hear and become familiar with literary structures such as 'A long, long time ago there lived a very beautiful princess'. My grand-daughter began, at 3 years old, to live in a fantasy world fed by the stories she feasted upon several times a day. 'I am just like the boy in *The Snowman*' Imogen would comment as she put on her scarf and boots to go out into the cold. On another occasion at around the same age, she told me with authority 'the horses in the field are very soporific'. Beatrix Potter has much to answer for! Research evidence is showing that there is a close link between the ability to narrate orally and competence in story-writing two or three years later. The researchers suggest that the same fundamental skills of structuring and sequencing thoughts are usefully developed in both the oral telling and later writing of stories.

Learning and Teaching Suggestions: Story Boxes

Story boxes are collections of artefacts either associated with a well-known and loved picture book or reflecting a theme, for example, dinosaurs or a treasure island. These act as a powerful source of motivation and prompt for children to create or retell their own versions of stories. These story boxes are a rich resource for all children but especially those for whom English is an additional language or those who can benefit from additional opportunity to narrate orally.

Influences of school on spoken language

Once at school, children become involved with a wider social community which requires them to communicate and function with many different people for a variety of purposes. Literacy has greater and greater impact on spoken language development. Speech structures become more complex and literary influences are evident in the child's oral language patterns and vocabulary. The presence of more elaborate connectives becomes evident, as does the awareness of cause and effect when the child experiments with constructions such as 'What I think is …' followed by 'because …', and 'When I get round to it I will …'. Ambivalence and uncertainty are expressed with 'maybe', 'perhaps', and 'probably', and the passive voice is understood but probably not used. Vocabulary expands with the acquisition of technical and subject-specific words through the need to meet the linguistic demands of school-based learning as the pupil now has the opportunity to experience specialist areas of the curriculum.

Summary

In Chapter 2 we have discussed the key principles which facilitate the development of spoken language and how this is achieved through adults maintaining the 'semantic contingency' of the talk. Language and also learning in general can be promoted effectively in school through adopting a conversational approach, which occurs more commonly at home. The value of capitalizing on a conversational approach to support language development, learning and thinking have been considered. Recent research evidence suggests that, while it is relatively rare, the notion of 'sustained shared thinking' as the 'gold standard' form of the conversational approach is a particularly powerful way of supporting learning in early years settings and classrooms.

   Discussion has focused on the way that books prepare children for the literary language that they will meet when they learn to read and write, as well as broaden and deepen their ability to story and develop their linguistic expertise.

Further reading

Clay, M.M. (1998) *Different Paths to Literacy*. Oxford: Heinemann.

Palmer, S. and Bailey, R. (2004) *Foundations of Literacy*. Stafford: Network Educational Press.

Riley, J.L., Burrell, A. and McCallum, B. (2004) 'Developing the spoken language skills of reception class children in two multi-cultural, inner-city primary schools', *British Educational Research Journal*, 30(5): 657–72.

Siraj-Blatchford, I., Sylva, K., Muttock, S., Gilden, R. and Bell, D. (2002) *Researching Effective Pedagogy in the Early Years. Research Report 356*. REPEY Technical Paper. London: DfES.

Whitehead, M. (2004) *Language and Literacy in the Early Years*. London: Paul Chapman Publishing/Sage.

Chapter **3**

Developing an Understanding of Written Language

> There has been great interest in recent years in children as cognitive beings, children who selectively attend to aspects of their environments – seeing, searching, remembering, monitoring, correcting, validating and problem-solving – activities which build cognitive competencies ... Because of what we now know about oral language acquisition we have to accept that children can be active constructors of their own language competencies. Too often we adopt teaching strategies which proceed as if this were not true.
>
> (Clay, 1991: 61)

Introduction

In this chapter we consider the links between oracy and literacy and the similarities between the ways that children learn both language modes. Research interest, as Clay points out in the above quotation, has moved to focus on how children grow to understand written language through observing and being engaged with its use, as they did a year or two earlier with spoken language. Over the past two decades researchers have come to view literacy as a social practice, as Hall et al. state: 'As a social practice, literacy learning is mediated by language and accomplished in a context in which social actors position, and are positioned by each other in verbal, non-verbal, and textual interaction' (2003: xix).

Hall sums up this research perspective by asking:

But how was all this work impacting on the emergence of childhood literacy?

- It demonstrated clearly that literacy cannot be divorced from language as a whole, nor from its wider cultural context. Literacy is given meaning by the cultural discourses and practices in which it is embedded and young children are from birth witnesses to and participants in practices.

- In uncovering young children's literacy lives in families and communities it drew attention to how young children are learning to mean with a wider notion of literacy than previously considered, thus opening the way for later investigation of broader notions of authorship, young children's relationship with popular culture, and their involvement in the new technologies of communication.
- It has raised powerful questions about the relationship beween literacy as a social practice and literacy in schooling at a time when in many parts of the world the autonomous model of literacy was being increasingly privileged by governments. (Hall, 2003: 7)

Alongside this view of the way children acquire literacy, the work of Marsh and Millard (2000) has raised awareness of children's abiding fascination with their popular culture and the role it has as a strong motivator into literacy. They argue that schools often see themselves as providing children with access to 'high' culture through experience of the classics and books such as *Wind in the Willows* while neglecting the interest that children have in material prominent in their peer culture such as videos, Disneyworld-type merchandise and television programmes (Figure 3.1). The concept of 'popular culture' is changing as the term itself is a construct and includes a wide range of cultural objects.

There is evidence that children read material which is related to their popular cultural interests (Millard, 1997) and anecdotally we know children will find their favourite cereal packet from a cupboard, the TellyTubbies video in the stack, ponder over Angelina Ballerina cards and games and avidly read the text on the computer game. Marsh and Millard (2000) suggest that parents are much more willing to capitalize on the learning effected by such materials while teachers are more reluctant. Suffice it to say here that learning occurs in many situations, contexts and through a variety of means. Out-of-school literacy is the generic term for the myriad ways that children and young people use texts to fulfil their own purposes and satisfy their interests. They are broad, rich routes into their meaning-making.

Understandings and skills that underpin the literacy process

Spoken language

In Chapters 1 and 2 we have seen how children acquire a remarkable grasp of spoken language from birth, and through their pre-school years the experience of print both in the environment and stories adds another dimension to their ability to communicate orally as children become aware that speech has a written form. Bielby says 'Learning to read and write is parasitic upon learning to speak' (1999: 16). This is demonstrated through the relationship

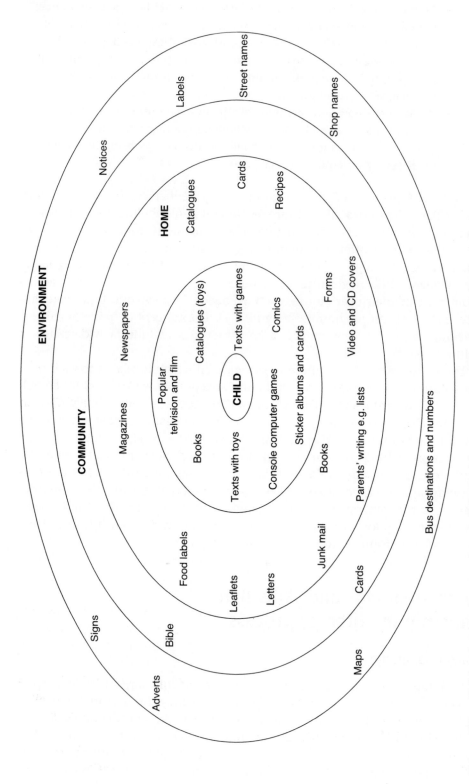

Figure 3.1 *Children's experiences of texts (adapted from Kenner, 2000, cited in Marsh, 2003)*

between learning to read and then coming to understand the way in which symbols represent speech. In addition, through the experience of literacy the child gains an explicit knowledge to add to her considerable implicit knowledge about language. This explicit knowledge about language is expressed as language about language (called **meta-language** – Clark, 1976) and includes the use of terms like 'word', 'sentence', 'phrase' and, with respect to writing, 'letter', 'capital letter' and 'full stop'.

Key Term

Meta-language: the technical term used to describe the properties of language. Thus, terms like 'sentence',' word' and 'morpheme' are meta-linguistic terms.

The level of this linguistic awareness is at both surface and deep structural levels. Through the development of spoken language and its primary focus on making meaning, structure (syntax) is nevertheless learnt. The awareness of the grammatical features or structure of language is accelerated as literacy is acquired. Fundamental understanding, also, of the sound system (or phonology) of spoken language and how it can be represented by letters and groups of letters has to be achieved next. This aspect of literacy learning will be considered in depth in Chapters 4 and 5. As Adams says;

> For purposes of learning to read and write ... sub-units [of language] must be dug out of their normal, sub-attentional status. Children must push their attention down from the level of comprehension at which it normally works. Not surprisingly, the deeper into the system they push the harder it is to do. Thus awareness of clauses or prepositions develops earlier and more easily than awareness of words. Awareness of words develops earlier and more easily than the awareness of syllables. An awareness of syllables develops earlier and more easily than the awareness of phonemes. (1996: 294–5)

As a result of attending early years settings and school, children's language develops and they learn to broaden their use of spoken language to accommodate new registers and functions with differing individuals in a variety of situations (Clay, 1991). Meanings become more precise and richer, vocabulary widens and sentence patterns become more complex. Children also become aware of constructions and literary conventions present in written language. They are exposed to complex structures particular to narrative discourse such as 'As I walked down the road, I noticed ...'.

Donaldson (1989) and Reid (1993) suggest ways in which the teaching of reading in the early years of schooling can capitalize on the learning that has occurred in the acquisition of speech. Reid describes these as bridges or links that can be established. They are described below.

Shared Reading

This idea has been formalized and used as one of the key approaches for the teaching of reading in the National Literacy Strategy, and will be discussed in greater detail in Chapter 6. The potential value of this activity of adult and child sharing books emanates from the research findings in the emergent literacy phase. The adult first provides the child with a **scaffold** of understanding through discussing the illustrations and the story, which enables the child to predict the situation and events of the story as a whole **(global context)**. Global context refers to the big picture or the overall sense of the story or passage. Three elements contribute to the context here. Two of the elements are local to the sentence: the emergence of the meaning within the single sentence and the developing grammar of the sentence. This is called **local context**. Thirdly, there is the wider context of the whole story: the context of everything that the child knows about life and pirates, for example, and about the structure, conventions and language of narrative.

Children are supported further by explicit and thorough knowledge of the **conventions of print**, if they have had the opportunity to become familiar with the literary language found in books. Adults share books in this way at home, and increasingly opportunities exist for books to be shared in school. This has proved to be valuable for pupils in the earliest stages of reading conventionally, and the use of enlarged texts enables teachers to adopt this approach with small and larger groups of children.

Key Terms

Scaffold: scaffolding is a metaphor to indicate the external support or cognitive help an adult can give children while they are internally constructing or developing schemas or concepts.

Global context: refers to the 'big picture' of the text. If a child is reading a story and is unable to decode a word, an understanding of the context may help to predict or guess the word. This is only one of the strategies available to the reader but nevertheless it is usually the first drawn upon.

Local context: refers to the elements that are local to the sentence – the emerging meaning within the sentence and its developing grammar.

Conventions of print: refers to the way written language and print (in our case English) is structured and organized, that is, words are separated from each other by spaces; print runs from left to right, sweeping back at the end of the line; print usually runs from top to bottom of the page, and so on.

Helping children to produce written language

Adults can help children to be part of the writing process, through their collaboration in the encoding of speech, by writing for the children and making books with them. The use of commercially produced materials to facilitate writing, such as *Breakthrough to Literacy*, (Mackay et al., 1970) can also be of great benefit. Pre-written words that can be selected and formed into sentences, short circuits the grapho-motor abilities of the very young child to make more smooth the link from thought to speech to print. Important understandings regarding the nature of a word as a unit of meaning, and letters as a representation of sounds, can be reinforced helpfully.

Use of print embedded in the environment

Children in the **logographic** stage of print processing (see Chapter 4) are able to recognize 'McDonald's and 'Weetabix' logos in context, through operating in a print-filled environment. At this stage, which begins typically before school, children begin to recognize familiar words as wholes or logograms without any notion of the alphabetic nature of their composition. In other words, they recognize words which are salient and interesting to them (their own name, Cadbury and Lego) without realizing as yet that the individual letters have a sound value.

Reid suggests that teaching in schools should take greater advantage of this developing skill and use print in an embedded form to maximum benefit, in the way that has been so supportive to children in their pre-school encounters with print. Use can be made in the setting or classroom of labels on packaging and storage containers, video titles, birthday cards, notices in work areas (for example, 'Only 4 children may play in the sand'), name lists and wall displays as a reading resource.

Key Term

Logographic: a term which designates the earliest stage of sight-recognition words.

A cross-curricular planning framework for literacy in the Foundation Stage

A learning environment

A learning environment which promotes literacy will also be supportive of the development of oracy. As has been discussed earlier, almost all children have acquired a competence in language with a wide vocabulary and have learned how to use a complex system of grammar before entry into mainstream school.

More importantly, they have engaged in the problem-solving, intellectual task of shaping language to express their own thinking.

Spoken language enables children to make sense of their experience and to communicate this to others. Talk will underpin all the purposeful activities in the setting and classroom. By the end of the reception year, written language increasingly supports intellectual development and extends understanding of the world and people. Therefore, it is essential that the early years practitioner or teacher views oracy and literacy as interrelated. He or she has the potential to offer rich experience, activity and stimulation that promotes the talk and discussion from which reading and writing will arise. Play is the vehicle through which much enabling language practice occurs in the Foundation Stage, and play can continue to be exploited as pupils move into KS 1.

Play is a vast and complex topic, and there are many different types of play. The following example is of a child engaged in solitary play through which she rehearses her own life experience, her own story.

Case Study 3.1

The child talks to her toys about past events and goes over what has happened in different ways of explaining and telling:

'This is my mummy house, my daddy house,
my Billy house, my granny house,
Houses, houses, houses, his houses,
and mummy goes to work and Billy ...'

For all that seems inconsequential, this early talk is by no means random. It performs many functions in children's language learning, but its relevance here is that it is storytelling, the beginning of knowing how to narrate. (Meek, 1982: 33)

Learning and Teaching Suggestions

What might a teacher want to discuss with the child if she observed such 'storying' occurring? What kind of supportive or modelling of language could the adult sensitively offer? Can you identify any occasions when you have observed children narrate in this way? What play materials are particularly valuable to promote this kind of language work?

The early years practitioner or teacher will harness the children's motivation to play, to talk, to story and to make-believe by providing many inviting opportunities to do so in the setting or classroom. The home corner can be converted into any of the current interests of the group to become a castle, a hospital, a post office, a Chinese restaurant, a travel agency, a bookshop, a hairdressing salon, a veterinary clinic or whatever else will stimulate engagement, fantasy, language and literacy. This provision allows children to enhance their language in order to play, and enhance their play in order to extend their language. Frequently, children will want to use writing and print in their play.

The benefits to a teacher of a well-organized setting or classroom are obvious, but the benefits to literacy learning perhaps need to be made explicit. Language is greatly enhanced, as indeed is all learning, by a setting or classroom with an organizational system that develops the autonomy of the children. This principle refers to the physical organization of furniture, materials and resources, and the way that the learning of the children is managed, for example providing opportunities for pupils to choose activities, and also to justify their choices. Two obvious benefits occur from a considered and well-managed classroom. The pupils' growth in confidence, independence and self-reliance is a valuable attribute when learning to read and write. This self-reliance also provides the practitioner or teacher with the time and opportunity to talk with children one to one, to observe and record literacy behaviours and thus to cater for individual differences.

A rich learning environment provides opportunities for children to express their ideas in a variety of ways. Successful settings and classrooms will share most of the following characteristics:

- attractive and inviting play areas designed with an emphasis on spoken and written language in mind
- furniture that is arranged to facilitate many organizational situations along with storage for materials that are clearly labelled
- well-maintained and well-equipped book area with a supply of high-quality children's literature and poetry (and possibly non-fiction if this is not stored centrally in the school library)
- a plentiful supply of high-quality reading books representing three different categories:

  - enlarged texts are crucial at Nursery and Reception levels for Shared Reading
  - individual reading books from a variety of commercial schemes to cover a wide range of interest. These should provide structure and progression in sufficiently small steps to support and allow consolidation for all levels of reading ability. Storage needs to be logical, clear and accessible to all the adults (that is, stored by the level of difficulty of the texts; see Book Bands colour-coded system in Chapter 7)
  - multiple copies of key reading books are essential for group reading (or Guided Reading as the NLS has named the approach; see Chapter 7 for a fuller description)

- an inviting, comfortable book corner
- a well-supplied writing area where children can express thoughts, feelings and ideas

- labels and notices that are at the appropriate height for the children and demonstrate a high standard of printing in order to provide a good model of typeface
- a variety of class-made books that are easily accessible
- use of information technology (IT) electronic, audio/visual equipment that is accessible and that the children are able to use, for example, language masters, audio-cassette recorders
- appropriate computers with concept keyboards and other appropriate software for literacy development including technology-assisted books and resources, for example, LeapFrog (see Chapter 11)
- reading support materials (including a variety of puzzles and games that encourage word play and specific focus on print) are ordered and accessible to the pupils
- a range of dictionaries, thesauruses and directories are available
- wall displays and charts that promote reading and discussion are placed where children can see them, including alphabet friezes
- a listening area with stories available on tape, plus puppet theatre, story boxes and storyboards for mini-dramatization (especially important for pupils with language delay and for whom English is an additional language)
- word banks of topic and high frequency keywords (see Primary National Strategy: Framework for teaching literacy, DfES, 2006)

The language experience approach

This approach is the time-honoured favourite used by most early years practitioners and teachers. It capitalizes on the current interests and activities of the children in order to record their experiences and spoken language by writing and drawing for themselves and others. Adults using this approach are able to demonstrate the word-by-word conversion of speech into written language (the encoding) as the child dictates. The approach is a powerful one, the process is as follows:

- The child is given an opportunity to have an ... *experience.*
- The adult encourages discussion and supports the translation of thought into ... *spoken language.*
- The adult writes the transcription of the talk ... *encoded into written language.*
- The adult reads the written text back to child ... *decoded by reading.*
- The child rereads the text ... *rereading.*

The power of the literacy learning in the language experience approach derives from the interest children have in the content and the written language that is generated by them and for them. An additional boost to the learning is that written language is in the natural speech patterns of the child. In the language experience approach the adult scaffolds both the encoding of the text and then its decoding, in carefully judged juxtaposition, to promote context-embedded learning. The writing of the short, learner-generated text is followed by a reading and rereading of the text, each process complementing and reinforcing the other.

A selection of the day-to-day class occurrences can be recorded and used as the talking, reading and writing focus of the day, whether it is the class topic or project, a visit to a place of interest, a visitor to the class, a science experiment, biscuits baked, or the arrival of a new baby – the possiblities are endless. The text can reflect the thoughts of the children or others, the recounting of a happening in the genre of journalism or the retelling of a favourite story using the appropriate literary language of the chosen narrative.

The resulting product could take the form of a letter, a note, a carefully considered, well-designed class-made book, or a large wall story to accompany a picture or model.

The practitioner's or teacher's role in the language experience approach

The practitioner or teacher needs to be aware of the individual stages of the children as learners and to support and extend both their spoken and written language as appropriate. She/he also needs to make explicit the links between reading and writing in order to effect the bridge that is so important for successful literacy development (Reid, 1993). For this reason the language experience approach has been embraced enthusiastically by early years teachers because it encompasses the support and reinforcement for all the interrelated aspects of the literacy process. With this approach to the teaching of reading and writing, the decoding of the child's own words makes the literacy task especially meaningful and memorable, particularly in the earliest stages of reading; prediction (that is, the ability to read a word through using global and local context) is made easier because the text has been initially generated by the child and so comprehension is unlikely to present difficulties. Working with children as they generate text enables explicit demonstration of sound–symbol relationships, letter by letter as the words are written (encoded). The quality of the child's language will be determined by the stimulus of the experience and the way in which it is discussed and developed into learning activities. This way of working with children mimics the parent at home by asking open questions, encouraging the child to reflect and comment further, to hypothesize and, most importantly,' to share enjoyment and a sense of wonder. It begins with the child and what she is interested in and by extending her understanding. As Clay says:

> When we try to provide experiences … we must go beyond the usual bounds of spontaneous learning in a free play situation or group learning from one teacher. The child's spontaneous wish to communicate about something which interests him at one particular moment should have priority and he must have adults who will talk with him, in simple, varied and grammatical language. We should

arrange for language producing activities where adult and child must communicate to co-operate. (1979: 53–4)

It follows, then, for the practitioner or teacher to work with that spoken communication and transform the child's words into the permanent record of a text.

The value of literacy in developing thinking

Learning to read and write both depends upon children's existing (oral) language skills and extends them. Literacy extends children's language and thinking not only by opening up new sources of knowledge, but also by its nature. It does this in two ways. First, in speech, meaning is often implicit, depending on the speaker and listener sharing a situation. For example, in giving instructions, a speaker may say, 'Look, you do it like this'. The meaning is 'embedded' in the ongoing situation. But instructions given in writing need to be much more explicit and organized. In its written form, language is 'disembedded' from the immediate situation, creating its own explicit, language-dependent, conceptual world (as when you are engrossed in a novel). Secondly, in its written form, language itself more readily becomes an object of perception in ways that develop reflectivity: it can be seen, reviewed and inspected. So not only does literacy develop understanding of a real or imagined world, it also enables individuals to consider language itself as it becomes separated and disembedded from a context.

Summary

In this chapter we have considered how young children build on their considerable competence in spoken language to learn to read and write. They do this through living in a world with parents, carers and older siblings who use texts and print for a vast range of purposes, and who intuitively involve the pre-schoolers in this meaning-making.

Further reading

Weinberger, J. (1996) *Literacy Goes to School: The Parents' Role in Young Children's Literacy Learning*. London: Paul Chapman Publishing.

Cairney, T. (2003) 'Literacy within family life', in N. Hall, J. Larson and J. Marsh (eds), *Handbook of Early Childhood Literacy*. London: Sage.

Lancaster, L. (2003) 'Moving into literacy: how it all begins', in N. Hall, J. Larson and J. Marsh (eds), *Handbook of Early Childhood Literacy*. London: Sage.

Chapter **4**

The Emergent Phase of Literacy

It is less obvious but equally true that learning to read is also a social activity. Long before there is any 'story' to consider, children's early experiences with picture books set the stage for the activity of reading. During these interactions, children learn about the mechanics of reading (how to turn the pages and proceed through a book), the pleasures of reading (curling up with a parent in a quiet space), and the interest of reading (the story or talk that goes on around the book).

(Bialystok, 2001: 158)

It is absurd to imagine that four-and five-year-old children growing up in an urban environment that displays print everywhere (on toys, on billboards and road signs, on their clothes, on TV) do not develop any ideas about this cultural object until they find themselves sitting before a teacher.

(Ferreiro and Teberosky, 1982: 12)

Introduction

The first part of this volume (Chapters 1 to 3) considered in depth how young children learn that spoken language is about communicating meaning and then realize, over time and through experiences with print, that written language is the permanent equivalent of speech. Children learn how to make literacy their own reinvention, in similar ways that they previously learned to do with spoken language. Through literacy children are able to reconstruct the world for themselves. First there occurs a fundamental and global understanding at a conceptual level or 'the big picture' (Purcell-Gates, 1996) about the purpose of written language, which precedes the finer-grained and multi-layered insights regarding conventions of print and the meta-language that accompanies them. Later still, the reader comes to appreciate the nature and function of the symbols in an alphabetic system. These complex strands have to be unravelled gradually, in personally purposeful situations, and in sympathy with Vygotsky's belief that 'Literacy is not a unitary construct' (1978).

Emergent literacy – not pre-reading

This notion of a slow initiation into text and print has led to the use of the term 'emergent literacy'. It was devised by Marie Clay in 1966, and has replacing an earlier notion of a state of 'pre-reading', and is the term now used to describe 'the reading and writing behaviours that precede and develop into conventional literacy' (Sulzby, 1989: 84). Emergent literacy describes the journey from a very primitive starting point of looking at, and responding to, for example, nursery images in a board booklet in the 'Baby's first picture book' category. This level of understanding is followed by the recognition of recurring signs in environmental print, such as a supermarket logo (and beginning to make connections between both the logo on the building and the one on the carrier bag). This leads on to the awareness of alphabet symbols as repeated shapes in names, in books, on a frieze, on greetings cards, on the television, and when playing games and puzzles, and finally through to fully fluent reading of whole text in story books. Evidence from a wealth of research undertaken mainly through an ethnographic methodology (that is, data collected through in-depth observation and case studies) has informed researchers and early years practitioners and teachers of the many idiosyncratic twists and turns on this journey.

A great deal is now known about children's competence as they begin to understand:

- the links between speech and writing
- the unchanging nature of print
- its communicative function and its conventions.

Importantly, in direct consequence of these research findings through the 1980s, development in reading and writing began increasingly to be viewed as the complementary processes of literacy. This work has far-reaching implications for practice in early years settings and classrooms.

How do pre-school children acquire these understandings?

As Goodman (1980) claims, the 'roots of literacy' awareness develop through living in a world of story books, letters, lists and printed materials, and are the beginning of the child's fascination with print. The prime understanding that young children, acquire gradually from 6 months of age to approximately 5 or 6 years of age, is that print has a communicative function (Ferreiro and Teberosky, 1982; Goodman, Y.M., 1980). The child grows to understand the purpose of print in a personal and context-embedded way: typically through birthday cards, McDonald's signs and biscuit packets (McGee et al., 1988, as cited in Sulzby and Teale, 1991).

The sharing of story and picture books has received the most attention from researchers, which is not surprising, as it is most commonly children's main and most sustained and enjoyable literacy experience prior to mainstream school and the formal task of learning to read. The benefits of reading stories as a socially created, interactive activity (Heath, 1982) are now clear. The young child's independent but as yet not conventional reading of books grows out of shared interactive reading with a facilitative adult providing a scaffold to her literacy development (Sulzby, 1989). Wells (1985, 1988) found a strong positive relationship between the number of stories shared with pre-school children and their later success in reading throughout the primary and secondary school.

Two important features of this work

Two features of this body of work on the emergent literacy phase observation have particular relevance for early years teachers. First, the research findings view children as active contributors to their own learning. The meaning-maker of spoken language is at work here also. This learner-centred view of the pre-school reader and writer is greatly influenced by Piaget, Bruner and Chomsky, each of whom see children as being constructive, hypothesis-testing, rule-generating agents in their own learning. This stance has been emphasized extensively in Chapters 1 and 2.

Secondly, the studies cited highlight the role of the supportive, interested, interactive and experienced language user, who scaffolds the child's learning in order that further progress can be made. These two crucial aspects of literacy learning have implications for the later phases of development as a reader and a writer. The child has mastered an important lesson about how to learn, both about and through, spoken and written language. Teachers need not only to note the ways that such valuable learning has occurred but also to appreciate *what* has been learned in order to build appropriately on these highly individual foundations.

What the child has learned about literacy before pre-school

If we begin from the point of entry to reception class, it appears that the most essential (and hopefully commonplace) lessons about literacy that the young child can achieve before school are that:

- reading is both a pleasurable and useful activity
- print has a communicative function
- written scripts have a set of rules and conventions that need to be adhered to
- text has a meta-language with which it is necessary to become acquainted (a set of terms used to describe aspects and functions of print, for example, letter, word, sentence, beginning, end, full stop, comma).

The research literature into emergent literacy indicates that there are three main types of experience which lead to the print-related achievements above:

- home literacy experience
- story-book experience
- teaching by parents and carers.

Home literacy experience

It is within the home environment that young children have the opportunity to develop most fruitfully their understandings of literacy. The learners are able to practise the language systems, both spoken and written, through interactions with others in a personal, secure and very specific cultural context. Gee (1992) refers to this as the **situated dialogue** of the **cultural practice** in the home community. By this is meant that children begin to learn about reading and writing in their homes and within their communities through observing and participating in culturally situated literacy practices (Ferreiro and Teberosky, 1982). This seminal work has been built upon and refined by Purcell-Gates (1996) in order to clarify the nature of the different emphases placed by various communities on particular literacy practices. It is recognized that literacy practices differ between communities in a variety of sociocultural dimensions and it is known that the child's pre-school and deeply personal experience profoundly influences success at school (Dyson, 1989; Riley, 1995a, 1995b).

Key Terms

Situated dialogue: dialogue that is 'embedded' and given meaning by its context in a shared situation, for example, 'Don't!' More widely, dialogue embedded in life-style and value system.

Cultural practice: value embued activities and situations characteristic of a cultural or sub-cultural life-style, for example, the birthday party, the stag night, the dinner party, the bedtime story.

Research into pre-school home literacy experiences

Once at school, concern about the wide range in the levels of success experienced by children of various socio-economic groups has fuelled recent research projects. Several studies from the USA have documented that while literacy is integral to the lives of both high and lower socio-economic groups, the experiences and therefore what the children make of them differ. As a group, pupils from lower-income families continue to achieve lower levels of literacy skills once at school than children from higher-income groups. It has been assumed by the research community, that one of the most salient factors causing this differential in success is associated with the range of educational levels of the parents. This in turn, it is suggested, affects the nature and complexity of the literacy activities at home to which the children are party.

Teale remarked that the findings '... should prompt a reconsideration of traditional wisdom which has it that children from low-SES [socio-economic status] backgrounds come to school with a dearth of literacy experiences' (1986: 192). Taylor and Dorsey-Gaines (1988) conducted an ethnographic study into the lives of five low-SES families whose children were successful in school. These children were observed participating in story and Bible reading events, they saw their parents reading newspapers, magazines and writing to various social service agencies and to schools.

Investigations of the types of literacy experienced by the child

Further studies have attempted to separate the dimensions of the home literacy environment and to quantify the ways in which they influence the child's knowledge about written language. The three identified dimensions of literacy experiences participated in by children in their home environments were:

- interacting with adults in writing and reading situations
- exploring print on their own
- observing adults modelling literate behaviours (for example, reading instructions/writing lists).

After many hours of detailed observation in the homes of lower SES families, completing a **data narrative** or description, the presence of varied literacy activities were indeed confirmed by the Purcell-Gates (1996) study. The types of literacy events that the children were likely to participate in or to witness were systematically coded. These categories covered aspects such as literacy connected with:

- *daily living routines*, for example, shopping, cooking, paying bills and so on
- *entertainment*, for example, reading a novel, doing a crossword, reading a television programme schedule, reading rules for a game
- *school-related activity*, for example, letters from school to home, homework, playing school
- *work*, for example, literacy used in order to secure or maintain a job
- *religion*, for example, Bible reading or study, Sunday School activities
- *interpersonal communication*, for example, sending cards, writing and reading letters and story reading.

In addition, the texts used by the adults were analysed for the linguistic complexity at vocabulary, sentence and clause levels.

Key Term

Data narrative: diary, coding and recording behaviours of subjects.

Purcell-Gates found that there was considerable variation in the quality of the print experiences to which the children were exposed and this she attributed to different levels of the **functional literacy** present in the 20 families studied which was clearly related, as was suggested earlier, to the educational status of the adults.

Key Term

Functional literacy: the level of literacy needed to operate reasonably effectively in a literate society.

The adult competence in literacy ranged from low literate ($n = 3$) to functionally literate ($n = 17$). These levels of competence were estimated in the study through the application of a broad definition of functional literacy as being the: 'possession of, or access to, the competencies and information required to accomplish transactions entailing reading and writing [in] which an individual wishes or is compelled to engage' (Kintgen et al., 1988: 263).

Then the study, using an innovative methodology, linked the home literacy experiences of children to their knowledge of written language in an attempt to unravel the connections between pre-school experience and success with literacy at school.

In the lower SES families the most frequently observed print event was literacy being used in the domains of entertainment and daily living routines. These rich data make compulsive reading as the fabric of the families and their daily existence emerges from the journal pages. Purcell-Gates says:

> Pre-schoolers whose home lives included more instances of people reading and writing texts at the more written level of discourse demonstrated more conventional concepts of writing as a system and Concepts about Print. They also showed a higher degree of knowledge of written register the more their parents

read to them. Children's storybook text was considered the most complex text for this study. Kindergarten and first grade children who experienced people in their home and community lives reading and writing at the most written level of discourse also demonstrated a more advanced understanding of writing as a system. (1996: 423)

It would seem that homes at all levels of socio-economic status and education offer many and varied opportunities for children to develop understanding about spoken and written language. What appears to differ is the quality of the encounters and the extent to which they are capitalized upon by the adults. It is not productive, therefore for early years practitioners and primary teachers to make professional judgements about the ways in which pupils will approach the task of literacy once at school, on the basis of socio-economic status and the educational level of parents. Much depends upon the children's **transactional stance** to learning, that is, their ability to make sense of the learning opportunities offered by school and the extent to which it builds on the home experience. This in turn is affected by the practitioner's or teacher's ability to assess the child's prior knowledge at school entry and thus to be able to provide well-matched learning activities.

The development of this issue will be addressed later in this chapter.

Key Term

Transactional stance: attitude and approach, preparedness and receptivity to the task.

Storybook reading and parent teaching

A Canadian study (Senechal et al., 1998) attempted both to quantify and differentiate between the particular contributions that the reading of stories, and the direct teaching of pre-school children, make to the level of success at school with oral and written language skills. This is currently a much debated area in the field of research into emergent literacy in North America. It reduces down to the relative importance of young children's understanding of 'the big picture' about literacy and their grasp of the alphabetic principle. This, in turn, is a more recent and focused version of the 'whole language' versus 'phonics' debate that has raged, in a counter-productive manner, through at least two decades of literacy research on both sides of the Atlantic. Also, on a note of caution, much depends, as always, on the research design for such studies. The results are dependent upon the nature of the outcomes to be measured, both at the conceptual level of the outcomes being investigated and the assessments used to measure the outcomes. However, these studies do have important implications for early years practitioners and teachers.

In summary, the findings from other studies and the following are that

> parents distinguish between two different kinds of experiences with print at home. Some experiences provide more informal or implicit interactions with print such as when parents read to the child. In this kind of experience, children are exposed to written language, but print per se is not the focus of interactions. Other experiences provide more formal or explicit interactions with print such as when parents teach about reading and writing words and letters. (Senechal et al., 1998: 109)

The distinction between the informal and the formal, it would seem, is whether the focus of the experience offered to the child is on the message contained *in* the print or *about* the print itself. The analyses of the data from the Senechal et al. (1998) study indicate that the different kinds of literacy experiences are related to the development of different kinds of literacy-related skills, perhaps not surprisingly. There is a need for further research to be conducted with greater numbers of children across the socio-economic continuum, but at a basic level this work is revealing to practitioners and teachers that children learn from the experiences they are exposed to and from what they are taught. Educationalists need to be clear about what is important in order to advise parents appropriately.

It would seem wise to suggest that young children are given broad, balanced and meaningful experiences with written language in order that they can be successful at school. They need, as stated earlier, to become aware of the purpose of print and its rules and conventions in meaningful and contextually rich situations.

The nature of these understandings when beginning mainstream school prepares the way for a successful start to conventional reading.

The beginning of conventional reading

The precise point at which the reader moves from emergent literacy into beginning conventional reading is not clear-cut. Sulzby (1992) defines this transition point as being when the child is able to use three aspects of reading in a flexible and co-ordinated way, they are:

- letter-sound knowledge
- the concept of a word
- comprehension.

Sulzby states that the transition point is blurred, as the child's imperfect understanding regresses and advances through many print encounters before finally moving into print processing in a conventional way.

For a detailed explanation of the developmental path of fluent reading, it is necessary to draw upon experimental psychology to shed light on young children's print-processing abilities as they enter the phase of beginning reading. These developing abilities have been described by several researchers as phases or stages during which the child learns to process the print in *qualitatively* different ways. Frith (1985) and Ehri (1995) propose a phase theory of progressively more refined print-processing abilities of the beginner reader. These theories are compared and discussed fully in Chapter 5.

Research evidence on the nature of children's knowledge of the alphabet

A study of literacy development that followed 191 reception children through the first year of school has shed light on the way in which the child gets to grips with the complexity of the task of reading, and how teachers can have insight into the print-processing abilities of the new pupil (Riley, 1994, 1995a, 1996). This research project provides further important evidence to indicate the value of the young readers' refined print awareness shown in the ability both to identify and label letters of the alphabet and to write their own name before formal instruction begins at school.

The three literacy-related skills, concepts about print, the ability to write her/his own name, and the ability to identify and label the letters of the alphabet, assessed by the researchers in the September, were all shown to be positively related to the ability to read in the following July. But by far the most powerful predictor of later success in reading was the child's knowledge of the alphabet, acquired pre-school, incidentally and informally.

This work adds considerable weight to the body of evidence that recognizes that speedy word processing is essential for progress in reading, the first stage of which is an understanding of the alphabet system. A recognition of the individual letters along with an ability to hear the sounds in words are the first steps in the development of the orthographic (print) and phonological (sound) processing capability essential in the literacy task.

The importance of capitalizing on what children know at school entry

We have discussed how children come to school with different types of literacy-related knowledge acquired through a variety of experiences in their homes and communities; it is argued therefore that teachers need to be aware of those understandings. But why exactly does it seem crucial for reception teachers to harness this hard-won pre-school knowledge as quickly and effectively as possible?

The most striking reason is that there is robust longitudinal evidence that reveals the long-term benefits of an effective early start to mainstream school. The earliest study to point to the first year of school as being of special importance is American and nearly 20 years old (Pederson et al., 1978). These researchers found that a group of children who had been taught by a particular first-grade teacher, 'Miss A', seemed to have been given an initial boost to their education that gave an advantage to these children throughout the rest of their school lives. The research methodology was an unusual and retrospective one. The researchers used the school annual report cards to track the academic progress of the groups of children in 'Miss A's' school (that is, the annual scores over many years, of all the classes from entry in elementary/primary through to exit from high (secondary) school). It seemed that this exceptional teacher achieved results with her pupils in early literacy and numeracy far beyond those of her colleagues with parallel and comparable intakes.

Large-scale longitudinal studies

More recent evidence comes from the findings of the Infant School Study (Tizard et al., 1988). This interesting project followed a cohort of children in 33 Inner London schools from the end of nursery through to the end of infant school. The main aim was to investigate the progress of children in order to explain the reasons for their differing rates of educational achievement. The most important finding is that it was only in the reception year that certain classes made statistically significant greater rates of progress than others. Also, the project showed that those children who had made the greatest amount of progress in reception remained the highest achievers all through infant school.

As Tizard says, 'We had evidence that the reception year has a particularly large effect on progress' (1993: 80). Tizard et al. followed up part of the sample of children at the end of primary school (at 11 years old) and the rank order of the children's scores had not changed. So, over seven years of primary school an early positive start appears to be important.

Another influential study, a junior school project (Mortimore et al., 1988.), confirms this research finding. This parallel project explored the organization and the teaching and learning processes of Years 3, 4, 5 and 6 (or ages 7–11). Among many other important findings, Mortimore et al. found that the rank order of children's test scores remained constant over the four years. In other words, how well the children were doing at the start of junior school predicted powerfully how well they would be doing at 11 years of age. This once again confirms the benefit of a successful, early start to school. These children were followed up to the end of secondary school (Sammons et al., 1994). The pupils who had been the highest achievers at the end of primary school were those who gained the best GCSE results. We know from the large body of research into school effectiveness, that school *can* make a difference to children's academic progress. It is suggested, also, that a positive start is especially important if an educational career is to be successful. Learning to read early and fluently will be a crucial part of that valuable beginning.

Studies that focused on the reception year of school

An explanation as to why it is the first year that is quite so important has begun to emerge. Two studies exploring the teaching and learning processes in the reception year of school have complemented each other in a fruitful way that adds to our understanding. Aubrey (1993) and, the work mentioned before (Riley, 1994) point to the fact that the new pupil brings a rich store of knowledge and skills to the task of learning mathematics (Aubrey, 1993) and acquiring literacy (Riley, 1995a) in school. Children have learned a great deal through their experience of living in a world operating with a number rule system and surrounded by print; both these studies show that the challenge to the reception teacher is to assess each child's stage of development in order to build on this and to enable further progress to occur.

Each study complements the findings of the other well. As Aubrey writes, 'While they may not possess the formal conventions for representing it, reception age children clearly enter school having acquired already much mathematical content' (1993: 26).

Riley found wide-ranging disparity in literacy development: some children were functioning, at school entry, at the level of a 3-year-old with only the haziest understanding of how books and print work, while other pupils were well on the road to beginning reading. Some of the teachers were aware of the differences in their new entrants and sought to design reading programmes that precisely matched the development. Other reception class teachers used a 'scatter gun' approach and randomly tried a variety of methods in the fond hope that 'something must work'.

The pupils who made the most progress during their first year of school were taught by experienced reception class teachers who were knowledgeable about literacy and able to match closely their teaching to the child's prior and developing competence (Riley, 1996). Aubrey had similar findings in her study regarding the children's progress in mathematics.

Implications for practice

Fisher says:

> [C]hildren starting school are already successful and active learners who bring considerable knowledge and experience to the task of literacy learning. Children learn best when they are able to relate what they are doing to their own experience. They also learn most successfully when the learning takes place within a social context, particularly from interaction with a caring adult or more experienced child. Home is a good place to learn and, although homes vary, there is much to be learned from the way the child has learned in the home. (1992: 36)

The essential role of assessment at school entry

As earlier discussion has revealed, early years educators working with young children need to be skilled practitioners capable of diagnostic assessment of their pupils' early literacy learning. At best they mimic the role of the parent or carer, who has facilitated so much valuable literacy progress before pre-school.

This information gathered at school entry for baseline assessment enables meaningful comparison to be made with attainment, as measured by the National Curriculum tasks and tests, at the end of Key Stage 1. Increasing accountability is required from schools, and evidence of effective teaching is sought by inspectors and governing bodies.

However, the main purpose of assessing the pupil on arrival at school is to provide insight into the child's abilities and understandings in order usefully to inform planning and teaching.

Information that the class teacher needs to record

General information on the child

Some of this information will be noted at school entry and updated as appropriate, with any progress recorded also. It is suggested that the following details are kept on individual children if they are not included in the current local education authority (LEA) 'Baseline assessment' data expectations.

- Relevant admission data including number of siblings, child's place in the family, and so on (it is especially important for bilingual children whose parents are not fluent English speakers, that the school needs to know if there are older English-speaking siblings who can help with literacy).
- Pre-school experience regarding length of attendance at nursery or playgroup.
- Relevant information about attitudes, concerns and expectations of parents or carers resulting from discussion with them.
- Relevant medical information regarding hearing, sight, and general health.
- Level of general physical and social development.
- Evidence of the level of the children's self-esteem and confidence.
- Ability to care for themselves regarding dressing, toileting, and so on.
- Evidence of children's level of adjustment to the class/school setting including their ability to integrate with peers.

Aspects of children's intellectual functioning

- Relevant information gathered from observing children at play in structured and unstructured activities.
- Children's ability to concentrate for periods of time at a task.
- Children's ability to represent the world and themselves (for example, draw themselves)
- The colours known.
- The numbers known (are letters and numbers confused?).
- The nursery rhymes known.

The assessment of children's spoken language

- Whether English is the first or additional language (and, if English is the additional language, the details of the home language/s; is the home language spoken at home solely or in addition to English? The level of the English fluency of parents/carers).
- The level of confidence when communicating with adults or peers.
- The ability to respond to questions, directions and requests.
- The ability to communicate needs, ideas and feelings.
- The ability to listen to stories and explanations.

The assessment of children's understanding of written language, its purpose and conventions

Concepts about print

- Do children demonstrate an awareness that signs and labels communicate a message (that is, show awareness of pupils' name labels, labels on boxes and equipment, signs in the home corner and so on)?
- When sharing a book, do children indicate understanding:

  - that the story starts at the front of the book
  - of the terms 'front' and 'back'
  - that the print tells the story
  - where the print starts, and which way it goes
  - the convention of the 'sweep back' (that is, the place of the next word at the end of a line)
  - of the meta-language of print – word/letter/sentence/full-stop
  - that within a word there are individual letters?

Print awareness is demonstrated by:

- the number of letters (by either name or sound, upper or lower case) of the alphabet that can be recognized and identified
- the ability to use some written marks in order to express themselves and to communicate.

Sound awareness is demonstrated by:

- the ability to hear *very* distinctly different words, that is, sat/chat/fat/Jane
- the ability to detect words that rhyme from non-rhyming words, for example, m -*at*/h-*at*/c-*at*/r-*ap*.
- the ability to detect words with the same onset, for example, *m* – an/*m* – at/ *m* – ap/*c* – an.

Positive attitudes to books and literacy are demonstrated by:

- voluntarily looking at books with enjoyment
- spontaneously writing notes, messages and stories
- enjoying and listening to stories read
- valuing and caring for books (developed from Riley, 1996).

The above lists convey suggestions of observations to be carried out and recorded by the class teacher on the reception child. Levels of functioning on arrival at school (or at a predetermined period soon after arrival) provide evidence of any specific needs regarding the provision for literacy teaching. In addition, these assessments will enable the reception teacher to provide appropriate experiences and opportunities within her/his class and the information will enable appropriate organization and grouping of the pupils.

Summary

In this chapter we have discussed:

- how the young pre-school child gradually becomes aware of the purpose and conventions of print and text
- that different children have had a variety of opportunities and a range of experiences with written language before coming to school
- how important it is for the reception teacher to be aware of each pupil's stage of literacy development in order to be able to support progress well.

This chapter has considered the understandings about literacy that are acquired by the pre-school child, and their importance for learning to read and write once at school. Research evidence suggests that not only are great strides made by the child in the emergent literacy phase, but that this knowledge contributes hugely towards success once at school. The importance of the role of the teacher has been discussed in how to assess this informal and personal knowledge in order that it can be capitalized upon.

Further reading

Neuman, S.B. and Roskos, K.A (1993) *Language and Literacy Learning in the Early Years: An Integrated Approach.* New York: Holt, Rhinehart and Winston.

Riley, J.L. (1996) *The Teaching of Reading: The Development of Literacy in the Early Years of School.* London: Paul Chapman Publishing.

Tizard, B. (1993). 'Early influences on literacy' in R. Beard (ed.), *Teaching Literacy Balancing Perspectives.* London, Sydney and Auckland: Hodder and Stoughton.

Chapter **5**

Learning to Read and Write: Print and Sound Awareness

[R]esearch indicates that the skilful reader's remarkable ability to recognise printed words derives from a deep and ready knowledge of their composite sequences of letters along with the connections of those spellings to speech and meaning.

(Adams, 1993: 207)

Introduction

In the above quotation, Adams is calling upon the huge body of research evidence that redresses the balance of the much quoted, but now discredited, claim that reading is a 'psycholinguistic guessing game' (Goodman, 1976). It is not, unfortunately and quite evidently, as straight forward as that. We have seen from the previous chapter that this 'top-down' processing or meaning making is an important part of the literacy process but there is a crucial and complementary aspect that the child has to get to grips with.

The Independent Review of the Teaching of Early Reading in the UK (The Rose Report) affirms Adams's statement and says:

It is widely agreed that reading involves far more than decoding words on the page. Nevertheless, words must be decoded if readers are to make sense of the text. Phonic work is therefore a necessary but not sufficient part of the wider knowledge, skills and understanding which children need to become skilled readers and writers, capable of comprehending and composing text. (DfES, 2006: 4)

The way in which spoken and written language are learned

There are similarities between the acquisition of both spoken and written language. The active engagement in the construction of meaning is an essential aspect that is present in both modes of language development; both are used, initially at least, to fulfil immediate and personally satisfying purposes.

Common features

Features common to both learning to speak and learning to read are as follows:

- The motivation to become involved is gained through the purposefulness of the spoken or written encounters.
- The learning of spoken language is essentially about learning to mean as is learning written language, which draws on the earlier achievement of oracy; children work out the rules of speech for themselves through interacting with experienced conversationalists and they use this problem-solving ability as they continue to work towards the generation of rules when puzzling out printed text.
- When interacting with text, children form 'hypotheses', that is, they predict (or guess/expect/anticipate) words through selecting the most productive cues to confirm the meaning of the text. These strategies have been learnt through understanding speech.
- The support of facilitative adults is vital, albeit in different ways, to the successful achievement of competence in both language modes.

The differences between written and spoken language

There are, however, distinct and important differences between oracy and literacy. Purcell-Gates (1996) lists features of written language.

- It is used to communicate over time and space. Written language must therefore be shaped so that meaning is conveyed in the absence of a shared physical context between writer and reader; conversely with conversation there is the support of the situation and presence of the speakers, meaning is negotiated through gesture and repetition, and confusion can be immediately clarified.
- It makes thoughts and emotions permanent. When writing there is time to express these ideas and feelings precisely. The opportunity exists to reread in order to establish clarity. This results in vocabulary (for example, the use of literary language such as *entrance* instead of *door*), syntax (that is more complex and integrated), and reference conventions being used differently from speaking. We write sentences such as 'There cannot be anyone who, believing this to be true, will continue to purchase cosmetics that have been tested on animals' rather than the spoken version of 'Nobody who knows about the testing of cosmetics on animals will buy them'.
- It also accommodates different degrees of involvement between the writer and reader. The impersonal nature of text has to be considered by the writer in order to make the meaning clear.

When learning to use (**decode** and **encode**) written symbols, it is necessary to understand that the writing system is an artificial code. Certainly this new learning is grafted onto the 'embeddedness' of the previous learning of speech (Donaldson, 1993). In Bielby's (1999: 16) words 'learning to read and write are parasitic on learning to speak' and the many previously acquired skills (see the previous chapters) can be utilized. This understanding regarding the nature and function of the alphabetic code is crucial to successful literacy learning. But it can develop (through opportunities to engage with text and direct teaching) only after the secure establishment of the concept that print has a communicative function and that its use is governed by certain rules and conventions (see Chapter 4).

Key Term

Encode and **decode**: these terms relate to the alphabetic code. The sounds of a spoken word are encoded into graphemes (that is, by the spelling of a written word), and a written word can be decoded into the sound, thereby allowing access to meaning, of a spoken word.

Becoming aware that the alphabet is a code system

Children gradually become literate, over several years and through many thousands of exposures to texts and signs. The recognition that the alphabet is a symbolic system that represents the sounds of speech in a written code and from which the meaning of language can be retrieved is an exciting and life-changing event. Research evidence has informed understanding of the mechanisms at work in this journey of discovery as the child learns that spoken language can be represented by written symbols in order to create text.

Before any progress can be made on the path to literacy, the child needs to appreciate through a wealth of first-hand experience, that the message of a written text is permanent and unchanging. Story books are still the most common way that this concept will be acquired, rather than text on a computer or television screen. The development of this understanding regarding the permanent nature of print is shown clearly by the protest when a favourite bedtime story is brought to a premature close. Even a 3-year-old will know exactly when they have been short-changed on a rereading of a tale (see Chapters 3 and 4). Following the acquisition of this understanding, the awareness of the rules and conventions of print is the next intellectual task for the child to achieve before the complexity of the code-breaking part of the literacy processing can be tackled.

The importance of print and sound processing skills

In order to teach literacy successfully, early years practitioners and primary teachers need to understand fully crucial research findings:

> the tide has turned from approaches that discourage explicit teaching of the connections between sound units and print to those that incorporate systematic instruction in the alphabetic code as an essential component of the reading curriculum. Pendulum swings in teaching practices are, of course, not new. What is new is the extent to which research from the science of reading is being taken seriously as a guide for decisions about how reading should best be taught. Evidence accumulated over the past 30 years has led to near consensus among researchers that early awareness of the phonemic principle of alphabetic writing plays a central role in becoming a skilled reader of English and other alphabetic systems. (Shankweiler and Fowler, 2004: 483)

There is substantial evidence that young children find segmenting spoken words into discrete units of sound very difficult. But as the above quotation argues the ability to read and write successfully and fluently depends upon it, albeit, after the individual has recognized the deeper understandings of the purpose and nature of written language (see Chapters 3 and 4). Becoming an effective user of the **alphabetic system** is dependent upon the accurate segmenting of words into the constituent phonemes (which is known as **phonemic segmentation**) and then the complementary skill to map the sounds onto symbols. Phonemes are the smallest sound segments that make up a spoken word, and which allow it to be recognized. Change a **phoneme** and the word is changed. Phonemes roughly correspond to the individual letter and digraph (and other letter combination) sounds – thus, 'patch' corresponds to the three phonemes in patch thus, p/+/a/+/tch. By changing the middle phoneme to /i/ it becomes /pitch/.

This is only one aspect of the process of becoming literate, but it is an essential part and without it accuracy is denied to the individual.

Key Terms

Alphabetic code: alphabets are systems of symbols representing the constituent sounds within words; they are a system for encoding the spoken sounds of words.

Phonological awareness: the perceptual alertness to the constituent sounds within words, ranging from alertness to rhymes and alliteration to distinguishing the individual phonemes.

> **Phoneme**: the smallest unit of sound in a word. A phoneme may be represented by one, two, three or four letters, for example, t**o**, sh**oe**, thr**ough**.
>
> **Phonemic segmentation**: the skill of distinguishing the individual phonemes in words, for example, that there are four phonemes in both 'fox' and 'socks'.

Children's difficulties with phonemic segmentation

Early years practitioners and primary teachers have a vital role to play in enabling children to develop **phonological awareness**. Unfortunately for both parties, it takes some considerable time to develop!

The linguistic units of sound below the level of the word (called sub-lexical units) are syllables, onsets, rimes and phonemes. The research evidence regarding the difficulties that children have making explicit phonological judgements is well known in the field of psychology. The phoneme, being the smallest unit of sound, is the hardest for children to discriminate. Bruce (1964) found that 5-to 9-year-old children were not able to remove a phoneme from a given word such as the 'n' in this case from 'sand', in a 'subtraction' task. Liberman et al. (1974) gave 4-, 5- and 6-year-old children a 'tapping' task. They taught the children to tap out either the syllables or the phonemes of a word presented to them by the researcher. A syllable is a unit of sound centred on a vowel sound, which is a vocal pulse of energy. This vowel sound may, and need not, be accompanied by consonant sounds preceding and following it. A word must contain at least one syllable. This the children found very difficult also. They found the syllable-tapping task easier than the phoneme task but the 5-year-olds simply could not learn to discriminate between the different phonemes within even short, regular words.

It seems therefore that pre-literate children find breaking words into units of sound very hard, but that breaking words into syllables is easier than identifying phonemes. Children were asked to set out counters for the syllables that they could hear in a word in one case, and the phonemes in another. This study showed again that young children find the phoneme discrimination task problematic. Treiman (1992) suggests that people find it more 'natural' to segment **syllables** into onsets and rimes – the onset being the one or more consonant phonemes that precede the rime. The rime is the vowel (peak) phoneme and any succeeding consonant phonemes. For example in the word chick, ch/ is the onset and /ick is the rime. All this is very complicated, so is it important? What is the evidence that suggests that this skill is essential to learning to read?

Phonological awareness and learning to read

Research findings indicate that there is a very strong relationship between children's ability in making phonological judgements and their success in learning to read. In fact Stainthorp says:

The involvement of phonological awareness in the development of reading and spelling is now virtually unassailable … Children who do not develop an explicit awareness of, or ability to manipulate, the sounds in words find it difficult to develop fluent skilled reading and spelling (Snowling, 2000). Conversely, children who learn to read without direct instruction at a precociously early age show significantly higher levels of phonological sensitivity than age-matched non-reading children. (2004a: 753)

Over the past three decades studies have indicated this from three different sources of evidence. First, one category of investigation showed that there is a very strong relationship between the ability of individuals to break words into phonemes and their progress in learning to read, and this relationship holds even when the effect of intelligence is taken into account (Stanovich et al., 1984; Tunmer et al., 1988). Secondly, other studies have shown that children who are backward in reading also function poorly on grapheme–phoneme correspondence tasks. Graphemes are the alphabetic representations of phonemes – thus 'rough' represents the three phonemes /r/+/u/+/ff/, and 'cat' represents the three phonemes of /cat/. Grapheme–phoneme correspondence (GPC) refers to the regularities that constitute phonics.

Phonological awareness is tested with experiments that use pseudo-words (for example, *wem* and *tugwump*) that the children could not possibly have seen before and therefore arguably they cannot have them stored in their memory bank or as part of their sight vocabulary of known words (Frith and Snowling, 1983). Thirdly, there are the intervention studies in which pre-school children were given extra phonological experience in breaking words up into their constituent phonemes and building words from phonemes (Lundberg et al., 1988). In Lundberg's follow-up study it seemed that the children who had received the extra phonological training did indeed learn to read more successfully than those pupils who had received as much attention from adults but not on this specific aspect of reading. Treiman has shown that the most natural segmentation of the syllable into **intrasyllabic units** appears to be at the onset rime boundary.

Key Terms

Syllable: part of a word which is pronounced as a unit, which contains a single vowel sound and which may or may not contain consonants, for example, pa/per. Syllables can be segmented into units that are smaller than the syllable per se but may be larger than the phoneme.

Intrasyllabic units: the onset, the rime, the peak and the coda.

Onset and **Rime**: The two sub-units of a syllable. The onset (if present) precedes the vowel sound, and the rime consists of the vowel sound and any subsequent consonant sounds. The onset is the consonant or consonant cluster (phonemes not letters) that are at the beginning of the syllable. The onset is not obligatory. Thus there are words like AT (no onset); PAT (single phoneme onset); SPAT (consonant cluster onset). The rime is all the phonemes that come after the onset.

'Peak' phoneme: all rimes begin with an obligatory vowel sound which is the peak and may end with optional consonants which form the coda. Thus there are words like SPA with the rime peak /are/ but no coda; and SPARK which has the single consonant coda /k/.

The development of phonological awareness

Given that we have discussed that being able to segment words into sound units of various types, but crucially into phonemes, is essential for effective progress in literacy, it obviously is important that primary teachers, particularly those concerned with the early years of schooling, know how to enable pupils to develop progressively more refined levels of phonological awareness.

Understanding the alphabetic code

This is a paradoxical issue. It seems that individuals learn how to break words into their sounds *through* learning to read and yet this skill, it has been shown, is crucial for the successful acquisition of literacy. Children who have not made the connection that words are made up of sounds and that these sounds map onto graphemes (letters and groups of letters in various combinations) have not grasped the principle of the **alphabetic code**. They are then forced into two main strategies for decoding text. First relying on its distinctive shape in order to recall a word and, secondly, to back up this strategy by confirming accuracy through predicting the word from the context (see Chapter 3). Both of these strategies are useful but they become truly effective and allow complete accuracy only when complemented by the strategy of grapheme/phoneme (letter/sound) correspondence (GPC).

The findings of research show that illiterate adults have similar difficulties with separating words into phonemes as has been demonstrated with pre-literate children. This indicates that competent and functioning, but illiterate adults, do not naturally develop this very specific, and it would appear, literacy-dependent, ability. It seems that people become aware of phonemes when they use the alphabet to read and write. Interesting and complementary work provides further explanation of this issue as to whether phonemic awareness is facilitated by the use of the alphabet or by being literate. Read et al. (1986) have undertaken research with individuals who have learned to read and write with a non-alphabetic script, such as traditional Chinese; a logographic script in which logograms represent whole words. These studies replicated the early work of Morais et al. (1979, 1986) on groups of adults, some of whom were literate in an alphabetic script and some in a logographic script. The results show that individuals who are literate, but in a non-alphabetic script, have enormous difficulty with phonemic segmentation.

This point is developed further in Chapter 10 when addressing the issue of bilingual children learning to read. The task for this group of children is facilitated or hindered by whether or not their first language has an alphabetic script. This adds further weight to the evidence of the necessity for individuals to operate in an alphabetic system in order to come to understand fully that it is a code. This supports the paradox discussed earlier, that the ability to segment phonemes is essential in order to become literate in an alphabetic script and in order to be able to segment phonemes an individual has to be functional in a script with an alphabetic code! Unfortunately, it is not even as simple (or complex!) as that, because in addition the reader has to be able to build up sounds into words in order to access meaning. The Rose Report, referring to children who have English as an additional language and those who find literacy challenging, says 'However, all beginner readers have to come to terms with the same alphabetic principles if they are to learn to read and write' (DfES, 2006: 16).

Rhyme and rime

If phonemic segmentation is hard for young, pre-literate children, are there other units of sound that are easier for them both to identify and discriminate between? The answer is yes. Pre-school children are skilful at playing with and detecting sound, at the level of rhyme and alliteration (Bryant et al., 1989; Dowker, 1989). While there is a wide variation between 3- and 4-year-old children in their ability to distinguish words that rhyme from words that do not, it is clear that this sound-unit is easier for them to identify and discriminate between than syllables or phonemes. There is also evidence that being able to identify rhyme at nursery school is a very good predictor of early success with reading at school (Bradley and Bryant, 1983). The way this works has been much debated. It seems odd that being able to detect rhyme is useful if the main and most important goal of phonological awareness is to be able to phonemically segment so that accurate grapheme/phoneme (letter/sound) correspondences (GPC) can be made when encoding and decoding print. Being able to hear and discriminate rhyme, while related, is a different skill, it would appear, and is layered with the myriad complexities relating to aural and visual rhymes and the vagaries of English spelling rules.

The point appears to be that phonological awareness develops in stages. First, children are able to distinguish rhyme, then syllables and, later still, individual phonemes in words. If rhyme is the first sound-unit that young children are able to detect, it is useful because it demonstrates that phonological awareness has begun to develop and can be built upon.

Another reason why rhyme may be so useful in the early stages of learning to read is that the ability to detect rhyme is a short step from the ability to identify the sound-units of **onset** and **rime** to which the identification of rhyme is linked. To be able to appreciate the rime of a word has been shown to be useful for early readers (Goswami and Bryant, 1990). For example, if children realize that the rimes of 'l-ook', 'b-ook' and 'sh-ook' have something in common, namely, both a sound element and a related visual element, in other words the spelling pattern, they are beginning to realize that spellings and sounds relate in a regular and specific way. In particular, that it is possible to work out new words on this basis, for example, words such as 't-ook', 'c-ook', 'cr-ook', and so on. This ability also then enables the distinction between dissimilar onsets of 't-----' and 'c-----' and 'cr-----'. These understandings are well within the grasp of Year 1 children for example. It also becomes another cueing strategy for decoding when they need to read an unknown word but one that has a familiar rime. Goswami and Bryant (1990) found that even very young children can read 'l-**ake**' because they are able to read 't-**ake**' in another situation. That is, they are able to use the analogy of the intrasyllabic unit of the rime of a word to decode accurately a new word not currently in their sight vocabulary. Their significance is that they are the smallest phonological units that children seem spontaneously to be alert to without being prompted by adults or by being taught alphabet letter sounds.

Learning and Teaching Suggestions

The following stories in rhyme are a joyful way of developing phonological awareness:

Beck, I. (1998) *Five Little Ducks*. London: Orchard Books.

Giles, A. and Parker-Rees, G. (1999) *Giraffes Can't Dance*. London: Orchard Books.

Bush, J. and Paul, K. (1993) *The Fish Who Could Wish*. Oxford: Oxford University Press.

Orthographic awareness: recognizing print

If anybody, not necessarily a teacher or someone connected with early years education, were asked to make a list of the most important aspects involved with learning to read and write, high on that list would surely be a capacity to perceive graphic signs and to be able to discriminate visually between them. First, it probably would be agreed that a novice reader needs sufficiently developed visual discrimination in order to detect the differences (and some of the differences *are* very slight and mainly owed to the orientation of the letter, for example, **p, q, b, d, g**) between the 26 printed symbols of the alphabet, and, second, the ability to perceive and remember words as wholes and attach to the remembered shape of the word its meaning.

However, it has been discussed previously in considerable depth that the business of getting to grips with literacy is not as visual an activity as one might imagine. The importance of the ability to hear the constituent sounds in individual words in order to read fluently in an alphabetic script has been addressed in detail. Clearly though the sounds once identified and segmented (or separated out) have then to be mapped onto recalled symbols or letters. This is called **orthographic awareness**, the other interrelated, interdependent 'bottom-up' skill in the literacy process.

Key Term

Orthographic awareness: this is roughly the visual equivalent of phonological awareness. It means the alertness to the spelling sequences that constitute written words. Thus, a child may learn that '-ing' is the common spelling of the endings of a number of different words and is a reliable guide to pronunciation.

Developing orthographic awareness

The intricacies of the cognitive mechanisms that enable readers to recognize words instantaneously and automatically is debated by psychologists (as helpfully summarized and explained by Ehri, 1992; Stuart, 1995). However, what is clear is that this facility develops over time and through many exposures to print and text. It is also incontrovertible from the research evidence that children process print in qualitatively different and increasingly complex ways en route both to becoming fluent in reading and being able to write coherent, accurate text.

In order for whole or sight words to be stored in an individual's **lexicon** (word memory bank), the words have to be 'learned' or seen so often that a **logogen** is formed. Each word has a logogen. The term has changed meaning with changing theories, but can be thought of as a kind of mental template against which perceptual instances of words are checked in order to permit identification. This picture is created by the brain so that the entire image of the word can be *recalled* when writing or *recognized* when reading, so that the meaning is accessed from the individual's memory store also.

This process is achieved through developmental stages and is influenced by the refinement of phonological awareness to a greater or lesser extent depending on your viewpoint or theoretical stance.

Key Terms

Lexicon: means dictionary or, when used by psychologists, mental dictionary. It refers to the memory store for words, their spellings and sounds.

Logogen: refers to the mental construct employed by psychologists in discussing the ways words are represented in the mental lexicon in order to permit word recognition.

Several psychologists have suggested developmental stage theories of the print-processing abilities of early readers (Ehri, 1992; Marsh et al., 1980). Frith's theory (1985) will be discussed in this chapter on account of its accessibility and suitability for the declared purpose of this volume, as it provides appropriate insight into the complexity of print processing for those early years practitioners and primary teachers who teach very young children to read.

Frith's phase theory

The logographic phase of sight word reading

In the first of the stages of the ability to process print as described by Frith (1985) the young child perceives words as wholes or as **logograms**. The word is recognized by the child through personally memorable and highly distinctive visual features such as the typography in the typeface of the logo of *Coca-Cola* or *Pepsi*, the two 'dd's of *Daddy*, the 'sticks' in *lollipop* or the distinct shape/length/two dots of **j** and **i** in one's own first name e.g. *Benjamin*. The child has no recourse to phonological processing as both the letters of the alphabet and the associated sounds are not known or salient to the reader at this very early stage of literacy development.

Children differ in the chronological age at which they pass through this stage. McGee et al. (1988) conducted a study on pre-schoolers in the USA and stopped with the five thousandth 3-year-old as they all showed that they knew that the McDonald's logo stands for hamburgers or McDonald's. This indicates that with the context-rich support of the golden arch alongside the logo, children as young as 3 years old have no difficulty accessing the meaning of this symbol of contemporary culture. Without such support though, children are not always able to identify words in a traditional typeface, for example, *Coca-Cola* without the distinctive flowing red script or, similarly, emergent readers fail to notice the change in *Pepsi* to *Xepsi* if the typeface remains consistent with the distinctive logo.

Word identification is related to meaning (semantics) so heavily that phonetically regular words such as *but* and *dud*, which are both so visually and semantically bland, are virtually impossible to remember and their spelling remains a mystery unless decoded.

Key Term

Logogram: is a term that refers to written symbols that represent whole words, as in Chinese, or as with the ampersand (&).

Case Study 5.1

Some children remain arrested in this stage of print processing for some time after they go to school, for example, Peter in Stuart's study, when asked how he knew a word was 'television', replied 'Oh that's easy. It's got a dot. Actually it's got two dots, but anyway, I don't care' (1995: 47). The implications for teaching children in this stage are important and will be addressed at the end of this section.

Learning and Teaching Suggestions

What do you think the implications of this are? What do practitioners and teachers need to assess in order to know about their pupils' literacy development?

Why do you think it is important for practitioners and teachers to know how children are processing print?

The alphabetic phase of sight word reading

The child moves into the next phase of print processing as letters of the alphabet are learned either by their distinguishing shape, their names or sounds. Ehri (1992) maintains that it is this knowledge that provides the child with sufficient 'low-level phonemic awareness' that the beginnings and ends of words can be recognized and rudimentary sound–spelling connections can be made. Words are still remembered by their distinctive shape, and through the salience of the meaning, but a crude sound–symbol link is also attached to the recognition process for the word as it is effectively committed to the lexical memory store or sight vocabulary. Many complex research studies (for example, Ehri and Wilce, 1985) have been undertaken with children in this stage of literacy development and here is the evidence of only one. It is clear that very soon after exposure to formal teaching, novice readers find non-sense words but those with a logical sound–symbol relationship easier to remember than words with arbitrary letters used in them (for example, *MSK* for *mask* in the first case and *HE* also representing mask in the second case).

Early years practitioners and teachers have the advantage of being able to assess their pupils' writing in order to determine their phase of print processing. This is providing, of course, that the children have been encouraged to generate writing independently using invented spelling or emergent writing, so that meaningful diagnoses of print-processing ability can be made. Children in the alphabetic phase of reading development typically display *the semi-phonetic stage* of writing described by Gentry (1981) (see page 104), such as when in pupil's mark-making or writing there is evidence of some representation of letter/sound (grapheme/phoneme) correspondence, for example *wnt* for went, *hse* for house and *pse* for please. These children are demonstrating that they are in the beginning stages of understanding the alphabetic principle, and they are self-evidently getting to grips with the code. Not only is this crucial ability displayed conveniently for early years practitioners and primary teachers *through* their mark-making or writing but it is most powerfully developed into progressively more accurate phonemic segmentation and appropriate representation of the sound units by being explicitly *taught*. This is the most effective way of capitalizing on the relationship between phonological and orthographic awareness as both abilities develop side by side and complement each other. The ability to recognize sight words becomes more and more efficient through this stage of print processing as the lexical memory store (or word bank) expands.

The orthographic phase of sight word reading

Ehri (1992) defines her equivalent of this phase of sight word reading as the processing of sight words through making connections in memory between the whole sequence of letters in a spelling of a word and the phonemic constituents in the word's pronunciation. This might be further explained by the reader being able to short circuit the letter-by-letter phonological conversion of the previous stage through being able to process 'chunks' of print from sight memory. Frequently processed words and parts of words come to be retained in the lexical memory as recognition units that permit virtually automatic decoding and faster reading. Such 'chunking' also helps with writing through the encoding of spellings, which thereby become more conventional and therefore accurate. Phonemic segmentation is accurate, as is a near perfect understanding of the English spelling system. Fluency is achieved as decoding becomes almost instantaneous.

Table 5.1   *Two models of reading development (print-processing)*

Age	Frith (1985)	Ehri (1995)
3–5 years	Logographic phase	Pre-alphabetic phase
		Partial alphabetic phase
5–7 years	Alphabetic phase	Full alphabetic phase
7–9 years	Orthographic phase	Consolidated alphabetic phase

A comparison between Frith's and Ehri's phase theories makes the earlier explanation more accessible. Ehri's suggestions of terms of the phases are usefully descriptive of the processing available to the child in the different phases, but the terminology is very wordy for frequent reference in connected text.

The comparison presents a simplified picture of two phased models of the print-processing aspect of reading development and how they relate to each other. Frith developed her model so that she could compare the literacy development of dyslexics with normal developmental patterns. She also included writing in her model, being interested in the way reading and writing developed slightly out of step but interactively. Ehri developed her model in relation to the contribution of alphabetic skills to the development and changing nature of sight word recognition.

Although their use of terminologies and some of their interests and inter-pretations are different, their accounts are compatible. Both researchers start with recognizing logographic/pre-alphabetic sight word learning and show how, through developing alphabetic/graphonic processes, letter-by-letter decoding is replaced by a more sophisticated form of sight word recognition in which words are perceived in terms of known spelling patterns or chunks.

For both models, the term 'phase' is perhaps preferable to 'stage' because progression is seen as cumulative and not clear-cut. Earlier modes of print processing are retained in the learner's repertoire of reading strategies, and used when needed.

Large-scale studies and reading progress

Further evidence (Tizard et al., 1988) about the progress children make in becoming literate comes from the findings of the Infant School Study. This project followed a cohort of children in 33 inner London schools from the end of the nursery class through to the end of infant school. The main aim was to investigate the progress of children in order to explain the reasons for their differing rates of attainment. Variables such as home background, ethnic origin and factors both within the school and between teachers are also explored, and their varying influences accounted for in the analyses of the data. At this level of complexity, it becomes a challenge in itself to explain the relationships between the different variables. The finding most relevant to this book is that of the positive relationship between a child being able to identify and label letters of the alphabet at the end of nursery and later progress in reading.

A study about literacy development that followed 191 reception children through the first year of school has shed light on the way in which the child comes to grips with the complexity of the task of reading, and how teachers can have insight into the print-processing abilities of the new pupil (Riley, 1994, 1995a, 1996). This research project provides further evidence to support the value of the young reader's refined orthographic knowledge indicated by the ability to both identify and label letters of the alphabet and to write her/his own name before formal instruction at school begins.

The most important finding is the relationship between the literacy-related skills assessed at school entry and reading (as measured by the raw score of the Neale's Analysis of Reading Test; Neale, 1989) at the end of the first year of school.

The three literacy-related skills, concepts about print, ability to write her/his own name, and the ability to identify and label the letters of the alphabet, assessed by the researchers in the September at school entry, were all shown to be positively related to the ability to read in the following July. However, the most powerful predictor of later success in reading was the child's knowledge of the alphabet. This was shown by the ability to identify and label the letters of the alphabet which had been acquired incidentally and informally pre-school.

This work adds considerable weight to the body of evidence that recognizes that speedy word processing is essential for progress in reading, the first stage of which is an understanding of the alphabet system. A recognition of the individual letters, along with an ability to hear the sounds in words, are the first steps in the development of the orthographic and phonological processing capability essential to the literacy task.

The predictive value of the knowledge of the alphabet and the ability to write own name, is not a new finding: it reaffirms the views of Wells and Raban (1978) and the findings of the Infant School Study (Tizard et al., 1988) regarding the strength of the association of orthographic knowledge and later reading. What is perhaps less appreciated is an explanation of these findings regarding the nature of the child's orthographic knowledge, which is shown by the continued influence of concepts about print in the statistical analyses.

Applying alphabetic knowledge

This finding suggests that it is not *knowing the alphabet* but *knowing how to apply* the knowledge of the alphabet that is important. In the next few paragraphs the evidence for, and significance of, this claim will be discussed.

The series of studies that followed the early finding, some 30 years ago, of the connection between knowledge of letters of the alphabet and early reading development (Bond and Dykstra, 1967; Chall, 1967) were disappointing. When Gibson and Levin (1975) and Ehri (1983) set out directly to teach children the letters of the alphabet, prior to school entry, there appeared to be no positive link with successful reading later.

Blatchford et al. (1987) suggest in their Infant School Study that the strong relationship found between letter knowledge on school entry and later reading probably reflects pre-school children's general acquaintance with written language.

I argue elsewhere (Riley, 1994, 1995a) that the connection is more complex than that. Children who have shown that they can identify and label the letters of the alphabet probably come to school with an understanding of the alphabetic code (that is, how the alphabet operates in words), and they are clearly further along the path to reading.

Arriving at the levels of understanding that a child possesses about anything is not easy. The distinction between the various levels of understanding of the alphabetic code is still more challenging. As children move from emergent literacy (see Chapter 4) to conventional reading, they develop through several levels of understanding from conceptual, to formal, through to symbolic understanding of letters. The symbolic relationship between letters and sounds is the basis of the English writing system, as discussed earlier. Vygotsky states: 'A feature of this (writing) system is that it is second order symbolism, which gradually becomes direct symbolism. This means that written language consists of a system of signs that designate the sounds and words of spoken language, which, in turn are signs for real entities and relations' (1978: 106).

Bialystok (1991) conducted a study that explored this gradual shift in understanding of children between 3 and 5 years of age. She designed labelling and spelling tasks using plastic letters. Of all the assessment techniques, her 'moving word' task proved to be the most powerful predictor of success.

In this task Bialystok used a 'naughty puppet' to move letters in words and it was the extent to which the children became concerned about this that she was able to ascertain the nature of their understanding of the alphabet.

Through this, she concluded that the most essential insight is the symbolic relationship by which letters represent sounds. This clearly needs to be built and capitalized upon in school with those children who show an early awareness of letter–sound correspondence and develop it into a gradual appreciation of the English alphabetic system and its complexities.

Bialystok writes:

> Children's first achievement with letters is as part of a procedure, namely reciting the alphabet ... Reading requires symbolic knowledge of letters. The representation must include the relation between the letter and its sound. Objects *have* meanings; symbols represent meanings. Objects can *make* sounds; Symbols *stand for* sounds. Meaning is somehow *in* objects; it is not in symbols. For this reason formal knowledge of the alphabet is not sufficient for learning to read. (1991: 78)

This explains why the studies mentioned earlier, which set out merely to teach the alphabet by rote, had no enduring value and failed to guarantee an early successful start to reading. The appreciation of the symbolic representation of letters for spoken sounds occurs slowly over time and with exposure to meaningful experiences of print and text.

In Bialystok's experimental group those children who could read were more successful in all the word tasks undertaken, they were the same age and there was no significant difference between their levels of spoken language as shown by their receptive vocabulary scores as the non-readers in the study. Bialystok suggests that: 'the difference between those children who could read and those who could not has something to do with the way in which they understand the letter–sound correspondences' (1991: 87).

Knowing letter names *or* sounds on entry to school indicates experience with print, cognitive and perceptual maturity and the requisite attention span, in addition to a symbolic understanding of the alphabet. The child's knowledge of spoken and written language offers access to the symbolic system. Downing (1979) provides a 'cognitive clarity' model which leads to a clearer appreciation of the alphabetic system. He asserts that superior letter-name knowledge is a symptom of a greater understanding of the technical features of writing and is one of the prerequisite concepts for fluent reading. Altogether these are the concepts of:

- the continuous flow of speech that can be segmented into parts
- the spoken word
- the phoneme
- code – that an abstract symbol can represent something else
- the written word
- the grapheme
- the letter.

Bialystok's study provides insight into different levels of awareness when identifying letters. These levels denote more advanced understandings of words and the symbolic nature of language. Children who have learned to identify thier letters, incidentally as it were, over time and through many meaningful encounters with print, have developed a deeper, more refined appreciation of the role of letters in the representation of sounds. Children who have this understanding at school entry are further along the road to reading than children who are merely able to recite the alphabet. The level of the child's understanding and knowledge is of great importance to the early years practitioner or teacher.

Adams hints at the transition phase of reading development when she writes:

> For children who, on entering the classroom, do not yet have a comfortable familiarity with the letters of the alphabet, finding ways to help them is of first order importance. Even so, knowledge of letters is of little value unless the *child knows and is interested in their use* [my emphasis]. Correctly perceived and interpreted, print conveys information. In keeping with this, children's concepts about print are also strong predictors of the ease with which they will learn to read. Before formal instruction is begun, children should possess a broad and general appreciation of the nature of print. (1993: 207)

Implications for practice

Working with the individual child in a supportive and diagnostic way

Nursery and reception class practitioners and teachers need to be aware of the precise stage of literacy development of their young pupils. Concepts about print are acquired slowly through the emergent literacy phase; they develop through rich and meaningful encounters with print in the twin processes of early reading and primitive message writing. These crucial understandings are the prerequisite to the acquisition of conventional literacy and are discussed fully in Chapter 4. An integral aspect of this understanding is the growth of the child's gradual appreciation of the symbolic nature as distinct from the formal understanding of written language (Bialystok, 1991) of which the ability to identify and label non-sequential letters of the alphabet at school entry is an early indication. This is very different from the ability to recite the alphabet by rote as has been shown earlier.

Practitioners and teachers working with young children need to be skilled, diagnostic facilitators of their early literacy attempts. At best they mimic the parent or carer who before school so powerfully assisted valuable literacy progress. At worst, nursery and reception class practitioners and teachers cut across the child's rich but highly personal prior learning to confuse and dishearten (Baker and Raban, 1991) (see Chapter 4 for further discussion).

Teachers need to know how children are progressing in terms of their understanding of how texts and print work, their grasp of the alphabetic code and how their word recognition skills are developing. Finally, and crucially, how is this underpinning reading and comprehending texts? Clay promotes careful, recorded observation of reading behaviours, in the very early stages of literacy, in order to inform the next step in teaching. 'Sensitive and systematic observation of behaviour is really the only way to monitor gradual shifts across imperfect responding' (Clay, 1991: 233). She goes on to list her signs of what she describes a 'developing inner control' in the areas of:

- using language (both spoken and 'mark-making' written language)
- gaining concepts about print
- attending to visual information
- hearing sounds in sequence.

The beginning reader gradually learns how to integrate the processes and the practitioner needs to monitor and analyse the progress systematically. Clay displays clearly the monitoring of the child's reading by the teacher to assess the extent to which the child can process text to access meaning through both word recognition and decoding (see Figure 5.1).

Teaching follows the sensitive observation. The initial assessment of the child will occur on entry to school and is covered in Chapter 4. All aspects of the child's reading can be supported with great benefit, through sharply focused teaching appropriate for the developmental stage and level of competence the child has in processing text.

Realistically, it is recognized that children will be taught in a variety of situations: whole-class, in groups and as individuals. However, it is crucial that practitioners are aware of the development and learning needs of each child in order to provide the appropriate experiences that will ensure that progress

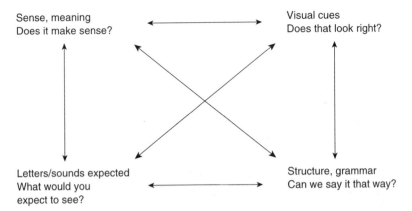

Figure 5.1   *Sources of information about text (Clay and Cazden, 1990: 207)*

will be made. The Rose Report adds, 'Hence assessment for learning is vital for planning work that is matched well to children's needs' (DfES, 2006: 22).

Learning and Teaching Suggestions (developed from Riley, 1996)

Children at the National Curriculum (pre-Level 1) stage

Observation of children reading

The following lists cover some of the literacy behaviours that are characteristically displayed by children at this stage of development.

Literacy behaviour displayed by children through:

- the enjoyment of books
- attempting to read known texts (acting like a reader)
- concentrating on the literacy activity in hand.

Understanding of the literacy task is shown through:

- knowing that print has a communicative function
- demonstrating awareness of environmental print, that is, recognizes labels/notices/ messages
- knowing the conventions of print, that is, can point to where you start reading/knows sweep back on line/knows where to go to on the following page.

The following are teaching approaches suggested to support the development of children's print and sound awareness at each learning stage.

Children at the National Curriculum (pre-Level 1) stage

Children at this stage are in the 'emergent literacy' phase of development, (see Chapter 4). They will be able to recognize a few highly distinctive, personally relevant words as logograms (or as whole words).

Sound awareness (phonological awareness) can be encouraged by:

- attention being drawn to sounds in words (bilingual learners should be encouraged to do this both in their home language and in English) to develop phonological awareness, for example, 'All those children who have a name beginning with "P" go and sit in their places' or playing games like taking out of a 'magic' bag a selection of objects all beginning with the same initial sound
- listening to and reciting poems, rhymes, jingles, songs and nursery rhymes
- explicit teaching of rhyme through learning of the written (class) rhyme of the week (using a commercially published chart or written on a large piece of card), working from books with rhyming text, brainstorming additional rhyming words on a flip chart
- introduce letter–sound correspondences through alphabet identification and learning (use of commercial materials and computer software, for example, Fast Phonics First from primary.marketing@harcourteducation.co.uk or visit the website www.fastphonicsfirst.co.uk for a preview or from Letterland Living ABC available from www.r.e.m.co.uk) to recognize, learn and name letters and sounds. This can also be done very effectively with a synthetic phonic scheme such as 'Jolly Phonics'
- having book bins of multiples of high-quality alphabet picture books (for example, those of Brian Wildsmith or Shirley Hughes) permanently available for children to browse through
- ensuring that alphabet friezes are on the walls around the room (at an appropriate height for children be able to easily see them) and also fixed (with plastic seal) to the pupils' tables or Oxford Reading Tree 'alphabet mats' for use on individual work tables
- having containers of plastic letters (upper and lower case) for constant use in relation to grapheme–phoneme (letter–sound) correspondence (GPC) work, this is especially valuable when children are writing at this stage of development
- oral games such as deleting initial phonemes or onset of a word, for example, **c**-ar, **P**-at, **d**-og, **st**-op.

Print awareness (orthographic awareness) can be encouraged by drawing attention to:

- distinctive words in familiar texts, for example, the names of characters in books
- familiar words in environmental print, for example, labels and notices
- children's names in the class through a variety of approaches, for example registers, lists and labels on trays and pegs
- opportunities for mark-making and 'invented spelling' both with adults and independently, for example, making cards, writing letters and notes, labels and notices, provide literacy activities in the home corner and adaptations of it such as a McDonald's, a hospital or a bakery
- class-made books with familiar, repetitive text from combinations of photographs of the children incorporating their names in the text or familiar logos, for example, 'For breakfast Jane likes *Rice Krispies*' 'Ahmed likes *Cocoa Pops*'.

Children at the National Curriculum Level 1 (early) stage

Observation of children reading

The following list of literacy behaviours that denote progress are characteristically displayed by children at this stage of literacy development.

Literacy behaviours are displayed through:

- reading known texts with much adult support
- pointing word by word as she/he or adult reads, that is, approximate one-to-one correspondence of written to spoken word, or stabbing with finger at known words and sliding over unknown words
- will substitute unknown words with no graphic accuracy but with sense in the context (for example, house for flat).

Understanding of the literacy task is shown through:

- being able to discuss books and plot at literal level
- beginning to appreciate that long words when spoken will require a correspondingly long symbol when written, that is, noticing that it must be *bicycle* not *bike*.

Print-processing skills of children are demonstrated by:

- accurate knowledge of the alphabet through regular, but brief teaching sessions using *one* synthetic phonics scheme such as 'Jolly Phonics'
- ability to recognize a few high-frequency words out of context
- being able to point to a letter in a word (this skill often starts with letters in the child's name)
- being able to read back own caption under a painting
- having, towards the end of this phase, acquired a small sight vocabulary linked to own interests/the reading scheme/and Primary National Strategy: Framework for literacy teaching high-frequency words.

Teaching approaches to support children in this stage

Children at this stage are moving from the emergent literacy phase towards the beginning of conventional reading. They have a sight vocabulary of a few words that they recognize as logograms, and they now need to be supported into the 'alphabetic' phase.

Sound awareness (Phonological awareness) can be supported by:

- encouraging recognition of and ability to write each letter of the alphabet by emphasizing the letter's shape, its correct formation *and* its sound, 'Jolly Phonics' are helpful for this (always teach letters in handwriting sessions in shape families for example, *c a g d*)
- using a flip chart to reinforce the above for whole-class handwriting, making shapes in the air first

- helping awareness of grapheme–phoneme (letter–sound) correspondence (GPC) through initial sound work starting with children's names
- free writing for a range of purposes and the child is encouraged to use 'invented spelling' in order to represent the sounds in words with a symbol. With adult support (most usefully in a small group situation) the segmentation (separation) of sounds in words can be reinforced and linked to the alphabet friezes on the wall and on the table or with plastic letters. This is a very important activity and should be carried out very frequently at this stage of reading, as it is the most effective way of teaching GPC. The adult provides feedback (that is, emphasizing phonemic awareness and its corresponding grapheme explicit) on what the child needs to understand about the alphabetic system
- work in groups on awareness of onset (beginning phoneme of word for example, **b**-at or **ch**-at) and 'rime' (end or following sound, including the vowel, for example, b-**at** and br-**at**) both aurally and visually.

Print awareness (orthographic awareness now word recognition)is supported by helping children to:

- make their own books with repetitive texts using photographs/names/familiar words to represent their own or class interests
- recognize their own name from a list of names
- write their own name correctly with an emphasis on both letter formation and the constituent letters
- identify and read high-frequency words through writing and games located in a meaningful context
- recognize that its length and shape is a cue for identifying a word (that is, what the word *looks* like)
- play games matching word cards to pictures, for example, photographs to children's names, name cards to characters in reading schemes and so on.

Children at the National Curriculum Level 1 (later) stage

Observation of children reading

A list of literacy behaviours that denotes progress characteristically displayed by children at this stage of literacy development.

Progress in reading is displayed by:

- slowing down when reading as children work hard at processing the text
- starting to show awareness of mismatch by self-correcting plus evidence of scanning ahead
- spelling is becoming more conventional when writing, using 'invented spelling' on own text.

Understanding of the literacy task is demonstrated by:

- beginning to be able to meaning-make and recognize words – through context (including picture cue), *syntax*, and the *look of the word*, that is, length/distinctive

features, *phonic analysis*, (see Figure 5.1). Meaning-making and word recognition will be imperfect as the decoding print is developing
- beginning to consider the plot and character of the story in greater detail.

Word recogniton skills of children are demonstrated by:

- having an increasing sight word vocabulary (approximately 50 words).

Teaching approaches to support children in this stage

Activities as appropriate for the earlier stages. Children will have moved from the logo-graphic through to the alphabetic phase of print processing and will have both strategies at their disposal for reading and writing.

Sound awareness (phonological awareness) is supported by:

- making explicit the grapheme–phoneme(letter–sound) correspondence when reading and writing
- listening to dominant phonemes (including consonant digraphs ch, sh)
- blending phonetically regular 2/3 (C/V/C) letter words, for example, m/a/n (including nonsense words such as w/u/g)
- identifying words that rhyme with familiar sight vocabulary, for example, can, fan, tan, pan, ran
- using knowledge of initial sounds to act as a cue to make a choice between two or three words within the sight vocabulary when reading connected text
- using analogy to help write new words from known ones, for example, *t-ook* from *b-ook*.

Print awareness (orthographic awareness/word recognition) is developed by:

- practising sight vocabulary with games, context sentence cards (both commercial and teacher-made), with and without pictures, or whole stories
- using correct spellings of a few common words in the course of their own writing. Attention can be drawn to the standard spelling (of one or two words only) with word lists in the classroom or personal word banks when appropriate and in context.

Additional teaching note: handwriting practice not only develops formation of letter shapes, but grapheme–phoneme correspondence can be reinforced. Also note that it is at this stage that print and sound awareness become more strongly linked and mutually reinforcing.

Children at National Curriculum Level 2

The following is a list of literacy behaviours that denotes progress characteristically dis-played at this stage of literacy development.

Observation of children reading

Progress in literacy displayed by:

- being able to read known text independently
- beginning to attempt unknown text, and well motivated to try.

Understanding of the literacy task is demonstrated by:

- reading more fluently
- being more able to integrate cueing strategies when decoding an unknown word
- being able to discuss stories with insight of character and plot.

Print-processing skills are demonstrated by:

- having a sight vocabulary of approximately 100 words.

Children will now be moving to the orthographic stage of processing text from the alphabetic stage, that is, they are able to recognize groups of letters by their spelling patterns and without needing to decode letter by letter. At times readers still use processing abilities of earlier stages (logographic and alphabetic).

Sound awareness (phonological awareness) is supported by:

- helping children to perfect understanding of grapheme–phoneme correspondence (GPC) in both their reading and writing, using 'invented spelling' and:
  - rhyming words
  - consonant digraphs and blends
  - phonograms (onset and rimes)
  - synthesis of words into syllables.

Print awareness (orthographic awareness/word recognition) is supported by:

- learning a sight word vocabulary in text, games and environmental print
- helping children to spell known words in the course of their own writing by drawing attention to use of word banks, key word lists, high-frequency words for the current topic, and so on
- encouraging familiarity with letter strings and patterns in words (this can also be done during handwriting practice)
- drawing attention to words with common prefixes and suffixes
- helping the decoding of unknown words by analogy with a known word, for example shook/look.

Additional teaching note: handwriting is taught concurrently with the above but not when the child is writing freely and using invented spelling, and when composition is the focus.

Summary

The similarities and differences between learning to speak and learning to read and write were discussed. The main focus of this chapter has been on the decoding skills of reading. For young children to become fluent, accurate and fast readers they have to be able to break words into their constituent sounds (that is, to segment phonemes) and to map accurately those sounds onto the relevant letters or groups of letters. This aspect of literacy requires an understanding of the alphabetic code which takes several years to achieve through exposure to print and text as well as through focused, direct teaching.

Further reading

Funnell, E. and Stuart, M. (eds) (1995) *Learning to Read: Psychology in the Classroom.* Oxford: Blackwell.

Oakhill, J. and Beard, R. (eds) (1999) *Reading Development and the Teaching of Reading.* Oxford: Blackwell.

Riley, J.L. (1996) *The Teaching of Reading: The Development of Literacy in the Early Years of School.* London: Paul Chapman Publishing.

Chapter **6**

A Holistic Approach to the Assessment and Teaching of Literacy

Teachers themselves have to be more knowledgeable and skilled about reading in order to teach it successfully.

(Ofsted, 1996: 8)

It is hardly surprising that training to equip those who are responsible for beginning readers with a good understanding of the core principles and skills of teaching phonic work … has emerged as a crucial issue.

(DfES, 2006: 5)

Introduction

This chapter brings together, in summary, for the reader the most relevant theoretical issues which have been explored in depth in Chapters 1–5 so that the reader can make direct connections between fundamental theoretical concerns and classroom practice. Modes of assessing literacy are viewed as the 'building blocks' on which informed planning and teaching are based, indeed, the embodiment of the current term 'assessment for learning'. The stance taken sees the teaching of reading as interrelated and dovetailed with that of writing, and, crucially, literacy is seen as integral to and interdependent with speaking and listening. The inter- and intra-related nature of oracy and literacy is acknowledged throughout this chapter and indeed the book as a whole which is reflected in the order of the chapters.

The purpose of this chapter

The two documents, the Early Years Foundation Stage Consultation document (DfES, 2006) and the Primary National Strategy: Framework for teaching literacy

(DfES, 2006) provide early years practitioners and teachers with a curriculum for teaching literacy throughout the Foundation Stage and Key Stages 1 and 2 in the primary school. The content of the PNS is handled in detail and stipulates both when (in terms of the year group and at which point in the academic year) and how it is to be taught. So, given there are such specific directives from the government, why is there a need for this book? The reasons, I believe, are these. I have argued elsewhere (Riley, 1996), in line with the two quotations above, that teachers have to be knowledgeable about the processes involved in the acquisition of literacy so that they are able to support children to become effective users of spoken and written language. Teachers are not merely technicians, they are professionals making complex and finely tuned judgements that underpin their teaching. They need to be informed about the 'why' of teaching literacy as well as the 'what' and 'how'. This volume aims to flesh out the theories implicit in the two documents which underpin current thinking about the teaching of reading and writing, and in so doing attempts to fill the theoretical gaps that are unarguably present in both the Early Years Foundation Stage Consultation document (DfES, 2006) and the Primary National Stategy: Framework for teaching literacy (DfES, 2006) in order that practitioners and teachers should be better able to implement effectively both documents with confidence rooted in professional understanding.

This chapter aims to bring together, in summary, as suggested earlier, the relevant theoretical understandings and the modes of assessing literacy, alongside which, further, complementary practical approaches to teaching literacy in early years settings and classrooms are discussed. There will inevitably be some intended repetition from earlier chapters in order to avoid the need for the reader to move back and forth in the book to obtain the necessary information.

Revisiting theories that underpin the teaching of literacy

First and foremost, this chapter reaffirms that children are immensely curious about the world. They are efficient and active makers of meaning as a result of the experiences they have and their attempts to make sense of those experiences. The mastery of spoken and written language are extraordinary examples of this apparently innate disposition to strive for meaning. It has been discussed, and at length, how not only does the meaning-making drive the acquisition of language and literacy, but that the different modes of language, namely, speaking, listening, reading and writing, facilitate higher levels of thinking as children strive to make sense of everything around them. Language enables the individual to abstract, categorize, generalize and through the generation of grammar, permits the acquisition, organization and reorganization of complex concepts.

Secondly, and because children are effective agents in their own learning, it is essential that practitioners and teachers are very skilled diagnosticians concerning the overall development of each child in their professional care, and regarding their specific language and literacy stage in particular. This is crucial so that teaching does not ignore previous learning and in so doing alienate and confuse children, and waste time. In order that early years educators are able to assess accurately children's literacy development , practitioners and teachers need to be knowledgeable about the literacy process and the developmental stages of literacy through which the reader/writer must pass. In other words, both the psychological processes involved and the stages in the learning of literacy need to be thoroughly understood. There are two prerequisites that need to be outlined before successful teaching and learning of literacy can occur. One is a task for the child, the second is a task for the practitioner or teacher.

The child's task

The beginning reader has first to understand the purpose and the conventions of print and then to recognize that the alphabet is a code system.

Research into the emergent phase of literacy has charted the child's journey from the first glimmerings of print awareness to fluent reading and writing (see Chapters 4 and 5). Pre-school children become aware of writing as a rule-based system, and they realize that the purpose of written language is to communicate, that writing is a permanent and unchanging record of meaning and has a particular format, rules and conventions. These principles come to the awareness of the literacy user as a result of experience with texts of many different kinds. The 'why' and 'how' of print, this gradual making sense of written language, is followed by the realization, acquired through both teaching and experience, that the individual shapes, squiggles, curves and loops of the letters of the alphabet are distinct from each other and represent the different sounds of speech. The understanding of the symbolic nature of the alphabet is so crucial that no progress in literacy development can occur without it, however structured, colourful, imaginative and energetic the teaching of grapheme–phoneme (letter–sound) correspondence (GPC) might be.

The adult's task

The practitioner or teacher needs to understand what is involved in the literacy process and how best to support the development of its separate components.

The stance taken in this book is that the reader makes sense of text through the means of a complex system of mutually assisting and interrelated psychological processes (see Introduction and Chapters 3, 4 and 5). Readers, both novice and experienced, need to recognize words either as whole words (as a part of the individual's sight vocabulary) or by decoding them in order to make sense of and to decode a text. The influence of the separate aspects of the processing system is more pronounced at different stages of proficiency and with different types of texts. An overreliance on the use of one process seriously reduces fluency and the ability to make sense of the text. In order to read and write speedily and fluently the reader has to be able to employ all the complementary processes, simultaneously and automatically.

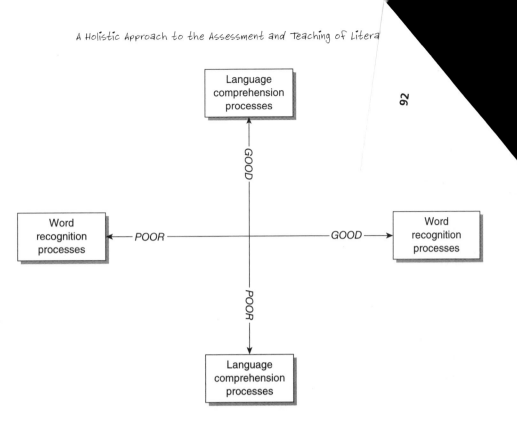

Figure 6.1   *The simple view of reading*

A psychological explanation of reading

In Appendix 1 of the Rose Report (DfES, 2006) Stuart acknowledges that read-ing is a complex activity, with two main aspects to it: 'decoding' and 'com-prehension'. While not the whole story it makes good and practical sense for teachers to think of these two components and that children need to be sup-ported with both. Decoding is the ability to 'recognise words presented singly out of context, with the ability to apply phonic rules a crucial contributory factor to the development of this context-free word recognition ability' (DfES, 2006: 76).

Comprehension refers to the linguistic comprehension (or understanding) by which the individual processes the meaning of words, sentences and texts to access the meaning. Psychologists consider there to be a set of linguistic principles which govern the comprehension of oral and written language.

Stuart goes on to say:

We believe that the simple view of reading [see Figure 6.1] provides a valid con-ceptual framework that is useful to practitioners and researchers alike. Clear dif-ferentiation between the two dimensions of reading provides a conceptual framework that:

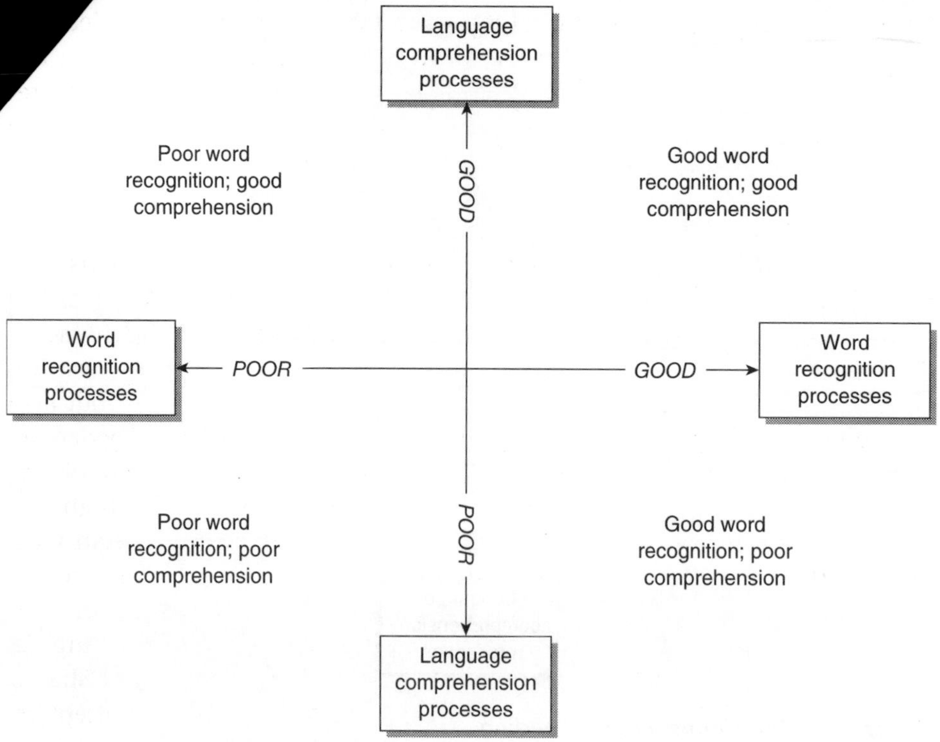

Figure 6.2   Different patterns of performance

a) encourages teachers not necessarily to expect that the children they teach will show equal performance or progress in each dimension;
b) offers the possibility of separately assessing performance and progress in each dimension, to identify learning needs and guide further teaching;
c) makes explicit to teachers that different kinds of teaching are needed to develop word recognition skills from those that are needed to foster the comprehension of written and spoken language; and
d) emphasises the need for teachers to be taught about and to understand the cognitive processes involved in the development of both accurate word recognition skills and language comprehension. (DfES, 2006: 78)

Figure 6.2 describes how children can vary and be imbalanced in their developing competence in both these dimensions.

The decoding skills and ways to develop them

Sound awareness

To learn to read, the child has also to be able to hear and distinguish between the different words and then to discriminate between the constituent sounds in each word (phonemic segmentation). These are then decoded from the letters and groups of letters on the printed page. The child who has this ability is said to understand grapheme–phoneme (letter–sound) correspondence (GPC). This aspect of reading is demonstrated clearly in Figure 6.1. An appreciation of both the visual aspects of print (orthographic processing) and the identification of the aural sounds of spoken language (phonological processing) develop side by side, the interrelationship ensures that each complements the other. The development of one supports and reinforces the development of the other. This processing is referred to as the decoding skills. These skills can be developed not only through the adult sharing picture books with children, and so implicitly generating meaning from the printed text which includes drawing on the illustrations, but also through directly supporting the decoding aspect of reading. The experienced reader assists the novice by pointing to words as they are read aloud, directing attention to different words and pointing out those that are high frequency, distinctive or highly patterned, for example, words that begin with the same letters as those in children's own names and are therefore memorable and easily identified. These approaches are incorporated in and described fully in the Primary National Strategy: Framework for teaching literacy (DfES, 2006) under the term Shared Reading. An adaptation of Shared Reading is appropriate in some nursery settings, and certainly in reception classes, but taking place with smaller groups of children and lasting a shorter length of time.

Key Term

Shared Reading: in a group situation, as recommended by the PNS, Shared Reading is reading (usually with an enlarged text) where an adult and children work together on a text, with the adult demonstrating, modelling and encouraging reading behaviours and skills. This approach to teaching reading offers children the experience of being supported in reading texts that they could not manage alone, with the support of both teacher and the peer group. (See Chapter 7 for a fuller description.)

These skills of phonological (sound) and orthographic (print) awareness are developed through both reading *and* writing as the new school entrant gets to grips with both decoding and encoding as a literacy user. But a model of a teaching approach that takes into account and is appropriate to the child's literacy stage can powerfully assist progress (see Chapters 4 and 5).

Sound (phonological) awareness work will begin in the nursery, as suggested in the the Early Years Foundation Stage (consultation document, DfES, 2006) and the Primary National Strategy, Framework for teaching literacy (DfES, 2006) both of which provide details of the order in which adults should teach the content. As discussed fully in Chapter 5, phonological awareness develops slowly and the child passes through stages on the way to being able to break up words accurately into phonemes (phonemic segmentation).

The first linguistic unit that young children appear to be able spontaneously to distinguish is rhyme (see Chapter 5). Working with a small group of early readers, at approximately the same stage of phonological development, in order to focus on rhyme such as the breaking of words into the 'onset' (initial phoneme) and 'rime' (end phoneme), for example sh-**ook**, and then considering other words with the same endings b-**ook**, l-**ook**, t-**ook**, should take only a few minutes, and mainly when the children are writing. This can be very valuable, and perhaps undertaken when Shared Writing is taking place during group teaching. Commercial and teacher-produced card and board games can usefully promote phonological awareness if available regularly, or even daily.

Key Term

Shared Writing: an equivalent writing situation to Shared Reading, with the adult and child(ren) eliciting wordings and spellings by appropriate prompts. The children are offered the model of an experienced writer making decisions on both compositional and transcriptional aspects of writing. (See Chapter 8 for further discussion.)

Print awareness

The direct teaching of *print (orthographic) awareness* has to be first encouraged by thorough learning of the alphabet, perhaps through a published synthetic phonics scheme such as 'Letterland', 'THRASS' or 'Jolly Phonics', with games, rhymes and also through plentiful, varied, attractive alphabet books and friezes. There are also digital versions such as 'Fast Phonics First' available from primary.marketing@harcourteducation.co.uk, or 'Letterland Living ABC' available from www.r.e.m.co.uk. See also Chapter 11 for other suggestions. The Rose Report recommends adherence to one chosen scheme.

By the end of the reception year, children need to be able to both recognize and identify the upper and lower case letters of the alphabet, and to reproduce them when writing, without constant recourse to an alphabet chart. The Rose Report builds on this and suggests that:

> Because our writing system is alphabetic, beginner readers must be taught how the letters of the alphabet, singly or in combination, represent sounds of spoken language (letter–sound correspondences) and how to blend (synthesise) the sounds to read words, and break up (segment) the sounds in words to spell. They must learn to process all the letters in words and 'read words in and out of text'. Phonic work should teach these skills and knowledge in a well defined and systematic sequence. (DfES, 2006: 18)

Building of a sight vocabulary

The acquisition of a sight vocabulary follows through, and for, reading and writing of high-frequency words of interest, those from the early reading books or relevant to the current topic. The PNS Framework for teaching literacy (DfES, 2006) provides high-frequency word lists and a suggested sequence of introduction to pupils in Reception and Years 1 and 2. The memorization of words that children will frequently meet in reading scheme books, and also those that will be needed when writing, has great benefit. An increasingly large sight vocabulary speeds up reading and writing fluency, providing a basis of known words whenever a new text is met or is to be written. Energy is then released for decoding unknown words, and employing all available cueing strategies when doing so. These key words can be stored in individual word banks or folders for each child, or in card pockets on a wall display, and they should be in constant use for reference, cross-checking letter order and the patterns of letter strings in words, as practice exercises and games.

Key Term

Sight vocabulary: the rapid and accurate recognition of an increasing repertoire of the common key words of text will speed progress towards fluent reading once the child has grasped the purpose and usefulness of the literacy task. However, it is of *no value* whatever to begin too early or before the child has grasped conceptually what reading and writing are for, what the purpose of literacy is, and what it can do for human beings. Teaching words out of context, particularly before children have any alphabetic decoding strategies at their disposal, results in the old hazards of the despised 'flash card' work from the cherished practice of the 1960s and 1970s. It leads to stories such as the one about a 5-year-old child playing the 'flash card' game with the teacher; when defeated by the proffered card she is unhelpfully prompted by an equally confused friend with 'Try DOG – it sometimes works!!'

Teaching to support print recognition

Practitioners and teachers of children in the early stages of learning to read have traditionally taught a list of high-frequency words in order to promote print awareness and to increase speed and fluency in both reading and writing. This practice went out of fashion for a while as it was seen to be too mechanistic and joyless an activity compared with the excitement of devouring challenging, stimulating texts!

Now, however, learning a sight vocabulary of high-frequency words or those of personal interest, words from the core reading scheme or the vocabulary of the class project, is enshrined in the practice of the PNS Framework for teaching literacy (DfES, 2006) along with its lists of words to be memorized in progression through Reception and Years 1 and 2. Recent research evidence suggests that this is sound practice.

In Chapter 4, it was discussed that in order for whole or sight words to be stored in an individual's lexicon (word memory bank) the words have to be 'learned' or seen so often that a logogen or 'image' is created of them by the brain. The shape of the entire word then can be recalled when writing or recognized when reading, and the meaning is accessed from the individual's memory store. This process is achieved through developmental stages and is influenced by the refinement of phonological (sound) awareness. There are stages through which the child passes on the way to fluent print processing, which have been discussed in depth in Chapter 5 but are here outlined again as a reminder of their importance.

Frith's theory: the logographic phase of sight word reading

In the first of the stages of the ability to process print as described by Frith (1985) the young child perceives words as wholes or as logograms. The word is recognized by the child by its personally memorable and highly distinctive visual features. Children in this stage have no recourse to phonological recoding, as both letters of the alphabet and the associated sounds are not known or salient to the reader at this early stage of literacy development.

At this stage of sight word reading it is helpful if the teacher draws to the child's attention the salient features of text rather than relying on idiosyncratic mnemonics, as in the case of the child who knew a word was 'television' because of the two 'i's or the two sticks in 'lollipop', which is hardly the most useful or sustainable strategy to use. Focusing attention to the letter–sound relationship (GPC) with distinctive letters encourages the use of more transferable strategies.

Learning and Teaching Suggestions

A practitioner is working with a group of 4-year-olds on a large poster (A3 size or larger) of the nursery rhyme of 'Humpty Dumpty'. After several joint 'reading/recitations' along with pointing and one-to-one matching of sound to word, she will draw children's attention to the two distinctive words H-**umpty** D-**umpty**. The words have different onsets and a common rime and, by drawing attention to the sound units matched to the written language, children's print awareness develops.

What other activities to promote print and sound awareness could the practitioner generate from the nursery rhyme 'Humpty Dumpty'?

Are there any pitfalls with words that are an aural rhyme but not a visual one ... and so cause confusion? for example, ch-**air** and p-**ear**.

The alphabetic stage of sight word reading

The child moves into the next phase of print processing as letters of the alphabet are learned by their distinguishing shapes, names or sounds. Ehri (1992) maintains that it is this knowledge that provides the child with sufficient 'low-level phonemic awareness' to allow beginnings and ends of words to be recognized and rudimentary sound–spelling connections to be made. Words are still remembered by their distinctive shape details but a crude sound–symbol link is also attached to the recognition process for the word, and this is then effectively committed to the lexical memory-store of sight vocabulary. The pupil's early writing can be a useful indication that this stage of print processing has been reached (although production lags behind recognition).

At this stage children will need to learn to recognize on sight the common function words such as 'went', 'play', 'on', 'in' and 'but' which make up 25 per cent of all text that they will encounter at this stage of reading. These words tax the visual memory as they present no visual image to the child and are best learned by games that match phrases or sentences on a card to a reading book. Written on strips of card, phrases are matched under text by the child and then can be cut up, read, learned and reassembled as a phrase.

The orthographic stage of sight word reading

The reader is able to short-circuit the letter-by-letter phonological conversion of the previous stage through being able to process 'chunks' of print (in the form of clusters or patterns of letters) from sight memory. Parts of words are automatically processed from the lexical memory for both encoding and decoding, and children speed up when reading and spelling become more regular. Fluency is greatly enhanced as decoding becomes almost instantaneous and, with it, comprehension is improved.

The more reading children do and the more fluent they become, the greater their sight vocabulary or memory bank will be. Fewer words will need decoding afresh each time they are encountered. Sight words are stored in the reader's lexical memory bank and can be recalled instantly when perceived, and are often recalled along with the phrases and patterns of written language in which they occur. This literacy knowledge is not acquired simply through learning by rote, perhaps particularly not by learning by rote! Reading is an active process and the brain has to process words thoroughly by perceiving, comprehending and using, and not by memorizing. A parallel example might be the learning of vocabulary lists of a foreign language. These can be remembered after a period of time only with actual use, and that is most powerfully achieved in the country where it is spoken and when used to fulfil a variety of purposes.

The further ways a sight vocabulary is acquired

Early years practitioners and teachers can support print awareness and the development of a sight vocabulary by offering their pupils opportunities to:

- read many types of text on different subjects with rich patterns of language and which capitalize on repetition and rhythm
- use the language experience approach to literacy (see Chapter 3) which converts spoken language into writing in the child's presence and explicitly reinforces letter–sound relationships (GPC) and the patterns and structures of words
- write with adult support on a variety of topics for many purposes (see the section on Shared Writing in this chapter)
- attend to words in and out of context, common words in environmental print, children's names, labels, notices and signs
- use word folders and word banks when writing and when playing word games
- have the words from the PNS high-frequency word lists drawn to their attention, when appropriate and not to interrupt the story, when reading continuous texts.

Assessment: the starting point for teaching

An awareness of the beginner reader's development – what the child understands and can do – is essential before effective teaching can occur. Given that reading involves a system of perceptual and cognitive operations, it is the task of the adult working with the child to analyse the outward, observable signs that indicate the processing that is occurring.

The Rose Report states:

> Good assessment should track performance in all four strands of language: speaking, listening, reading and writing, and identify strengths and weaknesses in children's knowledge, skills and understanding, especially those related to mastering word recognition skills. Hence assessment for learning is vital for planning work that is matched well to children's needs. (DfES, 2006: 22)

Clay has described how through knowledgeable, skilled observation of the child when reading, the teacher is able to assess the behaviours displayed and the strategies the child employs in order to read an unknown word. For the purposes of this book an unknown word can be described as one that is not in her/his memory bank of sight words and has to be decoded or worked out. Clay (1991: 232) describes this notion as sensitive observation while teaching. This is not a principle that is new to early years teachers; the adage observe, support, extend is a fundamental part of their professional repertoire.

Assessment for learning

Regarding *literacy-related behaviours,* the teacher should note the complex and fleetingly demonstrated repertoire of different reading behaviour which shows understanding on the part of the child is vast and takes experience and practice on behalf of the teacher to both notice it, and to know how to interpret it.

The consideration of the language that is used by the child

Most children bring to the task of literacy a competence in spoken language which includes:

- an understanding of the meaning of the words
- an ability to manipulate the sounds of the language
- an ability to construct sentences to order to communicate
- a wide range of vocabulary.

In addition to these impressive achievements, the child will be beginning to be aware of the conventions of literary language and the patterns and rhythm of oral language. Teachers will notice the influence of the children's oral language in their early attempts to read and write. Competent use of oral language has within it the basis of the children's ability to predict words when reading, through their deep knowledge of language structures and meanings.

Understanding of the conventions of print

The early stages of learning to read involve becoming aware of concepts about print and the realization that it is necessary to pay attention to them. These include:

- the appreciation of directionality of text
- the spaces between words and lines
- formats, punctuation and the general features of continuous text.

Consolidation of these understandings occurs, for most children, slowly over the first year of school and leads on to more refined understandings of meta-language and the understanding of a letter, a word and a sentence.

Awareness of visual information

This includes early orthographic awareness of children exploring patterns of print in highly personal ways.

Hearing sounds in sequence in words

This involves the development of phonological awareness.

The sources of information about text that the child is able to employ in order to make sense of it, as described above, are demonstrated clearly in the Clay diagram in Chapter 5 (Figure 5.1).

Assessing and recording literacy progress

A well-developed diagnostic ability of literacy development and assessment of progress is essential when working with a child who is delayed in reading development or confused about certain aspects of literacy. I would argue, however, that the observant and knowledgeable practitioner and teacher has a huge advantage over less well informed colleagues when teaching beginner readers. The potential for the young child's progress to be erratic or unbalanced is immense, given the complexity of the literacy process. This is before the issue of individual learning styles or particular difficulties are considered. Therefore the monitoring of development of all pupils is very important.

The main reasons for a class teacher to regularly monitor the literacy progress of the pupils are to:

- establish what each individual can do
- identify what strategies each child is using
- assess the individual child's stage and rate of development
- enable the teacher to provide appropriate teaching and tasks for the individual and/or small groups of children
- inform the choice of the appropriate materials and resources
- ensure appropriate organizational strategies are used, for example, for different groupings of children.

Monitoring follows the assess–plan–teach–assess cycle of primary teaching and is integral to the programme for literacy. Monitoring needs to be carried out at regular intervals; many theorists suggest every three or four weeks in Reception and Year 1 for those pupils making average progress. Children with difficulties will need to be assessed more frequently.

Monitoring can occur at different levels during normal teaching sessions. Class organization can be arranged so that there is an opportunity to assess one or two children daily.

Formal monitoring follows assessment on arrival at school (see Chapter 4). Experienced teachers constantly observe children across all types of activity in order to monitor learning, and this diagnostic observation informs teaching.

More formal monitoring involves assessing and recording the child's development regarding:

- the attitudes to literacy and ability to concentrate
- the essential understandings about print and its conventions
- the processing evident when reading continuous text;

Specific skills and abilities that need to be assessed are:

- how well directionality and one-to-one matching are established (that is, written word to spoken word)

- the extent to which the child can predict, confirm and self-correct
- the ability with which the child is able to reconstruct meaning of the text
- the range and extent of the child's sight vocabulary
- the child's ability to hear sounds in words (that is, whether she/he can segment phonemes) and to map the sounds onto a symbol or group of symbols, with increasing accuracy in appreciation of the vagaries of the English language
- the stage of the child's writing development in particular with invented spellings.

Holdaway's advice is still sound: 'the best policy is to monitor actual behaviour as the child carries out the task in a meaningful situation – such as normal reading and writing within the programme – and to compare such observations with those taken for the same child at some previous time' (1979: 168).

A teacher's observation of one or two children daily through undertaking a **miscue analysis** or a **running reading record** ensures that all the pupils in the class are formally assessed approximately every half-term. Such records, when completed regularly and systematically, monitor reading (processing) behaviour as the reader is working on an unfamiliar text, in order to build up a picture of development. Pupils who cause concern may need more frequent monitoring. Children progress at different rates from each other and are at different stages of development. Class teachers need to be aware of the variations within and between pupils, in order to ensure that the class provision matches their constantly changing literacy needs.

Key Terms

Miscue analysis: a procedure for recording a child's reading verbatim and analysing the miscues (mistakes) diagnostically in order to understand the strategies the child is using and the child needs.

Running reading record: this gives a quantitative and a qualitative analysis of the child's reading in order to inform the progress the child has made and the cueing systems the child is able to employ.

Running reading records and miscue analysis

Miscue analysis and running reading records are methods of assessing reading behaviour, largely unaided, and recording the level of accuracy on an unfamiliar text. In addition, the assessment uses children's errors, or, the more appropriately named, miscues, as the focus for analysis in determining the processing abilities of the reader as they utilize the cues available to them. In other words these assessment tools are systematic frameworks for observation that enable the knowledgeable teacher to capture and record the behaviours that are an indication of the print processing that the children are able to employ when reading a text.

Issues regarding the choice of texts

When undertaking an observation of the child's reading, the choice of the text is important. If it is a text that the child finds too easy this will mean that most of the words are being read from the sight vocabulary. If the text is too difficult it will mean that the child is not able to read a sufficient number of the words to be able to benefit from the meaning-making processing to inform the decoding processing of the text. In other words, if the text is too difficult and many of the words are ignored, there is no opportunity for the child to be able to predict a word using overall sense, context or syntax cues.

The levels of text difficulty

Difficulty of texts can be determined through the child being able to read the following proportions of the passage:

- an easy text (95–100 per cent correct)
- an instructional text (90–94 per cent correct)
- a hard text (80–89 per cent correct) (Clay, 2002: 55).

The running reading record is most useful for teachers of children at the beginning stages of reading because it provides opportunity both to analyse the errors or miscues, for the reasons cited above, and to estimate the child's performance quantitatively and so monitor progress. This is achieved only if a school has the reading books organized in a structured progression of difficulty, which enables teachers to determine the appropriateness of the reading book in terms of a match between a child's reading ability to text difficulty in a systematic way (see references to *Book Bands* in Chapter 7).

Taking a running reading record

The approach to taking a running reading record (not a running record as my students call them – as if we are fitness freaks!) is to practise and then to practise some more. The conventions are the most difficult aspect of the record to use well and the observation aspect requires expertise, obviously, but mainly experience. Practice makes perfect! The more records that teachers undertake the more subtle the behaviour that will be noticed.

The conventions used can be found in Clay (2002) Chapter 5.

Assessment: grasp of the alphabetic code through writing

Early mark-making attempts have huge value for the practitioner or teacher as, unlike reading, they are a permanent record of the child's print-processing abilities. Writing is the mirror image of reading in that it is the encoding of the sounds within words into written language. In reading, the goal is to access meaning which is achieved through the following strategies:

- the shape of a word as a whole
- its context
- decoding by grapheme–phoneme correspondence (GPC)
- orthographic processing (or chunking groups of letters through sight memory).

Writing is often letter-by-letter grapho-motor production. Both processes contribute to literacy acquisition, writing development occurs slightly later than reading, although they are interrelated and complementary to each other.

Clay talks about very early mark-making as being an exploration of literacy and describes the process that children go through as a pathway 'from scribble to letter-like forms, to letter like shapes, often part of their own name, to favourite letters and particular words ... all the time invented forms and invented words intrude into productions as they explore possibilities' (1993: 11). These early attempts demonstrate the child struggling to grasp the conventions of print as well as the beginnings of letter–sound knowledge.

As children write they actively struggle with the orthographic and phonological processing as they map one onto the other. They represent the sounds they can hear in parts of words with symbols on the paper, using invented spelling (that is, the beginning writers are inventing and working out the sound–symbol correspondences (GPC) when *not* provided with words to copy write, or one at a time, with a personal dictionary, or with a *Breakthrough to Literacy* folder). This approach to writing provides the adult with a crucially important opportunity to analyse literacy development.

When inventing spellings, children tend to move through the following stages of development (Gentry, 1981), which gradually become more refined and conventional.

Pre-communication

At this stage the young writers indicate that they know that symbols can represent speech for a given purpose. The writing will be a rough approximation of known letters or numbers. Often the letters of their own name are used repeatedly and in random order.

Semi-phonetic

One-, two- and three-letter spellings, at this stage, show some representation of letter–sound (grapheme–phoneme) correspondence, for example, wnt = went, dg = dog, p = please.

Phonetic

Now the writer has almost perfect grapheme–phoneme match as the child develops the ability to phonologically segment words, for example, becos = because, wot = what, sed = said, wen = when.

Transitional

At this stage of literacy development, children are in the orthographic stage of reading and able to process groups of letters without letter-by-letter conversion, in writing they are able to move gradually towards conventional spelling. The ability to process 'chunks' of words enables a recognition of the 'look' of a word to be remembered, and familiar patterns from a working sight vocabulary can be utilized, but imperfectly, for example, huose = house, eightee = eighty, thay = they. In this stage children begin to appreciate that in English the same sound can be represented by different groups of letters, for example, *ay, ai* or *a … e.*

If children are encouraged to use invented spelling, they will demonstrate developing awareness of

- alphabet and letter names
- letter–sound relationships.

When writing on their own children demonstrate other understandings such as:

- directional rules
- concepts of a letter or a word
- the functions of space
- the ordering of letters in a word
- the sequence of sounds within a word
- punctuation.

Implications for practice

The teaching approach of Shared or Guided Writing capitalizes on the experimental and self-directed nature of this mark-making and early writing. It is necessary to teach, and therefore support further progress by scaffolding children's encoding at exactly the appropriate moment. An early years practitioner or teacher working either on shared texts or with children working on their own texts in small groups with four or five pupils at similar stages of development is an effective way of enabling print–sound connections (GPC) to be emphasized and reinforced. Modelling writing with use of a whiteboard or an easel is helpful. Close observation of the writing as it is being generated letter by letter enables support to be given at exactly the right moment. Too early intervention and essential problem-solving is curtailed, too delayed and the child has moved on to the next word and the moment of focused attention and decision-making is lost. Assistance with breaking a word into its constituent sounds and then support and direction to the symbol or grapheme (that is, letter or the choice between two letters) on an alphabet strip that represents that sound are very valuable.

For some children, support at this stage of writing is only needed for a very short time; for others such directed and focused teaching is required for longer until they genuinely have grasped the alphabetic code as a system. For these children this activity should be a frequent one and planned within the Literacy Hour group activities well into Year 1.

Assessment of attitudes to reading

Assessment of the child's developing ability to process text (taking into account all the component aspects) is only part of the picture of literacy development that the early years practitioner or teacher must be aware of for each of her pupils. Early years practitioners and teachers will want to observe how enthusiastic children are about reading, which books they choose to look at or work with, and which types of books they enjoy. Length of concentration span and levels of motivation need to be noted too. This insight into the child's informal knowledge, skills, interests and attitudes about reading is important from the perspective of the child as a reader in a wider sense.

Awareness of the overall literacy profile is achieved through the observation of the child in many different circumstances and situations. These might include:

- noting enjoyment of and involvement with books, stories and storytimes
- noticing the books the child chooses to look at when not directed
- talking to children about particular books and seeking their views of their own reading development (such self-evaluation is often very informative)

- observing a child during shared or group reading, and noting levels of engagement and participation
- asking parents about children's level of interest when reading at home
- noting the type and frequency of written records kept by parents in connection with the home–school reading scheme. This will reveal a great deal about the emphasis placed on literacy and the messages given daily to children at home about the value of learning to read.

Record-keeping

The comprehensive set of observation data of the type described will be informative and useful for the early years practitioner or class teacher to inform planning, teaching and grouping of children for teaching purposes. All documentation kept on individual pupils needs to be manageable and of potential value to the class teacher. The frequent review of records needs to be built into the school policy in order to establish the pupils' rates of progress. Systematic and regularly kept records ensure that progress is monitored for all pupils and provides evidence on the fast, average and slower literacy learners.

A language and literacy profile

A language and literacy profile might take the form of a folder for each pupil containing the following records:

- school entry checklist/baseline assessment
- running reading records (completed approximately every three weeks), which need to include the analysis of the observations and notes on levels of comprehension and discussion of the stories read
- title and level of difficulty of books read
- notes on any discussion with parents and home–school records
- dated, annotated samples of the child's writing
- brief notes of conversations with children about their reading, especially those that denote interests and attitudes.

Summary

This chapter has revisited

- the theoretical background that underpins the teaching of literacy in order to supplement the picture presented by the Early Years Foundation Stage (Consultation document, DfES, 2006) and the PNS: Framework for teaching literacy (DfES, 2006)

and has discussed

- how an understanding of the literacy process can be translated into informed practice in the classroom
- the implementation of a holistic, balanced literacy programme in an early years setting or classroom
- the value of teaching to develop a sight vocabulary and sound awareness
- the place of assessment and monitoring of progress which informs planning and teaching.

Further reading

Clay, M.M. (2002) *An Observation Survey of Early Literacy Achievement.* 2nd edn. Auckland, NZ: Heinemann.

Chapter **7**

A Creative Approach to Planning Communication, Language and Literacy

[W]e must become universally committed to developing their [children's] appreciation of and familiarity with text ... in our society, their lives depend upon it.

(Adams, 1996: 91)

Introduction

The research literature illustrates that, while there are features in common, learning to read and write is not a natural process comparable to learning to speak, but is a demanding and, for most young children, a hard-won undertaking (see, for example, Donaldson,1978; Snow, 1983, 1991).

In this chapter, consideration will be given to planning for the effective provision for language and literacy learning throughout the early years. The chapter will build on the discussion in the previous chapter of the complex and interconnected array of psychological processes that occur when an individual is reading fluently, and suggest assessment techniques for each of the aspects. We have emphasized earlier (Chapters 3, 4, 5 and 6) how, with an alphabetic system, children must understand and use effectively multiple strategies in order to decode and fully comprehend written language. In the context of this web of attitudes, concepts and skills that children need to acquire in order to become fully literate, attention will focus now on how we can provide for the systematic development of these through planning rich and engaging literacy learning opportunities for children from 3 to 7 years of age.

Motivation to read and being a successful reader

It is almost so obvious that it goes without saying that, given the challenge that learning to read presents to young children, it will be accomplished more successfully if being literate becomes, or is seen as, a source of satisfaction and pleasure. Indeed, the research literature distinguishes between reading to please an adult and reading to please oneself, and shows different outcomes between the two. Oldfather and Dahl (1994) and Turner (1995) argue that intrinsic motivation is essential for full engagement in the process of learning to read. Guthrie and Wigfield (2000) claim also that motivated readers are strategic in their use of a range of approaches to comprehension, they are knowledgeable in their construction of new understandings from text, as well as being socially interactive in their approach to literacy. In consequence they argue, readers who are fully engaged with texts are more successful as readers. Research evidence suggests also that children who read frequently and are active in trying to understand texts, improve their levels of text comprehension as a consequence (Cipielewski and Stanovich, 1992). The nature and cause of intrinsic motivation is hard to unravel, some children while believing themselves to be good at reading also report that they do not enjoy it very much but, conversely, it is rare for struggling readers to report very much enjoyment from reading. It would appear then, that if pleasure is derived from books and wanting to learn to read makes a qualitative difference as to *how* children read, it behoves teachers to have motivating children in the forefront of their thoughts when planning their literacy provision.

The Rose Report also confirms the need for ensuring the pupils are motivated when it says: 'Obviously, developing children's positive attitudes to literacy, in the broadest sense, from the earliest stage is very important. In the best circumstances, parents and carers, along with settings and schools do much to foster these attitudes' (DfES, 2006: 4).

Developing a class of enthusiastic readers

Throughout the early years age phase, certain features appear to be conditional if groups of children are to become highly motivated readers. Practitioners and teachers need to:

- be informed and knowledgeable about the processes involved with literacy, an issue summarized in Chapter 6
- read for pleasure themselves, be up to date and enthusiastic about books for children and be familiar with texts across different genres

- know how to capitalize on opportunities for teaching literacy, employing multiple approaches from focused, teacher-directed literacy activities (such as Shared and Guided Reading in the Literacy Hour in KS 1) to include also cross-curricular approaches to their planning in order to authentically embed literacy learning opportunities in a meaningful context.

Towards a deep understanding of literacy

We have seen from the research literature that children need to become conscious of how language works in a deep sense in order to learn to read and write successfully. This will be achieved if an enticing and purposeful approach to the learning and teaching of language and literacy is adopted, such as the list above implies. This deep understanding is termed 'meta-linguistic awareness' and involves a conscious awareness of the components of language and how it is used and includes understandings of language at text, sentence, word and sub-word levels. Chapman (2004) summarizes what the term meta-linguistic awareness covers; children need to understand the nature and purposes of written language by being aware of the following:

The 'big picture' understandings –

- how language and literacy are used in the world
- the symbolic nature of language.

The more refined understandings –

- conventions of print (including directionality, spacing, spelling and punctuation)
- what print looks like (that is, the visual and perceptual features)
- meta-language (understanding the terms used to describe language such as 'letter', 'word' and 'sound')
- understanding the link between spoken and written language (these include the alphabetic principle, the phonetic principle, and phonological awareness moving into phonemic awareness)
- structural characteristics of written language at text and sentence levels.

It is common sense, from the awesome list above, that children do not and cannot achieve a thorough intellectual grasp of all the aspects of meta-linguistic awareness if exposed only to narrow exercises and phonic drills. Language development flourishes when the provision offers stimulating, first-hand experiences and where spoken and written language are used in a meaningful, functional manner to investigate and record topics and items of genuine interest, and when literature is savoured. So, within a rich literacy provision there will be access to a balance of quality fiction and non-fiction texts across the range of genre (see Chapter 9) for the children to become familiar and interested in how language works in many different situations for a variety of purposes. Finally, but importantly, as we have discussed earlier in this volume, effective and deep learning occurs most powerfully when children are active, when they are enabled to work collaboratively in a social setting and when they are supported, at precisely the opportune moment, by more experienced and knowledgeable language users.

Let us see what such provision might look like.

Language and literacy provision in the Foundation Stage

Case Study 7.1

This is a case study example of how a planning framework can be used to support the development of language and literacy within the class topic of pets. The Reception class at Thornhill Primary School, Islington, London, had become interested in the care and enjoyment of domestic pets. The pets being studied are of the types commonly kept by people in an urban setting – dogs, cats, rabbits, guinea pigs, hamsters, mice, gerbils, fish, tortoises and birds.

A parent brought for a morning visit to the class a recently acquired puppy, Smokey, which sparked the initial interest of the children; they were shown how to groom and feed the dog, discussion took place on how to house train him (much amusement occurred at this juncture!!) and the course of immunization he had been through before being allowed out onto the street.

When the dog fell asleep the children drew him with pastel crayons, and some did paintings. Lists of words which best described the puppy were written on A3 sheets of paper and put on display on an easel.

Class discussion at the end of the morning centred on the advantages of having a pet but also the disadvantages were considered and written down. The visit ended with a poem 'My Puppy' by Aileen Fisher.

The following morning, the parent-owner of the puppy stayed for the initial class discussion to tell the children that Smokey was unwell. The symptoms were of a hot, dry nose, and he was very uninterested in his food so he was going to be taken to the vet. Discussion then centred around veterinary surgeons and what they do. A class visit to the neighbourhood veterinary practice was suggested and considered by everyone to be an excellent idea. Cards were made and letters written to the vet to ask if members of the class could visit his surgery.

The visits occurred in groups of five or six children at a time to the veterinary surgery the following week. Productive use was made of the time lapse to undertake some research with non-fiction books about the work of vets and what types of animals a vet in a city might treat. While a group was visiting the vet, those remaining worked on converting the home corner into a veterinary surgery.

Transformation of the home corner

This was imaginatively constructed with one side consisting of a wall of sturdy cardboard boxes (wine case size!) covered in craft paper and stapled together with the openings outwards. The boxes became containers and cages for toy pets brought from home, mainly of the fluffy kitten and cuddly puppy variety. A hamster was loaned to the class for the duration of the topic and lived in the vet's office. The surgery also contained an examination table, boxes of files on the pets, a shallow plastic tray of the essentials for the treatment of sick pets, namely, a stethoscope, plastic syringes (minus needles, obviously), bandages, cotton wool, scissors, tweezers, antiseptic lotion bottles and pill cartons. A row of chairs opposite authentic posters on the walls reminded the waiting pet owners of the value of flea powder, certain pet foods and the necessity for immunization against various diseases.

A book display of a range of reference books (at both adult and child level) were placed strategically on a table near the veterinary surgery for adult and child use. This enabled the meaningful integration of first- and second-hand experience; the books of different levels and types on the subject of animals and vets were on hand to be used at key points when further information was genuinely needed.

With this topic as the purposeful context in which to embed the language and literacy, the following describes a morning's work. Mathematics, science and other subjects were integrated successfully, but here the focus for clarity was on English.

Opportunities for speaking and listening

Class discussion will take place on how to care for a cat. An adult will work with a small group to write books on caring for kittens, but this preliminary work will establish what the class knows and what needs to be researched. The teacher will scribe suggestions on the easel.

Opportunities for becoming aware of the 'big picture' of literacy

A group of children accompanied by the teaching assistant will work with a variety of informational material books and leaflets on the care of cats. Short sections are read to the children and some browse through the books looking at the illustrations, many of which are photographs of high quality. Exploratory talk will be supported. The use of non-fiction books will be modelled, looking in the contents and index for the topic and so on.

Opportunities to become aware of concepts about print

A group will go to read the poster of the poem that the class are learning about the puppy, they can point and 'read' half from memory of the learned poem with pleasure. Small black and white A4-sized versions will be available on another table for another group of children to illustrate and to 'read' together.

These will go home to be learned and read again with support from parents and carers.

Opportunities to develop phonological awareness

After the class discussion the teacher will work with a group on the class poem, drawing attention to the rhyming words and identifying similar rimes at the ends of words, the sounds they make, and writing them for the children with different coloured pens.

Opportunities to identify and name the letters of the alphabet and to learn the sounds they represent

Another group of children are working on an animal alphabet frieze, which will be used for the display on the wall.

Each child will choose a letter to illustrate with an animal the name of which starts with the letter. Felt pens will be put out to draw bright, clear pictures of the chosen animal to fill an A4 sheet of paper, each of which will be used to make up the frieze. Both the upper and lower case versions of the letters will be written by an adult with a large marker pen to accompany the drawing, illustrating the model of the handwriting style adopted by the school. The child will be present when this is done to reinforce letter shapes.

Opportunities to begin to become aware of GPC

In the nursery this enables the children to move towards secure knowledge at the end of reception class.

Suggestions for development of GPC as above and below.

Opportunities to mark-make for a purpose

After half an hour of investigation and research on the care of cats, the group who have researched with the reference books will work next with the teacher to write their own versions in small blank books prepared earlier for them. The teacher will first demonstrate the compositional aspects of writing, developing ideas and structuring them into sentences for which the writing is modelled in front of the group. The children will each attempt to write their own version on a page in their books. Any support needed with the GPC will be given by the adult as the writers attempt to convert spoken language into written text in an embryonic form of the instructional genre. As individuals identify each sound they can hear in a word (phonemic segmentation) they intend to write, support is given to find the relevant grapheme/s on the alphabet strip on the table in order to encode it. This scaffolded work is of immense benefit to learning how the alphabetic code operates in a functional and meaningful way.

The children will draw an illustration to accompany each sentence about the care of cats point made.

A few children will read their work and share it with the whole group at the end of the morning session.

Work continues

Further literacy opportunities will include listening to stories on the topic, such as *My Cat Likes to Hide in Boxes*, with children's own retelling using story props and enjoying the rhyme or to a poem or the collaborative rereading of the dog poem, 'My Puppy'. Shared Reading (Chapter 6) is appropriate only for very brief periods of time in reception unless, perhaps, at the end of the reception year or with a group of children for whom it is developmentally relevant. This makes the Shared Reading of a poem very suitable for this age group as children at this age should not be expected to sit for long periods in whole-class activities. The topic theme could be continued to include other pets and their care, story writing about adventures the pets might have and so on. The home corner play will continue in the vet's surgery, with appointment books and records kept on the pets. The theme of the topic might be expanded after a few weeks to investigate zoos and their animals, or animals that work, such as police or guide dogs.

Suggested resources

Burningham, J. (1994) *Courtney*. London: Red Fox.
Kerr, J. (2005) *Mog and the V.E.T.* London: HarperCollins.
Gene, Z. (1992) *Harry the Dirty Dog*. London: Red Fox; also published by. The Bodley Head.
Moore, I. (1990) *Six Dinner Sid*. London: Prentice Hall.
Sutton, E. (1978) *My Cat Likes to Hide in Boxes*. London: Picture Puffin.

The majority of practitioners in early years settings provide language and literacy learning opportunities integrated within a class topic or interest. The following planning framework, which can be used alongside the planning for an overall topic, incorporates the main aspects of meta-linguistic awareness and covers the requirements of the *Curriculum Guidance for the Foundation Stage* (DfEE/QCA, 2000).

A planning framework for communication, language and literacy within a topic or theme

Opportunities for speaking and listening
Opportunities for becoming aware of the 'big picture' of literacy
Opportunities to become aware of concepts about print
Opportunities to develop phonological awareness
Opportunities to learn to identify and name the letters of the alphabet and to learn the sounds they represent
Opportunities to begin to become aware of grapheme–phoneme correspondence (GPC) in the nursery moving towards secure knowledge at the end of reception

Opportunities to mark-make for a purpose
Permanent features within the literacy provision.

Naturally, the staple reading opportunities for individuals will continue through one-to-one sharing with an adult of the reading scheme 'little books' for both discussion and reading, and to be taken home. Assessment and record-keeping (Chapters 3, 4, 5 and 6) underpin the successful provision and teaching of language and literacy and will usefully inform the appropriate grouping of children.

Language and literacy learning in Key Stage 1

Language and literacy provision in Key Stage 1 becomes more teacher directed in group learning activities as children are able to concentrate for longer periods of time, but the provision should remain meaningful and always embedded in a real context. Guidelines from the Department for Education and Skills (DfES) on the 'Primary Strategy' encourages teachers to use the Primary National Strategy: Framework for teaching literacy (DfES, 2006) to inform planning of content to ensure coverage of the language and literacy curriculum, but without the pressure of the straitjacket of delivering a daily Literacy Hour. The pedagogical approaches of Shared Reading and Writing, and Guided Reading and Writing can be usefully adopted to great benefit and encompassed within a topic theme which offers rich and stimulating opportunity to use language both spoken and written for a genuine purpose. Worksheets and exercises are best avoided as much as possible if deep learning is to occur. With thought and imagination children can be offered the consolidation and practice they might need individually within the parameters of a meaningful topic context.

In Chapter 6, the issue of the need to offer children experience of texts which present varying levels of challenge was discussed. Throughout Key Stage 1 extensive progress in literacy occurs. It takes great skill and effort to manage this smoothly so that children are able to continue to improve steadily and do not either become complacent by being given too many easy texts or confused and disheartened by being faced with too great a challenge. For monitored and steady progress to occur Years 1 and 2 teachers will want to give children the opportunity to read both easy- and instructional-level texts for differing learning purposes. Texts termed 'easy' by Clay are invaluable for consolidation, confidence-building and practice. These books will accompany the child home and will be shared with parents, older siblings and carers. Children at this stage need plenty of experience to read texts on which they are able to employ all the four cueing strategies, of meaning-making and decoding. In this way, active, fluent reading is enjoyed and made secure. Sight vocabulary is also consolidated. The benefit of this 'over-learning' needs to be explained to parents as does the nature of their role in supporting this type of reading practice. Books at 'instructional' level are also useful for children when reading one to one with an adult and in Guided Reading. These texts are used for the following reasons:

- when undertaking a running reading record
- giving children sufficient challenge to ensure that problem-solving occurs and that the required meta-cognitive processes are put to use under the guidance of an supporting adult
- providing opportunity for praise and to raise meta-cognitive awareness through the fruitful discussion on the appropriateness of using a particular strategy.

Levelling of books

Most early years teachers agree with the value of using several commercial reading schemes in their classrooms, perhaps with one core scheme as the 'spine'. This provides children with an interesting range of content and type of book, to meet different settings, key characters, typeface and illustrators. Pupils thereby experience a variety of texts to read for both practice and pleasure; however, publishers' use of readability formulae differ and their categorizing and sequencing systems vary, so the levels across schemes do not match each other very precisely. Categorizing systems such as *Book Bands* (Reading Recovery National Network, 1998) offer help in placing reading scheme books in comparable difficulty levels. While this is a time-consuming task, it is well worth the effort. It takes the guesswork out of book provision and teaching children to read. Reading scheme books that have been systematically levelled for difficulty enable teachers to be confident about the level of challenge a book will present to an individual child. It helps teachers to make up sets of reading scheme books for Guided Reading when the match of book to child needs to be precise. And the great bonus is that teachers can monitor pupil progress easily and use time economically merely by recording those books she/he can competently cope with and noting the precise level at which the child struggles.

Planning for teaching reading and writing

All primary schools will have a policy which provides information on the progression of the teaching of different skills and aspects of literacy such as learning about a specific genre, presented as schemes of work or long-term plans. These largely adhere to progression and continuity suggested by the curricular content of the Primary National Strategy: Framework for teaching literacy (DfES, 2006), with its yearly objectives for the Reception Year, and the term-by-term teaching objectives for each year group from Year 1 to Year 6. Medium-term plans develop from the above, and can be thought of as three types identified by SCAA (1995) – 'blocked', 'linked' and 'continuous':

- Blocked planning refers to a discrete unit of work, such as, to focus and teach all Year 1 classes on the beginnings and ends of stories in narrative fiction writing over a period of three weeks.
- Linked planning might link English teaching with other curriculum areas, for example, to strengthen the understanding and use of the report writing through specific science work.
- Continuous planning provides for the ongoing routines of usually skill-based work which should occur regularly and frequently, such as the teaching of punctuation and providing teaching through guided reading.

Short-term plans are expanded from the medium-term plans, and provide discrimination between pupils with different learning needs through differentiation in the learning activities offered. Medium- and short-term plans can be woven into the overall topic or theme studied by the class and fulfil the School Curriculum and Assessment Authority (SCAA) category of 'linked' planning above. A worked example of this is given below. First let us consider the principles which inform 'continuous' planning for literacy.

Matching learning opportunities to the literacy stages of the children

Thorough assessment followed by meticulous record-keeping is the cornerstone of effective provision for all members of the class in Years 1 and 2, as we have discussed for nursery and Reception pupils (see Chapter 6). Knowing where children are on a developmental continuum enables the class teacher to:

- match a reading book precisely to the child's reading ability in order to offer a book at instructional level (Chapter 6). This is a reading scheme book with sufficient challenge for the child to make progress but not so difficult that it is not possible to use prediction as a cueing strategy. Put another way, if a text is so difficult for a child that more than 1 word in 10 is not within her/his sight vocabulary, the child is not able to capitalize on the global or sentence level context in order to predict the word
- place children with others at a very similar literacy level. Precise awareness of each child's literacy capability enables the grouping of children by reading level for specific activities, particularly Guided Reading and Writing in order to maximize the learning opportunities.

At the centre of the Primary National Strategy: Framework for teaching literacy (DfES, 2006) are the pedagogical approaches suggested for use in a daily

Literacy Hour, with its dedicated literacy and print focused activities. Emphasis is less on the daily element as the need for systematic provision. Four pedagogical approaches are suggested.

Shared Reading is a whole-class reading activity usually using an enlarged text (or software through an interactive whiteboard, discussed below) in which children are enabled to read jointly, a text beyond a level which they could manage individually. This has its roots in New Zealand where Don Holdaway (1979) developed an approach that he termed 'Shared Reading' that had the same qualities as the shared bedtime story, of supporting the young child's early reading attempts in a way that 'scaffolds' understanding and makes explicit to a young reader what the task of reading is and what is already known, in order to allow further progress to occur. Techniques such as using familiar, often repeated, texts coupled with interactive teaching are now also commonplace in this approach to supporting reading. The key features of Shared Reading are:

- the careful selection of the appropriate texts which should be just beyond the ability of the majority of the children to read independently
- the teacher models fluent, well-paced, expressive reading aloud, the children listen and on subsequent readings join in where they are able, particularly in the refrains
- the teacher also models effective reading strategies
- the Shared Reading offers opportunity for lively discussion and the use of effective questioning particularly using open questions
- the teacher is also able during a session to monitor children's literacy development particularly comprehension and attitude.

The use of interactive whiteboards to conduct Shared Reading is becoming more popular in KS1. Companies such as Smart Learning are offering 'interactive literacy' software programmes for use with whole classes with an electronic whiteboard and with individuals on a desktop computer. These programmes have text available for Shared Reading, alongside applications that will allow adults to highlight text, words or individual letters. Speaking and listening activities and animation are also included in the experience. However, the quality of the graphics still seems to fall short of those in most picture books.

Guided Reading can be viewed as a bridge between Shared Reading and Independent Reading, and is most valuable when small groups of children are placed with others of very a similar literacy level. In Guided Reading multiple copies of the same book are read by pupils simultaneously. This enables teachers to support and closely monitor literacy development with targeted teaching and assessment in a time-economic way. The key features of Guided Reading are that:

- it extends the opportunities provided by Shared Reading by focusing on the needs of children with similar reading ability
- the children read the same text which should be at instructional level (that is, a book the group can be read with 90–95 per cent accuracy)
- the teacher follows a teaching sequence of a book introduction, strategy check, independent reading, a return to the text and allowing time for reader response and discussion.

Independent Reading is self-evidently the backbone and the whole purpose of a balanced reading programme. Children are enabled to become readers through independent reading rather than children merely who can read. Independent reading builds confidence, fluency, enjoyment and reading stamina. It is highly motivating and builds personal habits and reading preferences.

Shared Writing (for explanation see Chapter 8).

Guided Writing (for explanation see Chapter 8).

Case Study 7.2

A topic encompassing provision for language and literacy in Year 1 – The Night and nocturnal creatures

The class had been working on Light and Dark for several weeks and this led into half a term's work on Night time. The introduction to the topic took place with a preliminary discussion of the children's experience of night time and the dark. This whole-class work establishes what the children know and gives status and value to their experiences. Reluctant speakers will be given space and time to contribute. Going to bed featured prominently, the children preferring to stay up with older siblings and adults, talking and watching television. Some children had memories of making journeys in the dark to visit relatives or getting up very early to travel on holiday. Complete darkness is outside the experience of many children, especially those living in cities, but the occasional power cut makes the point most dramatically. The storytime reading began of Jill Tomlinson's *The Owl that Was Afraid of the Dark*, the picture book version being available along with its audiotape in the book area.

The topic moved into why and how night and day occur. The teacher taught that day and night occur as a result of the Earth's rotation on its axis: the half of the Earth facing the sun at any one time having daytime, while the other half, facing away from the sun, is in darkness and has night time. The children learned about the movement of the moon around the Earth every 28 days and the phases of the moon at different times of the month.

The complex science was handled appropriately for the age group with the use of posters and web-based resources. Details of the planning of the science are in the Appendix to this chapter. A suggested non-fiction book is *I Wonder Why the Sun Rises and Other Questions about Time and Seasons* by Brenda Walpole.

A poem ('Bully Night' by Roger McGough) was read in Shared Reading and the children moved into independent work with a cloze procedure and illustration of a poem on A4 sheets, while the teacher conducted Guided Reading with a group.

Each group worked in rotation with a teaching assistant on the non-fiction book, *Why Do Stars Twinkle? and Other Night Time Questions*' by Catherine Ripley. Savouring and spending time on well-produced information books with an adult, reading, discussing and poring over the illustrations is time productively spent. Concepts are formed, appropriate ways of using books for information are modelled, delight and interest are shared. New vocabulary is met. Positive attitudes to books and how to ask questions of them are experienced, along with a growing awareness of the power of independent learning.

Creation of a 'dark' make-believe area

The children were given the opportunity to choose the kind of 'dark' make-believe area they wanted in their classsroom. They discussed various possibilities of a cave in a dark wood, an animal's underground den, a planet with no sun so that it was permanently dark. The cave was decided upon. It was not prehistoric but a contemporary, truly magical cave … the home of a trendy wizard and his tame badger. The children made spooky artefacts and equipment for the cave dweller to use. The ceiling of the cave was covered in stars and became a favourite place to read in.

Researching nocturnal creatures

'Reading for information in the early years will not be directed towards the accumulation of knowledge as such, but to widening concepts about the environment, and towards ways of thinking which will include observation, hypothesising, comparison and classification …' (Arnold, 1996: 65).

Primed by the storytime book of Jill Tomlinson's *The Owl that Was Afraid of the Dark*, the topic then moved on to the theme of nocturnal creatures. Foxes, owls, badgers, dormice and bats were discussed. A supply of non-fiction books was readily available supplying information about each creature (for example, *Bat Loves the Night* by Nicola Davis) the children, placed now in their groups of similar literacy level, browsed and acquainted themselves with the books again and with adult support. Parent helpers were invited to provide additional help at this stage of the topic. The teacher and teaching assistant worked with the children in most need of support. Systematic research will occur at the next stage of the topic. Each group is given the choice of creature for investigation, which then becomes the adopted name of that group for the duration of the topic.

Formulating questions to be researched about each creature

In the next whole-class discussion the teacher asked the children to discuss with their talk partner what they want to find out about their creature. After a few minutes or so she asked for suggestions of the research questions, which she wrote on the easel. Examples of these were:

Where do … bats/owls/foxes etc … live?
What do they eat? What do they like best to eat?
How big is a … bat/owl/fox?
How does it move around?
What colour is it ?
What do its babies look like?
What type of creature is it?
What covers its body?
Why does it like to come out at night?

Considerable shaping of the suggested questions occurred in order to achieve a list of this nature and comprehensibility. This in itself is valuable teaching.

The production of a group book on each nocturnal creature was the intended outcome of the research. Individuals within the groups were allocated one question to research and answer and then report on, which would also be illustrated on a sheet of A4 paper as his or her contribution to the book.

This work might take place over the period of two weeks or so, the completed response sheets being incorporated into a teacher-made hardback book. The book had a printed cover relating to the creature being studied, designed and printed by a group member.

Researching the facts on each creature

The next stage of research needed intensive adult support. The groups of children worked in rotation with the teacher or teaching assistant to research the questions with the help of the appropriate non-fiction books. How to use the contents page and index was modelled, and then how to access the sought-after information. Lively and lengthy discussion followed.

When not working in an adult-supported group, the children worked on self-sustaining activities in the home corner, painting pictures of their creature, listening to the story tapes, working on the computer and on construction materials with a design problem related to the topic. On successive days, the groups were rotated and each had an opportunity to research with adult support and to complete their own page for the group book, again with help. Some children wrote one sentence in answer to their research question, others managed more. Some wrote conventionally, others, in an earlier stage of literacy development, used the encoding approximations of emergent writing. Each carefully illustrated their work.

Other outcomes of the nocturnal creature topic

A class display was generated by the children writing their own riddles for their nocturnal creatures, animals in other countries who preferred night-time activity were researched and individual books made. A movement and dance sequence was developed exploring the possibility of the animals' different ways of moving. *Fantastic Mr Fox* by Roald Dahl was read at storytime.

Suggested additional resources

Hutchins, P. (1998) *Goodnight, Owl.* London: Random House Books.

Kerr, J. (2006) *Mog in the Dark.* London: HarperCollins Children's Books.

Wadell, M. *(1998) Can't You Sleep, Little Bear?* London: Walker Books.

See Appendix below for additional resources and acitivites regarding the primary science content for the primary Night and Nocturnal Creatures topic

Summary

Stimulating class topics with a motivating and fun element to them are the perfect context to deepen understanding of texts as well as offering opportunity to use language and literacy for a genuine purpose. Knowledgeable teachers are able to ensure that progression and continuity are built into the provision, with all children's needs being met appropriately.

Rose writes:

> It is important for schools to offer a coherent reading programme in which 'quality first teaching' as defined by the Primary Strategy [is met] … While such work, from the standpoint of those who teach beginner readers, may not be 'rocket science', it does require practitioners and teachers to have detailed knowledge and understanding of its teaching content so that they can plan and implement a high quality programme. Imaginative and skilful teaching that engages and motivates children does not happen by chance: it relies upon well-trained adults, who are skilled in observing and assessing children's learning, good planning and preparation. (DfES, 2006: 5)

Further reading

Mallett, M. (2003) *Early Years Non-Fiction: A Guide to Helping Young Researchers Use Information Texts.* London and New York: RoutledgeFalmer.

Appendix: Background primary science activities for 'The night and nocturnal creatures' topic for Year 1 children

1. Learning objectives for day

Children should learn:

- that the Sun is the source of light for the Earth
- to make observations and to try to explain these
- that it is dangerous to look directly at the Sun because it is so bright.

Possible activities

- In the playground on a day of intermittent sunshine and cloud, work in the playground and ask the children to identify, without looking at the Sun, when it goes behind and emerges from a cloud. Ask the children how do they know? What are the clues?
- This experience can be used to reinforce the concept of the Sun as a source of light – even when it disappears behind a cloud – this could have been included in the original topic of Light and Dark. It is a common misconception among young children that night is caused by the Sun moving behind a cloud.
- Use this activity to explain that the Sun disappearing behind a cloud is not the same as the change that occurs as we reach nightfall.
- Look at shadows on the playground at different times of the day on some sunny days. This should not be handled formally before Year 3 and should be dealt with as an introduction to the movement of the Earth round the Sun and the position of the Sun in the sky at different times of the day.

Learning outcomes

- Identify changes that occur when the Sun goes behind a cloud and understand that these are different from changes at nightfall.
- Explain that the Sun is a source of light, even when it is behind a cloud.
- Understand why it is dangerous to look directly at the Sun.

2. Night

Teaching should not be directly about the Moon with Year 1 pupils, perhaps read stories and poems to familiarize the children with the concept. The reasoning is that many children may not have seen the Moon directly at this stage and it can be introduced through posters, pictures and videos. Later work on the Moon could include some work on 'shiny objects', for instance:

Learning objectives for dark/night

Children should learn:

- that shiny objects (such as the Moon) need a light source if they are to shine
- that shiny objects are not light sources
- to suggest how to find out about where a reflective strip will shine brightly
- to make observations and simple comparisons and to say whether what they found out was what they expected.

Possible activities

- The main investigation would focus on reflective strips on clothing and bags, asking children why they think the strips show up at night, but not in daylight. Encourage them to test their suggestions; try to include putting strips in the dark and shining a light on them and to make comparisons of strips in daylight, in a dark place with no light source and in a dark place with a light shone on them.
- Work could continue with objects that only shine when they have light shone on them – shiny objects do not shine in a dark room!

Learning outcomes

- Recognize that shiny objects need a light source in order to shine.
- Explain that a shiny object does not shine in a dark room.
- Say whether they expected the reflective strips to shine near a light source.

Other related areas for Night at different times of the year would be: fairy lights, fireworks, Halloween lanterns, lights at religious festivals such as candles, and so on. Discussion could occur about why these light sources are used at night.

Chapter 8

Supporting Writing and Developing Writing for Different Purposes

Across the world, the ability to write is acclaimed as one of the twin peaks of literacy and as one of the central gains from education. ... Writing helps to bring permanence and completeness to communication. These qualities give literacy certain advantages over oracy for communicating across space and time.

(Beard, 2000: 1)

Children should be taught written language, not just the writing of letters.

(Vygotsky, 1978: 119)

Introduction

The above quotation from Vygotsky (1978) expresses most perfectly my views on the teaching of writing throughout the early years of education and is one which I, unashamedly, admit to using previously (Riley and Reedy, 2000: xi).

Sadly, for those beginning early years teachers already struggling to get to grips with the processes involved with learning to read, this chapter will focus on the indisputably even more complex task of learning to write. About this Stainthorp says: 'Writing is an example of human information processing in action. It is a highly complex task, which requires the orchestration of a number of different activities simultaneously and thereby places great demands on the cognitive system' (2004b: 62). Before addressing the nature of the task of writing in all its myriad complexity, as referred to here, the following four principles are the starting point for this chapter.

The development of each language mode is interrelated and supportive of the other

The skills of reading and writing can only develop from a secure foundation and competence in oracy. As Bielby asserts 'Written language is parasitic on spoken language' (1999: 16). Successful literacy learning occurs in an oracy-rich environment where children are encouraged to use language in authentic and engaging ways in order to fulfil their individual purposes.

Writing is the complementary process to reading

For the past few decades research has viewed reading and writing as twin processes. The process of writing entails the encoding of the sounds of speech into permanent, printed forms, and reading entails the decoding. The ability to read supports children with their writing, and the reverse is true. In support of this claim, consideration in earlier chapters was given to the ways Foundation Stage pupils are enabled to acquire understandings of grapheme–phoneme correspondence (GPC) through puzzling out how the component sounds within words can be represented by a grapheme when writing a text. This activity encourages phonemic segmentation and reinforces accurate identification of letters, their shapes and the sounds that they most commonly represent. As a result these young writers develop awareness of the alphabet code as a system. As Ferreiro affirms: 'Let us accept that those children, when they write, make an approximate correspondence between sounds and letters. They may have to face orthography problems, but they do not have further problems with writing, because they are now functioning inside the alphabet system of writing' (Ferreiro, 1985: 84).

Below are examples of how reading and being read to supports learning to write through exposure:

- the conventions of written language (how writing is placed on pages, left to right directionality of print in English and the way spaces mark the boundaries of words)
- punctuation that supports meaning but cannot be read aloud
- the particular forms of literary language used in written discourse through experiencing words and phrases such as 'Laughing merrily, they ran down the lane' which differs from the structure of everyday spoken language
- the nature of different types of texts written for varying purposes.

Literacy develops the capacity to think

As children have access to texts they meet new vocabulary, rich, literary language and mind-expanding ideas and information about a world beyond their own experience. Learning to write also gives them opportunity to use language in novel ways in order to fulfil a variety of purposes. This written language will differ from the way they speak: the texts created are by their nature intended for an absent audience. They are systematic and precise. Donaldson argues that it is these literacy experiences that are 'the main road, for the child's mind, out of the situation-bound, embedded thinking and language of the pre-literate years into a new kind of mental power and freedom'

Figure 8.1   *A Reception child's writing mirrors her reading scheme book*

(1985: 240). Bereiter and Scardamalia (1993) suggest another important notion that there are two types of writing: one is knowledge-telling and the other is knowledge-transforming. I want to propose here that early years practitioners and teachers can support children to use written language in a way that transforms their understandings and promotes conceptual development as they compose and write texts to fulfil a range of purposes.

Writing is difficult

Elsewhere it has been written (Riley and Reedy, 2000) that writing presents huge challenges both to adults and children. Writing is intellectually and physically demanding. But it is worth the effort. It is the role of adults working with young children to provide them with opportunities that allow them to appreciate that making the effort is worthwhile; practitioners can try to ensure that writers view writing as an activity with intrinsic value and one that can be not only useful but also deeply satisfying.

Why is writing difficult?

Writing is multi-layered. While simplistic, it is useful for practitioners, when working with children, to distinguish between the compositional and the transcriptional aspects of writing. Composition encompasses the content of a text, how the ideas are organized, and the way that the argument or story is shaped and developed. Transcription includes the secretarial skills of spelling (that is, knowing how the alphabetic code works as a system) and handwriting. Punctuation is considered, by most academics, to straddle both aspects of writing as it serves both grammatical and semantic (meaning) functions. Psychologists have attempted to develop models that take account of the complexity and interrelatedness of the writing process.

Hayes and Flower (1980) have proposed a schematic model of expert writing. This explanation sees writing as dynamic and focuses on the productive inter-relationship of the different stages within the components, as initially, the writer has 'an idea, a turn of phrase, an emotion, an image and shuttle[s] back and forth between ideas, images, emotions and words' (Smith and Elley, 1998: 68). The text determines what is written during the process of writing. Each sentence shapes its successor, in the way its predecessor has influenced its shape. Within text production, Hayes and Flower suggest that there are three main components of composing: 'planning', 'translating' and ' reviewing'.

Planning is the prior organization of the content in a broad sense, 'forming an internal representation of the knowledge that will be used in writing' (Hayes and Flower, 1980: 372) Encompassed within this stage of writing is the research and reading which constitutes the gestation part before planning a text for more academic writing. Planning can be broken down into sub-sections:

- generating ideas or the search of the memory bank for relevant ideas
- organizing ideas, involves ordering the ideas into a coherent structure
- goal setting, by which Hayes and Flower mean the ongoing process whereby ideas are generated and the way writing is shaped to accommodate them, 'refining one's goals is not limited to the "pre-writing stage" … but is intimately bound up with the on-going, moment-to-moment process of composing' (1980: 373).

Individual writers vary in the extent to which they preorganize their text, and writing is an evolving process for mature and novice alike. But prior thinking is essential, and this is a stage often omitted by very young writers.

Translating involves the transference of ideas to paper or screen. This process requires the secretarial skills of handwriting or typing, knowledge of the conventions of print, the choice of appropriate vocabulary and sentence structures and spelling. It is at this stage that writing generates new ideas and thoughts. If too much effort is required for any or all of these skills, as is often the case with young children, there remains little mental capacity free to be expended on the content or the ideas being recorded. Stainthorp reinforces this: 'If the words one wishes to write do not have complete, accurate representations in the orthographic lexicon, the letter sequences will have to be generated in a controlled way rather than automatically. This will require more processing capacity and leave less available for the generation of ideas' (2004b: 5). This is a crucial point in the early years of education and we will address later how practitioners can best support children as they generate texts in order to ease the massive and multi-layered effort it requires.

Reviewing consists of two sub-processes: evaluating and revising. Writing has to be read and reread critically and then strategies put into place for revision. This can occur continuously, with the production of each sentence or at the end of the piece. Translating and reviewing are integrated in the knowledge-transformation, how they interact with each other depends on the writer's style of cognitive processing.

Finally, these processes are all monitored or overseen by a mechanism which controls the work as it is produced. The writer may move from translating, back to planning, and then to reviewing, several times before progress is made or the text is deemed complete.

This explanatory model of skilled writing is an insightful one for practitioners and teachers to consider, as they enable children to develop as writers. But the Hayes and Flower model neither encompasses a notion that the process of writing might vary for different types of text production, nor that it may differ from culture to culture; nevertheless, it provides valuable insight into the stages and the meta-cognitive activity that occur during the compositional process of writing.

The model takes no account either of writers in the very earliest stages of learning to write. Berniger et al., (1992) has amended the Hayes and Flower model to include additional features relevant to this group of pupils. She believes that developmental constraints affect writing capacity. Both the level of a child's fine motor control influences letter formation and grasp of GPC impacts on spelling ability. Another issue raised from Berniger that is valuable for this readership is the issue of motivation and the support that the social context can offer embryonic writers.

Supporting children to write

Bereiter and Scardamalia (1993) also suggest that certain challenges present themselves to children in the writing process. The move from oral to written expression reveals many difficulties. In the view of these researchers, the most fundamental and problematic difficulty is the absence of a conversational partner to give feedback and encourage perseverance. Further challenges to children are:

- making decisions about content
- staying on topic
- producing a coherent whole
- making choices appropriate to an audience not immediately present.

There are essential differences between spoken and written language which present the child with particular challenges.

Children learn to speak naturally (and at times we wish we could stop them!). Learning to write requires the need to learn a new set of artificial, culturally specific conventions and rules. Young pupils have to learn to hold a pencil, to know how to form the letters, to know whether the letter should be upper or lower case, to work out how to represent the sounds of speech with letters and groups of letters, to be able to spell words accurately and so on – all this before they come to organize the text into paragraphs, and apply the appropriate forms of punctuation.

When removed from a listening partner children have to engage in new types of thought processes; they have to be able to take the reader's perspective. With no feedback to convey the level of interest shown in what has been written or what has been understood, the writer has to anticipate any possible confusion. The message has to be clear, comprehensible and able to stand on its own.

Finally, and most importantly for these researchers, children have to be able to sustain their writing, without the prompts or the encouragement of listeners' comments during conversations. Writers quite literally 'dry up' through the lack of feedback in this isolated activity.

Bereiter and Scardamalia (1993) suggest that teachers have to support children learning to write through helping them to produce continuous text without a turn-taking partner. Further research was undertaken that explored the ways children might be supported through their stumbling blocks with writing. The following were found to be important.

Learning to search one's memory for content

The problems children have with recalling their passive information when writing is, self-evidently, not the case when they are engaged in conversation. Teachers need to support young writers by offering strategies which will assist a memory search for relevant information.

A pre-writing ideas-gathering session is a well-proven method for overcoming this hurdle. The researchers conducted experiments with several modes of using this approach, and it appears that strategies where children are prompted to think in several modes about the topic, in order to produce lists of key words that can then act as a prompt to the memory, rather than writing whole sentences, proved to be the most valuable. Discussion is also useful, as is conferencing, in order to further explore the child's thought process, to aid information retrieval and to extend developing ideas. All these approaches are only valuable if they are an explicit way of demonstrating the meta-cognitive process that writers themselves need to employ during the composition process. These strategies are merely exemplars of the way that mature writers prepare and organize their writing.

Learning to think ahead and to plan

Inexperienced writers, as they embark on the first sentence, frequently do not have any sense of the overall structure or goal for their writing. This lack of a plan is a key feature of the knowledge-telling model of writing. Part of the difficulty is due to the limitations within young children and their level of cognitive maturity, and not being able to think of more than one thing at once. To generate ideas, to translate them into text and to revise the product, which means critically reading for appropriateness of language expression, structure and content, is all just too demanding a task for young children.

Writing frames are one attempt to facilitate pupils into being able to meet these multi-demands. On this side of the Atlantic, David Wray and his colleagues have done much to make teachers aware of the possibilities of this way of supporting children's thinking while writing, albeit for a short period of time, until they are able to organize the text for themselves. We will discuss this in more detail later in this chapter.

In addition, the approach advocated by Graves (1983), to support writing through conferencing is a possible way forward, but in order for this technique to be valuable, as with all teaching, the teachers themselves have to be knowledgeable about the writing process and aware of the considerable demands it makes upon the child, in order to be able to place appropriate support where it is needed.

Learning to revise one's own writing

The ability to review what one has written is key if pupils are to develop successfully as writers. This also appears to be a stumbling block for primary-aged pupils. Numerous research projects, investigating an improvement in the revision aspect of the composition process, report on only developing the ability to proofread, at best, and that rather superficially. Redrafting does not occur in speech and requires considerable cognitive maturity for the individual to be able to 'decentre' and thus to envisage why a hypothetical reader might have difficulty with the text produced. This process is the ability to see the text afresh through a reflective stance rather than a generative one. Peer evaluation can be very successful here. The idea of assessment for learning that results from reading and commenting on another person's work provides insights to both partners.

All these approaches aimed at supporting pupils' writing can be developed beneficially in the early years classroom. Research evidence is useful in the way that it offers insight and helps teachers to focus on the difficulties that children encounter when writing. Through being able to appreciate the challenge and hurdles that writing presents, practitioners are in a better position to support progress. Professionally, it is not easy to know exactly how to move a child beyond the knowledge-telling position of writing shown so well in the following description:

> I have a whole bunch of ideas and write down until my supply of ideas is exhausted. Then I might try to think of more ideas up to the point when you can't get any more ideas that are worth putting down on paper and then I would end it. (Cited in Bereiter and Scardamalia, 1993: 160)

Aldous Huxley describes a very different process of knowledge-transforming writing, one that allows him to rework his thoughts. He says,

> Generally, I write everything many times over. All my thoughts are second thoughts. And I correct each page a great deal, or rewrite it several times as I go along … Things come to me in driblets, and when the driblets come I have to work hard to make them into something coherent.' (Cited in Bereiter and Scardamalia (1993: 160)

It has been shown that the path from conversation to writing in the knowledge-telling mode (and there can be many levels of quality and competence within this model) through ultimately knowledge-transforming writing is thorny for adult, teacher and pupil! Individuals need to be able to operate both modes of knowledge-telling and knowledge-transforming in order to function in an advanced and literate society. Later in this chapter, we will discuss how practitioners can offer opportunities for children to become acquainted with both modes of writing in their provision.

Supporting writing in the Foundation Stage

Supporting young children's literacy progress in the Foundation Stage, as we have seen in Chapter 7, is most valuable when it is provided through rich oracy and literacy learning opportunities woven within a topic. This ensures that the literacy activities on offer are both purposeful and engaging for the young learners. The approach begins with an informed practitioner who, mindful of the research evidence cited here, plans systematically for spoken and written language experiences within a cross-curricular theme. This replicates the way that children are supported in home settings where adults are seen using and producing texts in ways that are useful, where books, stories and writing materials are plentiful and can be experienced several times a day when so inclined, and where adults are ready to support or scaffold a child attempting to read, to mark-make or write at the opportune moment.

Planning for language and literacy in the nursery and reception class

In Chapter 7 the following language and literacy framework was offered as a way of ensure comprehensive coverage of literacy provision when planning a cross-curricular theme:

Opportunities for speaking and listening
Opportunities for becoming aware of the 'big picture' of literacy
Opportunities to become aware of concepts about print
Opportunities to develop phonological awareness
Opportunities to learn to identify and name the letters of the alphabet and to learn the sounds they represent
Opportunities to begin to become aware of grapheme–phoneme corre-spondence (GPC) in the nursery moving towards secure knowledge at the end of reception
Opportunities to mark-make for a purpose
Providing mark-making opportunities within the setting.

Writing areas will vary in emphasis between a nursery setting and a reception class, but much will remain constant. The physical location of this space will have been carefully considered and often the writing area will be placed near the quieter reading/listening area, and certainly as far away as possible from the construction, water play and art resources work spaces.

The resources in a writing area

Space will dictate the lavishness of the provision. At one end of the contin-uum there might be an area that consists of several square metres and is semi-partitioned, with wall displays (of alphabet charts, handwriting/calligraphy examples, spelling lists of key words in reception class, days of the week, months of the year, starting points for writing), shelving, sta-tionery racks, alphabet books, picture word books, first dictionaries, and at least one computer with word-processing and software packages for letter learning reinforcement ('Sheraton', 'Talking First Word' and 'Textease'). Alternatively, in very cramped conditions, the writing area might consist sim-ply of one piece of display boarding with a table placed in front, on which the resources are laid. Resources, also, will vary according to space, setting or class ethos and, inevitably, available finance. The following resources are essential:

- pencils (with different grades of graphite), felt-tip pens, crayons (pencil and wax) and highlighter pens
- paper of various types, surface quality (including rough paper), pre-cut in different sizes and colours
- various pieces of card as above
- ready made blank books of various sizes and colours from mini-books to A4

- envelopes and notepaper (even specifically class-designed headed notepaper)
- blank greetings cards (also class made as above) and envelopes
- blank official forms (for example, postal catalogue-type forms)
- clipboards, bulldog clips, paper clips, staplers
- erasers, pencil sharpeners, adhesive-sticks, sticky tape, masking tape, blunt nosed scissors
- handwriting cards, books, guidelines (in reception only) dictionaries for use in early years settings, for example, *My ABC Dictionary*, (Collins); *Collins' Rhyming Dictionary* (Collins); *DK Dictionary* (Dorling Kindersley).

The following resources might be included from time to time:

- postbox
- boards and chalks
- shallow trays with sand for letter formation tracing
- notice board or message board
- displays of poetry and story writing
- bins of alphabet books.

Role-play areas that encourage writing

Traditionally, early years settings have encouraged independent writing through role play, capitalizing as it does on the child's pre-school positive learning stance. Nursery and reception classes provide:

- home corners with telephones, message/list pads, notepaper and envelopes
- shops of various kinds with posters, labels, price lists of merchandise and bills
- hospital corners/baby clinics/veterinary surgeons with patient/pet progress cards and prescription pads
- cafés with menus and order pads.

All the above specialist areas demand writing of a particular 'genre' for a specific purpose or audience, and perhaps on specialist stationery designed for an appropriate use. Practitioners have a role here also, in the way that they are able to model how best to use the area and its resources. An adult joining in the dramatic action strengthens the involvement of the pupils and also demonstrates the expert literacy user during the play; for example, Goldilocks writing a letter or an e-mail to the Three Bears justifying her misdemeanours and developing a website for them, for example, www. Bearsite.com.

It is worth mentioning in this section, the widespread concern about the level of boys' literacy, which appears generally to be lower than girls', right from baseline entry through to GCSE. Boys tend to use writing areas less than girls (QCA, 1998) but respond well to the more activity-oriented role-play areas and where writing is seen to be meaningful. If practitioners take care and effort throughout the early years of education, to motivate boys and to encourage them to consider that writing is a useful and necessary skill to perfect, the situation may change. It is in the early years that enduring attitudes, both positive and negative, to writing are formed and become entrenched.

Writing after reading stories or in drama sessions

Writing can follow the reading of a story naturally and with great pleasure, or it can be included as part of a drama session. Sensuously illustrated *Peace at Last* and by Jill Murphy *Can't You Sleep, Little Bear?* by Martin Wadell are appropriate books to accompany or lead into work on light and dark. The books focus upon light sources at night in contrast to the day and can be imaginatively linked to science work. Lists can be made using A3 flipcharts or 'smart boards'. In *Can't You Sleep, Little Bear?* Wadell develops a picture book on the theme of one of the most common emotions – fear of the dark. Suggestions on how to cope with this fear, such as having a night light, leaving the bedroom door ajar, having a cuddly toy in bed, having a brother or sister sleeping in the same bedroom can be written with adult support and illustrated for a compilation in a class book or for a wall display. Making further investigation of the place of lullabies in babyhood, safely distances their benefit towards younger siblings. Mick Inkpen's *Lullabyhullabaloo* is written in the form of a lullaby with humour and flair. Writing a lullaby in a group and then recording it by an adult would smoothly follow a reading of this delightful picture book. There are wonderful examples of descriptive and onomatopoeic words to savour also. Additional examples of nursery rhyme versions of lullabies such as 'Hush-a-bye, baby, on the tree top' photocopied and available in individual A4 size for reading, singing and colouring so that those children not working with the practitioner can continue the investigation with individual, self-sustained work.

Supporting writing in Key Stage 1

In Years 1 and 2 children begin to gain control over the transcriptional skills of writing and teachers are able to place emphasis, in Key Stage 1, on developing awareness of how to structure sentences and texts. The pedagogical approaches of the NLS of Shared Writing and Guided Writing are effective, time-economic methods of organizing teaching. Through such approaches teachers are able to make explicit the meta-cognitive strategies of writing to whole classes and to groups of pupils of similar levels of literacy development, respectively. In the interests of clarity and accessibility, it is preferable to focus on one aspect of teaching in group situations. As Stainthorp says:

> A particular feature of writing maybe embedded in a specific text that the children are studying. It may be necessary to highlight that feature and to isolate it for some direct focused teaching. During the primary years children may not have the cognitive capacity to focus on word, sentence and textual features without specific teaching at each level. (Stainthorp, 2004b: 13)

Shared Writing

The ideas behind Shared Reading were explained in Chapter 6, from which Shared Writing is thought to have developed.

Features of this approach can be attributed to Donald Graves (1983) in the USA, who proposes a process approach to the teaching of writing, in which the pupil is given a constructive role as an active learner and encouraged to develop hypotheses about the nature of language and the writing process through writing. In this approach, errors provide opportunity for insight into the text and print processing that the child is able to achieve. This again is in line with the thinking behind miscue analysis (Goodman, 1973) and running reading records (Clay, 1993) discussed in Chapter 6. The key concepts of the process approach to writing are:

1. *Ownership*. Writing is a demanding and challenging task. In order to assure the high level of motivation which is required to overcome the taxing nature of the task, Graves suggests that children should be allowed to choose their own topic for a great deal of the time in early years classrooms.
2. *Drafts and revision*. Writing is seen as evolving, not arriving perfectly formed on the page with the first draft. Through revision, writers have the chance to operate the deeper mechanisms of the writing process and allow the advancement of ideas to be pursued through a reworking of text (for explanation see the Hayes and Flower model earlier in this chapter).
3. *Conferencing*. This is when in the Graves model most teaching takes place. The teacher provides an audience and gives feedback to the writer, thus the developing writers receive clarification, and in so doing the difficulty of one of the most challenging aspect of writing is solved, namely, the conceptual problem of writing for, and putting oneself into the position of, an unknown audience. With this mode of teaching, one particular aspect of writing can be focused upon and explicit help and advice offered.
4. *Publishing*. This important feature of the process approach provides purpose, motivation and feedback by making the product available to others. Importance is vested in the presentation of the product which is offered for public recognition (and wider constructive criticism?).

Implicit in the Graves approach to writing is the modelling of writing by the teacher for pupils. This modelling is the basic principle behind Shared Writing. The teacher demonstrates to children what experienced writers do and the mechanics of what has to be undertaken for a text to be constructed. In the earliest stages of learning to write, the adult will show, first, how the planning is done, to operating within the conventions of print, and to working out the sound–symbol system (GPC) of a particular word. Children are made aware of the challenges of writing and how to solve them, as well as its delights and satisfactions.

Shared Writing strategies can be used with benefit, with all age groups in the primary school, with the whole class or with smaller groups. In nursery and reception classes, at text level, the reworking of a favourite, well-known tale is a supportive way to re-enforce the structure of narrative at both text and sentence level. In Years 1 and 2 the modelling can include and make explicit the planning stage of writing with the adult thinking aloud 'I wonder how we should start our story?' 'What, then, shall we make happen?' and so on to 'How can we end our story? ... is that surprising enough? ... do we want it to end in such a straight-forward way? ... could we think of an unexpected twist for the end? ... as in such and such a book we read?'

When focusing on sentence-level work, ideas can be rehearsed orally before modelling the writing. Frequent rereading of the writing helps children to hear and see the developing text and to demonstrate how sentences flow on from each other. Punctuation can be used as appropriate to support the meaning of the developing text. Explicit modelling on the way expert writers make decisions which affect the structure, shape and effect of the text is the most insightful aspect of this approach to developing the writing of young writers.

As Washtell (1998) says, Shared Writing can be used to demonstrate:

- a sense of purpose and audience – voice (formal or informal), planning, drafting, revising, proofreading, presentation (publication)
- content and features of different types of texts – linguistic features, structural features, language choices for a specific genre, grammatical features
- transcriptional skills – punctuation, spelling, handwriting
- self-help strategies – correcting mistakes, discussing, peer conferencing, collaborating.

Guided Writing

Guided Writing is the counterpart to Guided Reading, when focused teaching occurs with small groups of children who are at similar levels of literacy ability. The following examples show how Guided Writing approaches might be applied in early years classrooms:

- In the reception class teachers may choose to support the development of grapheme–phoneme association through writing. This is a clear example of the way that the two processes of reading and writing support each other. We have written earlier in this volume and before (Riley, 1996: 88) on this approach to develop reading through enabling children to hear and identify the constituent sounds in words, then map those sounds onto letters and groups of letters.
- Year 1 – the teacher, by scribing for the group their own jointly constructed, dictated story, releases pupils from the burden of transcription; the mirror image version of this activity is when the teacher dictates a story to the group of children to write and so, conversely, they are freed of the task of composition. Modelling the construction of a sentence is a focus for teaching at this stage.
- Year 2 – in collaborative writing children are set an activity, the purpose of which is to support the writing capacity of each member of the group. The

task might be first to sequence, to write an outline (composed of brief sentences) and then to rework a known story by fleshing out the outline plot. This activity rehearses the narrative structure by using a well-known story, practises sequencing, and then provides, through collaboration, support with the transcriptional skills of spelling, paragraphs and punctuation.

Independent Writing, its development and support, will be discussed next. As addressed in Chapter 7, it is crucial that the teacher is aware of each individual's developing competence in order to target teaching precisely. While, it has been admitted, that writing is more complex and multi-layered than reading, it does have the big advantage of being easier to assess, as there is a product which lends itself to mulling over.

Assessment: what do children know and what can they do?

Teaching of quality only occurs when it is informed by knowledge of what children already know. The ability to support children in the compositional process of writing occurs through teachers first being aware of the distinctive features of each genre and then knowing:

- what the child understands of those features through the close analysis of the writing produced
- the decisions to be made about what the child needs to learn next and what she needs to do to be able to use independently regarding the features of the different genre
- how to provide meaningful and interesting experiences that make writing both necessary and purposeful; in other words, the creation of the context within which the intended development can be fostered.

Assessment of transcriptional and compositional aspects of writing

Teachers do not usually separate out the different and distinct aspects of the writing process when they assess children's writing, nor perhaps is it advisable that they should do so. Assessment can become mechanistic in consequence. But teachers will need to focus their attention on a particular aspect of the child's writing for specific teaching purposes from time to time. What assessment schemes are there and which aspects of writing do they endeavour to assess?

Educationalists in Australia and New Zealand (cited in Smith and Elley, 1998) do not separate the transcriptional aspects of writing from the compositional; they describe writing as being on a developmental continuum with stages referred to with targets set. Two schemes are worth considering.

- the Western Australian Education Department's Writing Developmental Continuum (Eggleton and Windsor, 1995)
- 'Written language: achievement objectives' as handled in the New Zealand Curriculum.

	Emergent level	Early level	Fluent level
Process-Focus	To have correct directional movement To leave spaces between words To use approximations according to the sounds heard at the beginnings of words To begin to use some high-frequency words	To use beginning and end sounds of words To use vowels To spell many high-frequency words correctly To use more correctly spelt words than approximations To begin using editing skills – to place full stops – to place capitals – to locate approximations by underlining To begin to correct approximations by using word sources	To use editing skills – thinking about the message of writing – using most punctuation marks correctly – dividing written work into paragraphs – recording and presenting information in different ways – using a dictionary and thesaurus
Product-Focus	To be able to choose a topic to write on To use own experiences for writing To begin to talk about some features of own writing To be able to present a piece of writing for others to share	To understand that words carry many kinds of information To know that writing must make sense To be able to select from a wide range of topics and genre To be able to choose an appropriate title To begin to make some corrections to meaning To begin to realize that writing can involve a number of stages To begin to record and present information in different ways	To use variety in sentence beginnings To sequence ideas To use an increasingly wide vocabulary To write spontaneously to record personal experiences (expressive) To write descriptively on a variety of topics, shaping ideas and experimenting with language and form To write instructions and recount events in authentic contexts (transactional) To begin to explore choices made by writers and apply to own writing

Figure 8.2   *Children's targets in early writing, classified by level and process/product (adapted from Eggleton and Windsor, (1995: 13–17)*

The Western Australian Education Department's Writing Developmental Continuum sets out the stages as follows:

1. Role-play writing
2. Experimental writing
3. Early writing
4. Conventional writing
5. Proficient writing
6. Advanced writing.

In the Eggleton and Windsor scheme (1995, and cited in Smith and Elley, 1998) children's targets are classified into both process and product, and the authors' suggestions are that they fall within three levels of development, 'emergent', 'early' and 'fluent' (see Figure 8.2). While these three stages are very broad, and inevitably encompass a wide range of development, the process/product distinction is useful. The step from 'early' to 'fluent' writing encompasses a huge amount of progress in competence which can be separated into more refined stages. However, the Eggleton and Windsor scheme offers usefully a separation of the features that are connected to the process and product aspects of writing. In the process aspect the growing awareness of the alphabetic system (referred to as spelling in the early stage), understandings of conventions of print and punctuation are focused upon. The product aspect involves planning and the organization of ideas in text, including a developing grasp of genre, and also reviewing and editing. These authors show how each of the two processes facilitate and augment the development of the other.

The levels of the New Zealand Curriculum, which are referred to as 'Written language: achievement objectives', makes a distinction between the expressive, poetic and transactional categories of writing (see Figure 8.3) in terms of the developmental challenges each presents to the pupil. This is an important issue. Children demonstrate variable degrees of mastery of the writing process, which is dependent upon the nature of the content and topic and their individual response to it. Together, the staff of a school might usefully consider the two schemes cited here in order to develop a school assessment framework for their own purposes. Having in mind a pathway of the potential literacy development of their pupils, is perhaps the most valuable aspect of the use of any assessment scheme which demonstrates progression clearly.

The developmental schemes outlined here are most useful in the day-to-day diagnostic, formative assessment of children's writing that is necessary in order to inform teaching, but not for the 'high-stakes' type of assessment. By this they are referring to the type of assessment of the National Curriculum tasks and tests in England and Wales. The English National Curriculum was designed to enable formal, summative assessment of each of the prescribed levels of achievement of pupils.

Evaluation of a range of samples of writing

The type of writing assessment that is being suggested here is ongoing and formative. It needs to be embedded in whatever system the school finds useful, and it is based on the teacher having a broad and comprehensive picture of the child's developing control of writing within which growing ability to compose texts will be encompassed. An understanding of the child's abilities to think through a piece of written text and to structure it appropriately certainly is not possible through the analysis of one piece of writing, as it might erroneously be thought is implied here. The other point to make is that all analyses of children's writing needs an awareness of the full details of the

	Expressive Writing	Poetic Writing	Transactional Writing
Level 1	Students should: • write spontaneously to record personal experiences	Students should: • write on a variety of topics, beginning to shape ideas	Students should: • write instructions and recount events in authentic contexts.
Leve 2	• write regularly and spontaneously to record personal experiences and observations	• write on a variety of topics, shaping ideas in a number of genres, such as letters, poems, and narrative, and making choices in language and form	• write instructions and explanations, state facts and opinions, and recount events in a range of authentic contexts
Level 3	• write regularly and with ease to express personal responses to different experiences and to record observations and ideas	• write on a variety of topics shaping, editing, and reworking texts in a range of genres, and using vocabulary and conventions, such as spelling and sentence structure, appropriate to the genre	• write instructions, explanations, and factual accounts, and express personal viewpoints in a range of authentic contexts, sequencing ideas logically
Level 4	• write regularly and with ease to express personal responses to a range of experiences and texts, explore ideas, and record observations	• write on a variety of topics, shaping, editing, and re-working texts in a range of genres, expressing ideas and experiences imaginatively and using appropriate vocabulary and conventions, such as spelling and sentence structure	• write instructions, explanations, and factual accounts, and express and explain a point a view, in a range of authentic contexts, organising and linking ideas logically and making language choices appropriate to the audience
Level 5	• write regularly and confidently to respond to a range of experiences, ideas, observations, and texts, developing a personal voice	• write on a variety of topics, shaping, editing, and reworking texts in an extended range of genres, selecting appropriate language features and using conventions of writing accurately and confidently	• write coherent, logical instructions, and factual accounts, and express and argue a point of view, linking main and supporting ideas, and structuring material in appropriate styles in a range of authentic contexts
Level 6	• write regularly, confidently, and fluently to reflect on a range of experiences, ideas feelings, and texts, developing a personal voice	• write on a variety of topics, shaping, editing, and reworking texts to express experiences and ideas imaginatively in an extended range of genres,choosing appropriate language features and using conventions of writing accurately and with discrimination	• write clear, coherent instructions, explanations, and factual reports and express and justify a point of view persuasively, structuring material confidently, in appropriate styles for different audiences, in a range of authentic contexts

(Continued)

Level 7	• write regularly, confidently, and fluently to reflect on, interpret, and explore a wide range of experiences, ideas, feelings, and texts,developing a personal voice	• write on variety of topics, shaping, editing, and re-working texts to investigate and explore ideas imaginatively in a wide range of genres, using the conventions of writing securely, and integrating techniques with purpose	• write clear, coherent explanations and reports, and debate a proposition or point of view, structuring well researched material effectively, in appropriate styles for different audiences, in a range of authentic contexts
Level 8	• use expressive writing regularly, fluently, and by choice, to reflect on, interpret, and explore a wide range of experiences. ideas, feelings, and texts, expressing complex thoughts in a personal voice	• write on a variety of topics in a wide range of genres, shaping, editing, and reworking texts and demonstrating depth of thought, imaginative awareness, and secure use of language, including accurate and discriminate use of the conventions of writing, and integrating techniques with purpose	• write explanations and reports on complex issues, and debate in depth a proposition or point of view, structuring well researched material effectively, in appropriate styles for different audiences, in a range of authentic contexts

Figure 8.3 *Levels of the New Zealand Curriculum: Written language –
achievement objectives*

context in which it arose and whether the finished result was aided or independent.

Teaching writing for different purposes

At Key Stage 1 teachers will want to continue to offer opportunities for writing in role play situations and to provide the space and materials to write for personal reasons in a writing area. Building on the resources already mentioned, provision should also be made of the following.

To reflect the current book being read at storytime the writing area should include publishers' promotional posters of the book, children's own illustrations , children's own version of the story so far, alternative view points of the story, that is, a different authorial voice.

• Thesauruses, more advanced dictionaries and word books, list of key words connected to the topic, days of the week, months of the years and the four seasons.
• Handwriting practice resources.
• Diaries, address and birthday books.

Examples of stimulating role-play areas which offer literacy opportunities in Years 1 and 2 classrooms are:

- offices with computers, 'photocopiers', stationery of all kinds, and dictation pads
- estate agent's office
- travel agent's office
- optician
- veterinary surgery
- hairdressing salon
- airports and aircraft flight deck
- post office.

Offering experience of texts in a range of forms

Given the close links between reading and writing, teachers will want to provide the children in their classes with opportunities and reasons for writing using a variety of forms. A rich context might be to create a newsagent's shop in the imaginative play area. This will enable pupils to explore the range of forms and functions of information texts. Initially, a few typical text items from a newsagent's can be brought in and discussed with the children. These might be:

- a newspaper
- a magazine
- a sweet wrapper
- a lottery ticket
- a video box
- a greetings card.

Most children will know the purpose of each of these items from a long acquaintanceship and show extensive knowledge about them. The teacher might ask the following questions about the text to focus thinking:

- What is it? What is the text for?
- Why do you read it?
- Do we know who wrote it?

Then the pupils' attention can be focused on to some of the textual features of each item. For example, if the greetings card is examined, what does the information on the front indicate:

- What type of greeting is the card is offering?
- What is the age of the intended recipient? How do you know?
- What do we know about the relationship between the sender and recipient? For instance, is it jokey, casual or formal? Is it a male to female or vice versa? Is it a loving relationship with a close family member or is it professional? And so on.

Inside the card the function and grammatical form of the printed message brings another layer to the discourse evident on the card.

A visit to a local newsagent might be organized in order to discover more about the types of texts to be found there. This could involve writing a shopping list beforehand, and so reinforcing the purpose, an aid to memory, as well as the form.

After the visit, children could be encouraged to stock their own newsagent in the classroom. They could conduct an ideas-gathering session to decide on the contents they wish to design and make and, then, having had their attention drawn to the different forms, can independently begin the tasks. The contents are likely to include a variety of the following: greetings cards, sweet boxes, invitations, comics, newspapers, notices and advertisements (of the type usually found in newsagent shop windows), video covers as well as the writing of shopping lists before going to play in the class shop.

Through this type of authentic experience with the potential to engage children with a real purpose, they will be encouraged and motivated to produce a variety of different types of writing showing how much they know not only about spelling and letter formation, and the relationship between purpose and structure, but also how much they know about the forms of writing.

Chronological writing

The recount

The recount is often the first type of independent writing attempted by children. It is typified by series of events, ordered sequentially and chronologically with the use of simple connectives, most typically a series of 'and' is followed by 'and then'. 'News' writing, the time-honoured favourite of Monday mornings, is a prime example of this, and used to be accompanied by the collecting in and counting of the dinner money in my teaching days! Primary teachers justified this practice by suggesting that it allowed reflection on and organization of an earlier experience. The truth of the matter was frequently rather short of this, with dreary accounts of going shopping, playing, having fun, frequently repeated Monday after Monday. Nevertheless, this genre is the most common first writing experience of children and, as such, deserves to be taught enthusiastically and supported appropriately.

Typically, the structure for these recounts is orientation–sequence of events–final orientation.

Writing of this type, often begins like this:

We all went to the museum. Some mums came with us.

continues with an outline of the events of the day:

We got given a talk about the things in the museum and I drew a big old book with metal bits on. We had to sit outside on a bench for lunch I had a sandwich and some crisps then it started to rain and we had to go in.

Figure 8.4 *A Year 1 child's recount*

And ends with the final event and possibly an evaluative comment:

> After we went back to school and my picture was showed to everyone. Mrs Mitchell said it was good.

The example in Figure 8.4 shows and gives evidence of how the recount records the fabric of children's lives, their activities, pains and pleasures.

The narrative

A recount of this type is an example of the 'observation/comment' genre. The recount can only develop into a narrative when, after the initial orientation, there is a disruption in the sequence of events. A problem needs to occur which leads to a resolution (followed sometimes by a moral or coda). It is not until children begin to introduce the dramatic action, the complication of an event or problem, that recount develops into true narrative.

Linguists offer sophisticated models to demonstrate the narrative fiction structure. Longacre (1976), for example, identifies the following elements:

Aperture	The 'once upon a time' type opening.
Exposition	Containing the information about setting (time and place) and characters.
Inciting moment	The point when the predictable exposition is disrupted and the story gets going.
Developing conflict	When the plot reaches a point when the confrontation or 'final showdown' becomes inevitable.
Denouement	A crucial event occurs that makes the resolution possible.
Final suspense	Details of the resolution are worked out.
Conclusion	Some sort of satisfactory end is worked out.

While many stories written by children will have a less complicated structure than outlined above in Longacre's model, the main features will need to be present for them to fulfil the criteria of a true narrative. Having an explicit knowledge of this structure will help teachers to be clearer in their understanding of how to teach children to write stories.

Why is narrative important?

We have discussed the role of stories and storying in Chapter 1, and we now consider again their importance. Linguists, psychologists and psychotherapists believe passionately that stories are an important way through which individuals come to know the world and their place within it. Barbara Hardy says:

> Narrative like lyric or dance, is not to be regarded as an aesthetic invention by artists to control, manipulate and order experience, but as a primary act of mind transferred from art to inner life. Inner and outer story telling plays a major role in our sleeping and waking lives. We dream in narrative, remember, anticipate, hope, despair, believe, doubt, plan, revise, criticise, construct, gossip, learn, hate and love by narrative. In order really to live, we make up stories about others, and ourselves about the personal and the social past and future. (1977: 12–13)

This frequently quoted phrase that narrative is 'a primary act of mind transferred from art to inner life' is central to this discussion. Storying, as we have seen in the earlier chapters on spoken language development, is our way of making sense of human experience. The more able we are to tell stories both to ourselves and others, the better equipped we are to understand the world. 'Storytelling is something we all do and understand. The habit is so deeply understood in us, historically and culturally, that we recognise our common humanity in all the tales we tell and hear, from childhood to old age, waking and dreaming' (Meek, 1996: 22).

Less poetically, the teaching of narrative is clearly placed in the statutory framework for teaching, whether it is the Programmes of Study in the English National Curriculum (DfEE, 1995) or the guidance of the Primary National Strategy: Framework for teaching literacy (DfES, 2006). The Cox Committee in its rationale for the original National Curriculum for English was firm about the importance of narrative:

> Young children hear stories either told or read from a very early age and, as soon as they have the skill, they read themselves. In this way, they internalise the elements of story structure – the opening, setting, character, events and resolution. Similarly, they come to realise that, in satisfying, well-structured stories, things that are lost will be found, problems will be solved, and mysteries will be explained and so on ... (DES, 1988: para. 17.28)

The development of narrative understanding

Story truly becomes a narrative when it has a plot, characters and a setting. The term 'plot' encompasses the unfolding of a story when a character is met with a dilemma or challenge, which has to be resolved through action in order to bring the story to a conclusion. Characters and settings are placed in a context to make the action come alive in our imaginations.

Foggin (1991) offers a sequence, which outlines development in terms of structure, vocabulary and includes the creation and manipulation of character. The insight that Foggin provides is that narrative 'becomes more complex and more mature as the writer becomes more imaginatively interested in the characters (as opposed to the events) in the narrative and, at the same time, becomes more intuitively aware of the needs of the reader' (1991: 14).

The developmental sequence from reception class through to the age of 11 (end of Key Stage 2) as suggested by Foggin is as follows:

1. The simplest form of narrative consists of a *main clause plus a list of objects*. For example: 'The girl's mum went to the shop and bought a satchel, coloured crayons, pencils and a notepad...'

2. Frequently featuring *a list of events*. This is marked by a heavy use of connectives such as **and, so, then, but**. These also typify the markers of oral narrative. for example: 'Maria went to her new school and she joined Class 3 and she made friends with a girl called Jessica.'

3. The next stage includes the development of *events causally linked, that is, plot*. The markers for this kind of narrative are words such as **because, although, when, where, since**. For example: 'Maria had many fears about going to her new school, her Mum had taken a new job in a city far away from their

old home. Would this school be very different? Although Class 3 seemed friendly enough would there be anyone who wanted to be her friend? … but there was and her name was Jessica.'

In order to develop to the next stage, Foggin states that as meanings become more explicit, events will be dramatized. The next level is:

4. *Dramatizing the story or plot events*, might include:
   (a) establishing a landscape or context
   (b) developing the use of dialogue
   (c) additional ways of establishing character such as description of appearance
   (d) developing more precise and appropriate vocabulary. for example: 'Jessica, the class loner, gazed at the small, thin girl as she looked anxiously around her, clutching her new satchel as if life depended upon it. Maria's shoulders were held stiffly as the teacher introduced her to the class, she and her Mum had moved from London to start a new life here. "She really looks OK" Jessica said to herself.'

This developmental sequence outlines the main teaching focus for early years practitioners, namely, the development of an understanding of plot through events that are causally linked. Progress can only occur when children achieve a firm grasp of narrative structure. The focus of teaching is to demonstrate to children how to move from writing a main clause and list of events (with the occasional affective comment) through to events being causally linked. This is not to say that the descriptions of character, the enrichment of vocabulary and the development of dialogue should be neglected but, in Key Stage 1, establishing an understanding of plot is the main goal. So, in relation to understanding the term plot, during Year 2, children's stories should show the following:

• an orientation or explanation of a situation
• a complicating action
• a causally linked resolution
• events are dramatized by establishing character through a simple description, actions and speech, and a setting, whether climate or place developed. The use of a vocabulary selected for effect.

The Primary National Strategy

The teaching objectives contained in the Primary National Strategy: Framework for teaching literacy (DfES 2006) lay out in detail a progression from the Reception Year to the end of Year 2. There is emphasis on oral retelling of known stories, and developing insight from reading and discussion of what is read, in children's own written narratives. The emphasis on the understanding of the components of narrative: plot, character and setting, is extensive and should be developed, again mainly through reading and discussion.

Teaching narrative structure

The following teaching approaches aim to teach children the component parts of stories, each of which has a particular function, and together they produce a coherent whole and a story worth the telling/reading. These teaching strategies release the story-maker from one strand of the task of narration to allow focus on only part of the whole. The approaches can be used together to help children compose and structure a narrative.

Reading and discussing stories

Story-reading is the starting point for story writing, through experiencing the pleasure of listening to many, many stories, discussing the features which make them satisfying, the seed corn of narrative writing is sown. Both story telling and story reading are developed further in Chapter 9.

Retelling a story

Learning how stories are structured is reinforced through the oral retelling of an incident, a happening or a favourite tale to a talk partner. It can start with the teacher telling a favourite story, and so modelling/demonstrating the oral tradition. This will need rehearsal, whether it is an incident drawn from one's own life or a folk tale. Before, during and after the telling of the tale, the practitioner or teacher will offer comment on what is happening, and so make explicit the content and the different components of the narrative.

Once the story has been retold the structure can be made explicit again orally ('Don't forget to begin by telling your partner the title of your story … ') or the structure can be written as three or four prompts on a flip chart, which the children are able to refer to if needed, particularly when rehearsing their story with a talk partner. This process can be repeated when retelling traditional stories such as fairy tales or favourite stories read at home or in class.

Story Maps and Story Boxes

Children can be supported further to understand the different components of narrative through the use of the prompts of a story box or a story map; a pictorial or concrete representation of the story. The most suitable stories are those which involve a movement of characters from one setting to another. Both of these devices help children to appreciate the sequencing of activity, and to move beyond beginning, middle and end of most story frames. Traditional tales lend themselves well to this approach, for example, 'The Hare and the Tortoise' story boxes give the story a concrete dimension with

(a)

25-2-06 The Pirate Adventure

I was asleep and I had a dream about
~~Sum~~ (some) children and twenty-r One pirates.
~~and~~ The children had a magic Key and
the key started to glow and When
they opened the door there
was a beach. ~~and~~ When
they got on to the beach
they saw s ~~um~~ (some) pirates and
the Pirats Wanted to have
a Party. ✓   ☺
I wonder what happened then?

(b)

Figure 8.5   *A Year 1 child has begun a promising narrative*

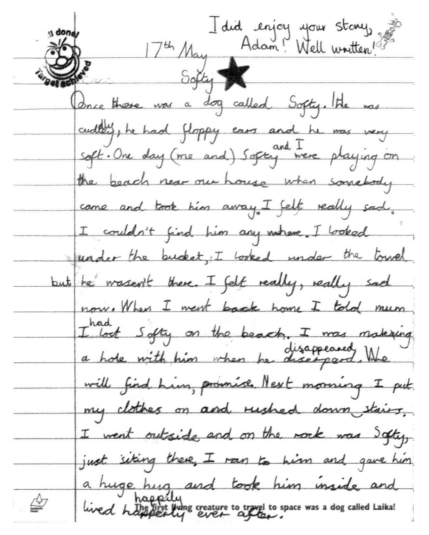

I did enjoy your story, Adam! Well written!

17th May

Softy ★

Once there was a dog called Softy. He was cuddly, he had floppy ears and he was very soft. One day (me and) Softy and I were playing on the beach near our house when somebody came and took him away. I felt really sad. I couldn't find him any where. I looked under the bucket, I looked under the towel but he wasn't there. I felt really, really sad now. When I went back home I told mum I had lost Softy on the beach. I was making a hole with him when he disappeared. We will find him, promise. Next morning I put my clothes on and rushed down stairs. I went outside and on the rock was Softy, just sitting there, I ran to him and gave him a huge hug and took him inside and lived happily ever after.

The first living creature to travel to space was a dog called Laika!

Figure 8.6   *A Year 2 child's story*

objects to manipulate during the retelling which either remains faithful to the original or with personal adaptations, for example, *The Cockerel and the Fox* retold and illustrated by Helen Ward.

Retelling a story in writing

Similarly, children can be supported into greater awareness of the components of narrative through a collective reading and discussion of written texts, and encouragement to use the understandings within their own written stories. A very powerful strategy for helping children to internalize these features is to read and discuss a text (see above) and then invite the creation of a different story while using the same characters, setting and basic structure (Figures 8.5, 8.6 and 8.7).

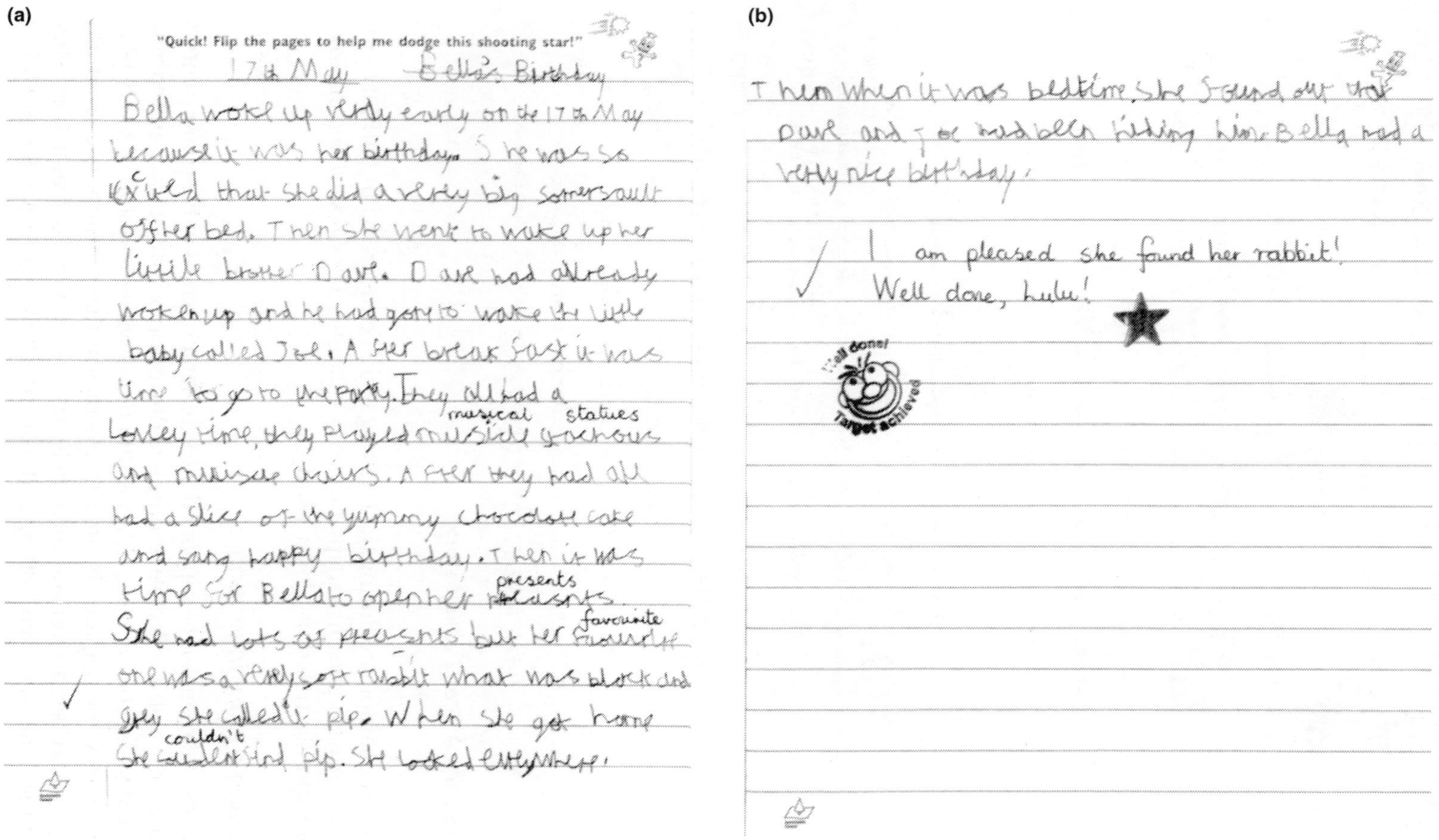

(a)

17th May
Bella's Birthday

Bella woke up really early on the 17th May because it was her birthday. She was so excited that she did a very big somersault off her bed. Then she went to wake up her little brother Dan. Dan was already awake and had got up to wake up their baby called Jack. A she broke first it was time to go to prepare. They all had a lovely time, they played musical statues and musical chairs. After they had all had a slice of the yummy chocolate cake and sang happy birthday. Then it was time for Bella to open her presents.

She had lots of presents but her favourite one was a really cute rabbit what was black and grey. She called it Pip. When she got home she couldn't stop stroking Pip. She loved everything!

(b)

Then when it was bedtime she found out that Pip had got out and I er she been hiding under Bella's bed a very nice birthday!

I am pleased she found her rabbit!
Well done, Lulu.

Figure 8.7   Lulu (aged 7 years) writes her story about Bella's birthday

Supporting children to write poetry

The poetic form is sometimes classified as a sub-category of narrative. Here we will discuss briefly what distinguishes poetry from other forms of text and suggest classroom strategies that will help pupils to understand the distinctive features of the poetic form. In many ways poetry is the form of written language to which young children warm the most. Infants play with the sound patterns of language and with rhythm as they learn to speak. Babies under a year, delight in rhymes with accompanying actions such as:

> Pat a cake, pat a cake, baker's man
> Bake me a cake as fast as you can
> Pat it and prick it
> And mark it with J ... and put in the oven for baby and ME.

Toddlers hardly able to walk will bend their knees and sway to a rhyme chanted for them. So children find hearing and reading rhymes, and even writing poetry, deeply satisfying all through the early years of education. Earlier chapters drew attention to the importance of distinguishing individual sounds within words, phonemic segmentation, in the early stages of learning to read and write and that this skill is supported by learning rhymes and jingles. While there is conclusive research evidence on this topic, here we consider the fundamental right of children to be given opportunities to appreciate the joys of poetry. Fry (2005) writes:

> I believe poetry is a primal impulse within us all ... I believe our poetic impulse is blocked by the false belief that poetry might on the one hand be academic and technical and on the other formless and random ...
>
> For me the private act of writing poetry is song writing, confessional, diary-keeping, speculation, problem-solving story telling, therapy, anger management, craftsmanship relaxation, concentration and spiritual adventure all in one inexpensive package (2005: xi–xii).

A poem is an oral art form, it is written to be read aloud and it comes alive, as it were, in the mouth. Verse uses the patterns and sounds of language through rhythm and repetition. A poem is consciously designed and composed as a poem, and important decisions have been made concerning the appropriate form, structure and vocabulary. Poetry through conjuring with images, communicates on many different levels and it embraces light-hearted and serious topics. A poem may be a joke, an anecdote or a profound reflection on love!

Dilemmas occur concerning the differences between prose and poetry. W.H. Auden merely says 'It is a sheer waste of time to look for a definition of the difference between poetry and prose. The distinction between verse and prose is self-evident' (1963: 23). And very young children will come to appreciate the patterning of language that is the key feature to be recognized in what counts as a poem through the experience of having poetry read to them every day of their lives.

The structure of poetic form

The 'Language in the National Curriculum materials' (unpublished, 1992) summarizes the four different areas which we should consider when looking at poetic language and its distinctive features:

> Sight
> Sound
> Structure
> Sense.

The way that a poem is written and shaped on the page is different from prose. The distinctive line breaks (that is, words do not continue to the right-hand margin as they do in prose) and the layout (the poem may be arranged in verses or regular stanzas each containing, for example, four lines indicated by a gap between each group) give a visual clue to how we should read the text. This point is well illustrated by Hull (1988). In his example, Rachel, has written her personal response to a film using a firework as a simile:

> I felt as if something had burst inside of me and trickled into all the parts of my body like a firework going off and sparks sprinkling everywhere.

This reads like prose, albeit with 'poetic language'. But, Hull suggests, if set out in the form of a poem, this transformation occurs:

> I felt as if something
> had burst inside me,
> and trickled
> into all the parts of my body
> like a firework going off,
> and sparks sprinkling everywhere.

We are able now to approach the text as if it were a poem, treating the language as condensed and compressed, and savouring the use of the firework simile.

There are many poetic conventions or organizations that influence the shape and form of a poem; there are the poetic forms of limerick, sonnet and haiku or, conversely, it is acceptable to reject any kind of internal structure and convention and write in free verse form. However, so wide a choice for children also creates difficulties. Introducing Year 2 pupils to a range of common forms of poetry enables them to begin to see the possibilities and if and when to choose to use them for their own purposes. For the youngest children the awareness that poetry is read differently to prose is sufficient as a starting point.

Sound – metre and rhyme

Sound is the key feature of a poem, and is the one that is most readily recognized and which distinguishes it from prose. It is this distinctive feature which leads us to say that poetry needs to be read aloud. The following technical key terms that teachers need to know, contribute to the tools or devices that poets use to create sound pictures and patterns in a poem.

Key Terms

Metre or metrical structure is a significant feature of most poetry. Languages have a natural rhythm and each spoken word is composed of syllables. For example, 'bus' has one syllable, 'garden' has two syllables, 'loll/i/pop' has three syllables and so on. **Stress** is placed on one or more of these syllables when speaking. In 'garden,' we place the stress on the first syllable with 'GARden'. Where the stress is placed is learnt as infants learn to speak and is a source of confusion to non-English speakers. It is **stress** and **metre** that give spoken language its patterns and **cadence**.

Rhyme is the repetition of sounds, usually the endings of words or the **rime** and not necessarily related to spellings, often at regular intervals, and most commonly at the ends of lines of poetry.

Poetry with no formal metre is called **free verse** and poetry without any rhyme but with a metrical structure is called **blank verse**.

The stressed and unstressed syllables form the natural rhythm of language and this is capitalized on by the poet to generate consistent and repetitive patterns. When a rhythm becomes regular and repeated it is known as **metre**. The use of certain types of rhythm depends on the type of poem and the effect that is sought by the poet. The most frequently mentioned metre in English poetry is 'iambic pentameter', where each line of the poem has the pattern of stressed and unstressed syllables repeated five times:

<u>Which</u>/**thus**/<u>presents</u>/<u>and</u>/**thus**/<u>records</u>/<u>true</u> **life**. (Elizabeth Barrett Browning)

bold = stressed syllable <u>xx</u> = unstressed syllable

Formal identification of metre is not the type of technically complicated work required in early years classrooms. But the point being made here is that repetitive rhythms are crucial to poetic writing and young children will gradually be able to appreciate this if inducted to many forms of poetry in the course of rich language provision in the setting or classroom.

Another contributor to the distinctive sound of poetry is **rhyme.** It is important immediately to make clear that it is not imperative for poetry to rhyme, even though young children (and some teachers!) are convinced that a poem is essentially a group of words which rhyme. Indeed, perhaps it is better to suggest that children avoid rhyme altogether, initially at least, when writing poetry. It is the added dimension of struggling to find words that rhyme that produces banal, contorted results. What is relevant here is that young children come to appreciate rhyme, that they can hear and identify it as one of the distinctive features of poetry and, in time, are able to incorporate rhyming words into their own poems for added effect.

So, basic building blocks of poetry are:

- the form and organization of the poem and the effects of and reasons for ending a line in a particular place
- the resulting visual form of the poem
- the features of the sound patterns of the poem, achieved particularly through repeated rhythms and rhyme.

With these fundamental understandings in place, the content or sense can be developed, including perhaps the use of imagery, metaphor, simile, surprise and ambiguity. Further structural features are the selection of words, with the shape and sound qualities of the words guiding the choice as well as the sense, and the way that these words are combined in a poem, which is the syntax. Sense and syntax are fundamental to all written language, of course, but they are not the springboard for the youngest children in early years settings and classrooms. Understanding of these technical aspects of poetry will develop through reading, enjoying and collaboratively writing many, many poems.

Crafting a poem

It is necessary to remind ourselves of the following underlying principles for teaching poetry in early years classrooms:

- A poem needs to be both seen and heard to gain both the aural and visual pleasure of poetry.
- Selecting a poem to be read aloud needs to be done with care to demonstrate its intrinsic qualities:

  - the organization and construction distinctly different to other forms of writing
  - a poem should intrigue, puzzle, dazzle, describe and play with language.

- Through collaborative poetry-making, distinctive poetic features are debated and considered and taught in a context. An understanding of rhythm and rhyme as well as the overall structure and line syntax will develop only through demonstration. Children are party to the decision-making of the choice of words; their aptness and precision are considered rigorously. Poetry is seen to be 'the best words in the best order', for that specific purpose, and rejection of some words is part of the process of selection.

• Children learn through discussing real poems, rhymes and rhythms and then applying their insights to composing their own, both in collaboration with others and individually.

These principles will inform and complement practice when implementing the statutory requirements contained in The National Curriculum for English and clear objectives outlined in the Primary National Strategy: Framework for teaching literacy (DfES, 2006) many of which are concerned with poetry.

Hearing and reciting poems

When adults read poetry aloud they model the distinctive rhythms and patterns, emphasizing the music in the poetic language. Deliberations on the meaning are best delayed till after the poem has been read and savoured, even after two readings. This may be through discussion on the subject or theme of the whole poem and in a way that relates the content to the young child's own experience. Similarly, consideration can take place on the effect of the particular words which combine with the meaning and the way words have been selected for their quality of sound in order to support the impact or atmosphere of the poem.

Children need access to poetry, stories and non-fiction books. Collections of poems that have been read, laughed over and learned by heart can be displayed in reading areas. Anthologies (rather than rhyming stories) placed in a bin box labelled poetry and referred to as poetry books, will reinforce the particularities of the genre. Multiple copies of anthologies of well-loved poetry is a manageable way to further support pupils' developing understanding of the poetic form. Such boxed collections can be used as a school resource and shared between classes of the same year group, whenever there is a focus on poetry. Reading aloud from enlarged versions of poems and drawing attention to differences in layout is also valuable. Owing to their central role in early adult–child interaction and popularity in playground culture, children and adults know many nursery rhymes and poems by heart (including the rude versions!). So this type of verse is fruitful for language play, developing awareness of rhyme, rhythm, alliteration and the sound patterns in poetry in general.

Nursery rhymes are the starting point with nursery and reception children, reciting and committing to memory favourite rhymes. 'Jack and Jill went up the hill', 'Mary, Mary quite contrary', and 'ring a ring o'roses', and so on are physically experienced through chanting, singing, clapping and joyfully dancing. Clapping emphasizes the repetition of stress in each line which forms the basis of the rhythm or metre in the nursery rhymes; the children will be encouraged to join in.

In addition, pupils in reception classes can be encouraged to listen for the words that rhyme. This is valuable for their appreciation of the poetic form, and for developing phonological awareness, the crucial skill in early reading.

Poetry and Shared Writing

Shared Writing was discussed earlier in this chapter and is a key teaching approach in the Primary National Strategy: Framework for teaching literacy. With Shared Writing practitioners model the way experienced writers of poetry compose or construct a poem.

The Framework for teaching literacy, as outlined earlier, conceptualizes texts as having three levels; whole text, sentence and word. When writing poetry the terms 'whole text', **'line'** and 'word' level might more appropriately be considered as a focus for teaching. Whole text refers to the way that the text is shaped overall and will include the layout and the final format on the page. It could also include features of the number of syllables and/or words that will be used (for example, in haiku and cinquains) if such conventions are being adhered to. Line (rather than sentence) level will refer to where line breaks occur, the metre/pattern of syllables within the line, and syntax. Word level encompasses the 'diction' (that is, vocabulary) which includes, obviously, the sounds of words, as well as their meaning and the possibility that they rhyme.

Writing poems on a theme

Most early years practitioners and teachers collect poetry that relates to identified themes for use at relevant times with their pupils. Photocopying has made box file collections of poetry a convenient possibility, with photocopied poems pasted onto cards and filed under categories such as Winter, Transport, Ourselves and Our Families, Emotions, Animals, Food, Festivals, Home, Water, and so on, but also the information details of the title and page number of additional poems within the themes from published anthologies. This takes the frustration out of a future hunt for a half-remembered but much enjoyed poem.

A worked example of writing a class poem

Using just such a collection, poems on bonfire night and firework displays had been read to a reception class over a number of days at the beginning of one November, including the poem 'November the Fifth' by Leonard Clark.

The children were asked to concentrate on the poem, to listen to the words and the way that these describe the subject matter well, and to enjoy the repeating sounds the poets used. **Onomatopoeia** and **alliteration** (Figure 8.8) were discussed (but not in those technical terms) as common features in the poem.

Wiggy Witch works
her ways.

Alliteration

Well done, Ella. I like your
12/1/05   picture!

Figure 8.8   *Ella (6 years old) uses alliteration to enhance her poetic writing*

Key Terms

Onomatopoeia: words which echo sounds associated with their meaning: clang, hiss crash, cuckoo

Alliteration: a phrase where adjacent or closely connected words begin with the same phoneme: one wet wellington, slithering snakes

---

Working with groups of about six children at first, discussion occurred about some of the meanings of the words, rhythms, repetition of words and sounds, as well as description. The poem was read again with children accompanying the reading as they were able, in order to 'feel' the poem. A firework display was taken as a focus of a movement lesson to deepen the experience of the fireworks. Using their bodies to represent the explosions, the swirling,

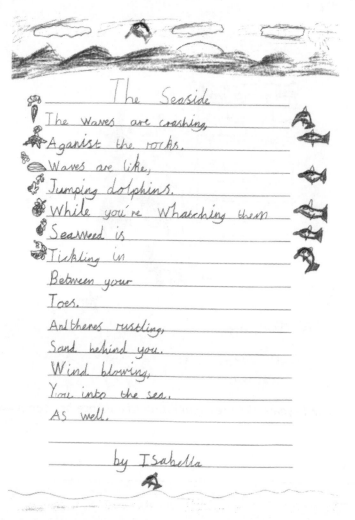

Figure 8.9 *A Year 2 child's poem about the seaside (1)*

zig-zagging, fizzing, stuttering trajectories of fireworks against the sky, enabled kinaesthetic experience of the fireworks to provide a way into words.

Secondly, the adult and children shared ideas of as many appropriate words as possible to describe the firework display, and the sight, colour and sounds of the fireworks as well as the actions that they make when alight. As the words were offered they were written onto a large sheet of paper attached to a flip chart (or a whiteboard or a 'smart board' could be used).

At the third stage, the adult scrutinizes the words to see how they can be shaped into a poetic form. Here the experienced writer demonstrates the way words can be shaped and crafted into the lines of a poem to achieve a desired effect, as in the case of a firework display earlier. Examples here have been inspired by a school visit to the sea side.

Figures 8.9 and 8.10 were the results.

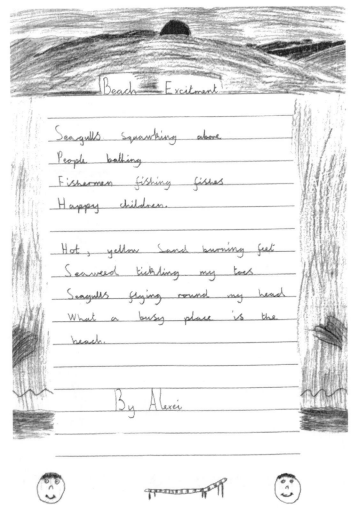

Figure 8.10   *A Year 2 child's poem about the seaside (2)*

Using poems as models

The final section of this chapter is concerned with using whole, or parts of poems as structural models for children's own poems and therefore substituting more substantial amounts of text into the structures already present (Figure 8.11).

Developing awareness of non-chronological and non-fiction texts

In Chapter 9, we address the importance of children meeting, using and learning to write non-fiction texts. Academics are beginning to place more

Figure 8.11   *A Year 1 child uses a structure*

and more emphasis on the value of being able to operate across a variety of genres, indeed some argue forcefully that to deny children access to non-fiction genre is to straitjacket thinking and curb intellectual development.

> We require of them (pupils) a kind of thinking that does not come sponta-neously to the human mind. The urge towards it is there, but the possibility of its mature development depends on a long cultural heritage; and of this heritage the special literate ways of handling language form an essential part. (Donaldson, 1993: 54–5)

So children, given opportunity, learn gradually, over the years of primary school, to participate in the impersonal modes of thinking and linguistic expression that are an important part of their cultural heritage. Donaldson goes on to give examples of the kinds of phrases that represent this 'language of systematic thought', such as, *'one reason is'*, *'what this means is'*. People who cannot operate within this type of language and the impersonal thinking it represents are at 'a gross disadvantage in every field of study from gardening to astronomy' (1993: 51).

It has been argued earlier (Riley and Reedy, 2000) that children in the early years of education should begin to have access to these modes of thought so that they are enabled to develop critical thinking, and to contribute in the most powerful discourses that shape our society. If they cannot they are excluded and relatively powerless.

Children need access to examples of these texts so that they can begin to incorporate the structural features of text organization, language, register and specific vocabulary, when writing their own. This is a very powerful connection.

Understanding non-fiction texts

Many children will have had experience at home of the kinds of texts they eventually meet, read and use at school. However, we need to be aware of those who have not. The different types of informational texts, can broadly be reduced to a small number of categories.

- Narrative:
  biography, information stories, and so on.

- Procedural:
  instructions, such as recipes, rules of card games, explanations on how to carry out experiments, and so on.

- Expository:
  illustrated books on one topic, usually containing structural guides such as contents, indexes and glossaries.

  Reference:
  dictionaries, encyclopaedias, CD-ROMs, and so on.

- Lists:
  shopping lists, telephone directories, and so on.

Littlefair suggests that 'perhaps the most important non-narrative text in school is expository ... it is this register of language which presents the greatest challenge to readers and which is ultimately of the greatest importance for their development as readers and competent language users' (1993: 131).

As pupils read explanations and descriptions they learn to understand that texts can be arranged quite differently from narrative. The differences are mainly the following.

- *The register* – this encompasses the grammar and structure of the sentences and the vocabulary used. In narrative texts, the language used can be complex and descriptive, while in expository texts it is often terse and concise with use of many specialist technical terms. Non-fiction texts are often written in the passive voice and abstract concepts are discussed.
- *The complexity* – the features of the expository texts that children have to recognize and use are cohesive devices which are less familiar to young children, such as conjunctions, for example, *however, although, therefore, consequently*. In narrative, the connectives are more linear and easier to understand, and the context and the flow of a story helps to support meaning.
- *The texts are read differently* – narratives are read from beginning to end. With expository and screen-based informational texts, readers read selected sections in order to access specific information (for example, the number of species of owl that exist in the UK).

So, the language of expository texts is unfamiliar and different from popular storybooks and the spoken language of many pupils, and the way that children approach it is also fundamentally different.

Appreciating the structural differences in non-fiction texts

First, we have to have a range of non-fiction texts in the classroom both to read to and discuss with children and allow them time to explore. As Meek says: 'The most important single lesson the children learn from texts is the nature and variety of written discourse, the different ways that language lets a writer tell, and the many different ways a reader reads' (1988: 21).

Secondly, we write these kinds of texts collaboratively with children, making explicit the structure and linguistic features of each, within the context of school activities.

The main generic types that are expected to be taught, by the PNS – namely the recount, the non-chronological report, instructions, labels, captions and lists. Next, we will address recounts and non-chronological reports as well as sequential instructions.

Recounts

Recounts we said earlier are the most common and familiar form of writing that young children are required to produce in school. The form is close to narrative, being chronological and the anecdotal recounting of events in our lives. Pupils take to this form of writing most easily.

Reports

Reports (or non-chronological texts as the Primary National Strategy terms it) do not neatly mirror our everyday conversations, and the conventions for structuring are not integral to most children's experience. Therefore, exposure to and using reports will be crucial in developing an understanding of their form and purpose. However, reports and procedural texts are not commonplace in the daily routines in early years settings other than, perhaps, recipes for cookery. Practitioners need to be imaginative in this area of provision, making use of fantasy to intrigue and stimulate.

Modelling using writing to fulfil personal purposes

People write constantly. We make shopping lists prior to a supermarket visit, we fill in forms, we send postcards, invitations and letters. We sometimes write a permanent record for others to read, enjoy or follow. In school, writing to display knowledge and to demonstrate new learning is well recognized as a valuable teaching approach. However, writing should always be purposeful, and teaching how to structure writing should never be the sole reason for children writing non-fiction. It is most meaningfully the means to an end.

Recounts are produced when it is important to make a record of a personal experience, whether an event outside school or a class trip or visit. Reports are the result when science experiments or natural phenomena such as plants and human physiology are described. Instructions are written with a particular audience in mind to tell them how to do something specific. New experiences and/or observations are offered to children, and then they will move through discussion and reflection, to summarizing and organizing their thoughts into a written form for an audience. Each stage in the process needs to be made explicit to children while encouraging them to keep in mind the reason for writing in the first place, namely, the audience and purpose. For young children the most challenging part of this sequence will be the organization of the writing, particularly the typical structural form associated with unfamiliar text types.

The use of writing frames

To help pupils learn how to structure various forms of non-fiction texts, Wray and Lewis (1997) suggest the teaching strategy of 'writing frames'. These consist of frameworks or outlines to scaffold and prompt the children's non-fiction writing. Frames provide a template of ways to begin the text; they offer connectives and sentence modifiers which give children a structure so that they can concentrate on communicating what they want to say, while scaffolding them in the use of the linguistic features of a particular generic form. (See Figure 8.11) for an example of a frame.

These explicit models for writing offer support at text level, sentence level and at word level. An overall structure of the text is supplied. The beginnings of sentences model the typical grammatical register for the children to continue. Vocabulary of appropriate connectives is also present.

Writing frames have been heavily criticized as formulaic devices that 'trick' children into writing in certain ways. This may be because the intended way to use them has been misunderstood. Wray and Lewis are clear that writing frames should never be given to children as an exercise in their own right. The same principles that are consistent with all effective teaching approaches guide the use of writing frames. The frame is most effective when introduced through discussion, with the teacher explaining the purpose, and modelling how the frames are constructed and used. Connections made between the texts children have read and the writing they are about to undertake establish the link. Teachers can then move to Shared Writing, using, adapting and modifying the frame as appropriate for a specific teaching purpose and bearing in mind the children's prior experience. Only then are children offered a writing frame that will help shape and structure their own independent writing. Once the frame has been used the structure should soon become internalized, and further explicit support is unnecessary.

The advantages of writing frames are that they:

- 'help maintain the cohesion of the whole text
- provide experience of appropriate connectives
- model the more formal "register" of non-fiction genres
- introduce more complex vocabularies
- scaffold the appropriate generic form
- prompt further thinking, for example, 'a fourth thing we noticed was … '.

Writing frames enable children to achieve success in producing a text and in doing so:

- improve self-esteem and motivation
- prevent children from being presented with a blank piece of paper – a daunting experience for some children who find starting a piece of writing difficult' (Wray and Lewis, 1997: 123).

The dangers inherent in the use of writing frames are that they can be seen as representing fixed overall forms as well as the only way of phrasing parts of the text. Frames may become the reason for using information to achieve a prescribed end product rather than through the means to engage with an opportunity to organize and connect thought. Thus the frames here are viewed as tentative and adaptable in their overall form, and should be used for a transitional stage in the child's writing capability. They are best incorporated within a purposeful context either for communicating information or for recording and reflecting upon knowledge.

Approaches to teaching how to write non-fiction genres

Whenever non-fiction books are read aloud, teachers and other adults are given the opportunity to do valuable teaching by discussing with children the content. This will include asking questions such as:

- What is this book about? (Looking at title, picture on cover, and so on.)
- What can you see in this picture?
- Do you think this book is about real things or not?

Such questions will lead in to discussing and categorizing books according to their intended purpose. Enlarged texts or 'big books' are particularly useful for this, with the initial question framed as 'Is this a story or information book?' Year 1 and Year 2 children can take part in a sorting activity, with two hoops placed on the floor, a mixed pile of books to be placed into one of two categories, namely, story or non-fiction. The children's attention should be drawn to the structural features necessary for information retrieval including:

- title
- the description of the book on the cover
- contents
- index
- page numbers for cross referencing.

With a text which is not read sequentially, pupils need to know how to frame the questions they have in mind as they use an informational text. Researching a particular issue or searching for a sub-section in the text, are both supported by formulating the appropriate questions. Retrieval devices help children to navigate a book until the information to satisfy the enquiry is found.

Expository texts are the most common type of non-fiction texts that children meet in school. However, children encounter other information texts beyond school which should be valued. One way of doing this is to make a collection of all the different types of information texts that can be found at home or in school. This allows pupils to demonstrate what they know regarding the use and purpose of information texts and the teacher is then in a position to build on this understanding. A 'lucky dip' bag filled with a wide range of texts is an excellent way to manage this opportunity. An assortment of texts including diaries, recipe books, bus tickets, maps, photographs and photograph albums, newspapers, food packaging, magazines, instructions from electrical goods, carrier bags, cheque books, video boxes, television listings, magazines, local trade telephone directories, and so on, will be in the bag. The children all have a 'lucky dip', and discussion follows. As each text is taken from the bag, the following questions can be asked:

- What is it?
- Where does it come from?
- Who uses it?
- What does it tell us?

Each of the following sections contains an example of teaching which results in a particular form of writing being produced by children. Each example is preceded by a brief outline of the purpose and the typical features of the text type.

Teaching how to write a recount

When supporting children to write a recount, the adult needs a clear idea of its purpose, structure and linguistic features. Recounts retell events to entertain or inform. The typical structure is as follows:

- an orientation to set the scene
- events in sequential, time order
- a final orientation which is optional
- an evaluation, which is also optional.

The important linguistic features are:

- use of simple past tense
- presence of cohesive words to do with time, for example, **later, after, then, before**.

The following are ways that this can be taught.

Oral recount telling such as 'My weekend' – one way to do this is to write three or four prompt words on the flip chart to remind the children what their recount should contain. This is usually:

Who?
When?
Where?
What happened?

Important vocabulary related to time can be introduced and talked about (for example, **first, next, then, after, finally**). These words, too, can be written up as a visual reminder for the children.

This process might be repeated when recounting other events by the teacher and when children are talking about their weekend to the class or to a partner.

Modelling through Shared Writing and with the use of pictures to structure and sequence a recount is also an effective strategy. The examples in Figures 8.12, 8.13 and 8.14 demonstrate this.

Procedural/instructional texts

As with recounts, when teaching the writing of procedural texts practitioners need to have a clear idea of the purpose, structure and the linguistic features. The features of procedural/instructional texts are as follows.

Instructions have a clear purpose which takes a reader through a series of sequenced steps in order to describe clearly how something is done (Figure 8.15). The structure usually is as follows:

(a)

20·6·0\

I Went to the sdool fete
on Sunday. My favourite
thing was the little
steam train. I Went on
il two times. My second
favourite thing was
haveing my face painted.
I chose to have a
rainbow painted on me,
After the school fete my
neighbours came round

(b)

for a barbeque. They had
a baby called James. We
had the swimming pool out
and James liked the wate
in it. ✓ ★ What a busy day, Martha

Figure 8.12   *A recount by a Year 1 child (1)*

(a)

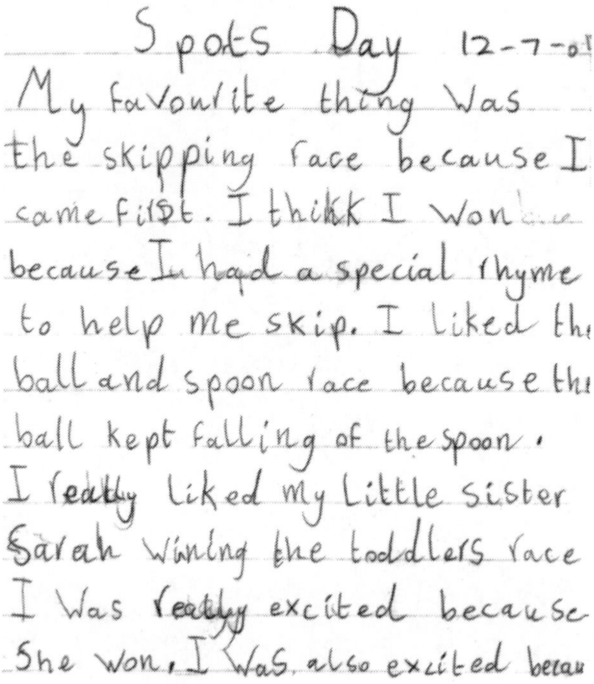

Spots Day   12-7-0?

My favourite thing was
the skipping race because I
came first. I thikk I won
because In had a special rhyme
to help me skip. I liked the
ball and spoon race because the
ball kept falling of the spoon.
I really liked my little sister
Sarah winning the toddlers race
I was really excited because
she won. I was also excited becau

(b)

Zoe came second. It was
funny when the dads did the
balloon race. It was funny because
the balloons kept squeezing
out.

Figure 8.13   *A recount by a Year 1 child (2)*

Figure 8.14   *A recount by a Year 1 child (3)*

- a statement of what is to be achieved
- any materials that are needed
- the method, usually set out as a series of sequenced steps
- the above is sometimes accompanied by a diagram or illustration.

The most important linguistic features are:

- usually in present tense
- use of cohesive words to do with time, for example, **next, after, then, now, first.**

   The following teaching sequence developing an understanding of the form and function of a procedural text was completed by a Year 2 class (6–7-year-olds). It exemplifies the teaching approach of moving from reading to writing with structured support from the teacher, including the use of a writing frame. This is well summarized by Beard (1999).

Figure 8.15 *Example of a Year 2 child's instructional text.*

There are three stages to this approach:

1. *Modelling* – sharing information about the uses and features of the genre (format, grammar, and so on).
2. *Joint construction* of a new text in the same genre by pupils and teacher.
3. *Independent construction* of a new text in the same genre by pupils, with drafting/editing consultation with peers and teacher and publication/evaluation.

Figure 8.16   *Thomas describes a Cateraffe*

Non-chronological reports

The purpose of reports is to classify and describe the way things are (Figures 8.16 and 8.17). The typical structure of reports consists of:

- an opening generalization/classification
- a description of the phenomenon, which will include some or all of the
  - qualities
  - parts and their functions
  - habits/behaviours or uses.
- summary (which is optional).

The most important linguistic features:

- are usually in present tense
- contain impersonal language
- contain subject specific vocabulary.

See the genre table in Section 3 of *Developing Early Writing* (DfEE, 2001).

(a)

The Catfly has a long
tail
tale.   The caterfly has nice
wings.   It has a big
round   tummy .   It makes
a miaow noise.   It likes to
fly   in the sky.   It has
pointy ears,

(b)

Caterfly

Figure 8.17   *Pippa's 'combination creature' the Caterfly is described here (A Year 1 child)*

Conclusions

The included examples show that young children can write in a range of straightforward non-fiction forms given an appropriate context and focused teaching and support. Lively learning environments provide reasons for making the Herculean effort to produce written texts, and as with developing reading to learn this needs always to be the starting point.

Summary

In this chapter I have suggested that:

- in school, children need to engage with a range of fiction and non-fiction texts
- children need to know the differences between fiction and non-fiction, including subject matter, language register and the way that they are read
- the characteristics of a range of different non-fiction genres can be taught explicitly to young children
- writing frames are a very useful support when children are writing in particular forms for the first time
- children's writing should always be set in meaningful contexts that are familiar to the experience of young children.

Acknowledgement

I would like to acknowledge the debt that I owe to David Reedy regarding the extent to which I have drawn in this chapter upon the book that we wrote together and which is suggested as further reading. I am grateful also to the children of Dropmore Infants School, Burnham for their examples of writing which enliven this chapter wonderfully.

Further reading

Department for Education and Employment (DfEE) (2001) *Developing Early Writing.* London: Standards and Effectiveness Unit/NLS
Riley, J.L. and Reedy, D. (2000) *Developing Writing for Different Purposes: Teaching about Genre in the Early Years.* London: Paul Chapman Publishing.

Chapter 9

Children's Books in the Early Years of Education

Poems and stories tap deep responses. Such processes take time and cannot be measured or tested by immediate questioning about the surface features of the poems and stories. However, the cumulative effect of our many experiences as spectators of fictive events, feelings and personalities is an enlargement of our imaginative sensibilities and understandings.

(Whitehead, 2004: 134)

[I]nformational texts can be powerful tools when emergent readers and writers explore the means and ends of written language.

(Richgels, 2002: 594)

Introduction

The inclusion of a chapter on both the value of and ways to use children's literature can need no justification in a volume focusing on the development and teaching of literacy. After all, books are both the means, and the chief purpose for, learning to read in the first place. Picture books and storybooks are the major source of pleasure and the motivation to learn to read: they foster concentration and galvanize the effort required for fluency. In addition, books represent a key resource for the adult in the early years setting or classroom: they offer the potential to delight, to inform, to instruct and to enrich. This chapter aims to cover the use and selection of both fiction and non-fiction books as children move from 'learning to read to reading to learn'. Discussion will take place also on how books can enhance pupils' overall intellectual, emotional, visual literacy, spiritual and moral development as well as their growing ability to use texts to fulfil a range of personal purposes.

Books and the development of language

Stories and poetry offer thoughtfully crafted models through which children's spoken and written language is enhanced. Whitehead says 'Language as art has been shaped, altered, chosen and carefully placed to produce the effects of just those words in just that particular order' (2004: 138). Early years practitioners and teachers capitalize upon the joyful potential of literature to support language acquisition (see Chapters 1 and 2). Not only is the volume and type of words we know increased through reading (or being read to), but through language we are able to escape the immediate and are provided with the tools to make sense of the present and to plan for the future (Tucker, 1993). As Whitehead again writes: 'We find in literature new words for new worlds and new words for old experiences, as well as meeting old words used in startlingly bright and fresh ways' (2004: 146). In addition, books present children with the engaging and continually reinforcing demonstration of the differences between written and spoken language (Chapter 3). So hearing stories read expands the child's vocabulary, and deepens understanding of written sentence structure and the cohesion of text. Exposure to high-quality books introduces children to a literary language, its conventions and its structures. Tucker continues with 'Good writing for this age group from a literary point of view should be fresh, direct and rhythmic – easy to remember and a pleasure to listen to. Short, spare sentences are preferable to long rambling structures, and a bright, lively vocabulary better than a dull repetitive one' (1993: 117).

Books are the pleasurable way a child can experience and read flowing, rhythmic language, language that is attractive to the ear when read aloud. On the nature of the language used, there has been great debate regarding the benefit of a natural language style and its ability to facilitate comprehension and reading development in young readers. Many texts for novice readers capitalize on the familiar spoken language patterns of the pupils but Perrera suggests that 'a more judicious blend of familiar and more literary grammatical structures will be just the right combination' (1993: 96) for some more knowledgeable and advanced readers. The particular writing conventions in the genre of non-fiction texts can present difficulties for young readers, as will be discussed later. Consideration will be given later also to the particular role that expository texts provide to support children's language development by offering them fresh ideas, new concepts and a richer vocabulary through exposure to a wider and wondrous world.

Written language and the development of thought

[L]anguage written down is thereby cut loose ... or disembedded ... from the context of on-going activities and feelings in which speech functions and on which speech thrives. *Once on the page, language is on its own.* This gives it a degree of independence which makes it particularly apt for the development of certain kinds of thought. (Donaldson, 1993: 50)

Books, we have said, provide accessible, engaging models of written language. If spoken language releases the individual from the 'here and now' (Tucker, 1993), Donaldson argues that the power of written language is that by its 'disembeddedness' it has the potential to develop in the child the ability to think in the abstract, as the quotation above suggests. She continues: 'I have in mind thought that is about general topics with no immediate bearing on the personal life. For instance, how do birds find their way when they migrate? Or why does concrete set so hard?' (1993: 50).

Donaldson suggests that while the desire to understand precedes and exists without literacy, it is greatly promoted by access to written language. This is achieved in two ways; first, by the individual having the opportunity and recourse to ideas and sources beyond her experience, namely, to look up information in books and on the Internet. Secondly, literacy has the life-enhancing capacity to enable individuals to order and to sustain their thought. Frequently, this is achieved through writing down one's thoughts and reordering them through systematic redrafting. In this way 'Thinking itself draws great strength from literacy' (Donaldson, 1993: 50) and books every day provide a model for this type of ordered, systematic thought.

This level and form of thinking is essential for success in any field of academic study and educational endeavour, as it lays the foundations of being able to follow or structure an argument, of the ability to go beyond the personal and to generalize from the evidence provided. Impersonal, disembedded thought and then its linguistic expression are part of the cultural heritage of all children as their educational entitlement: these are the key to success in the educational system and an advanced society depends upon them.

Fiction: concerning narrative

Early experiences of stories

From as early as 6 months old, infants begin to play with, hold, suck and gaze at books. Picture books are a source of sensory stimulation and emotional satisfaction, illustrations are touched, experienced and talked about while held safely close to their carers. Technical wonders of book production of hinged flaps, holes and pop-up devices intrigue 1-year-old babies and older toddlers, they fascinate, comfort and delight, depending on the circumstance. These early experiences sow the seeds for the deep enjoyment of stories and books through the whole of our reading lives and long before interest can be sustained by the unfolding of an entire story.

Initially, children delight in stories showing them everyday occurrences which connect with their own lives – instances of children playing, getting dressed, being fed and, frequently, being naughty. A little later, fantasy worlds begin and are populated: mice dance like ballerinas, rabbits live under oak trees, fairies, goblins, princesses have adventures. Even what might be considered by adults to be quite frightening books are sought out and requested over and over again, Whitehead says:

> One reason that young children (and older ones too) thrive on terrible tales is usually expressed as the reader or listener being an onlooker or spectator of literary events … non-participation gives us time and freedom to evaluate more sharply our feelings and attitudes about the events and characters represented – even very small children pick out the kind and the naughty, the dishonest and the brave in stories, but our ambiguous real life motives and complex reactions involve heart searchings, self-delusions and frequent misunderstandings. (2004: 134)

The influence of literature on the development of the child

The literary critics of children's books have for many years been aware of the power of stories to affect children's attitudes towards and perceptions of good and evil. That literature can influence individuals very deeply is self-evident from one's own experience. Most of us can remember vividly the effect of a particular novel on our emotions, on the formation of our views and on understandings of life. In my teens I avidly read historical novels, those of D.K. Broster (sadly now out of print!), Margaret Irwin, Rosemary Sutcliffe and Alison Uttley. I can still recall the excitement, fear and passion they evoked as I read far into the night of battles on windswept Scottish moors, the beheading of queens, and the privations of Roman Britain. Not only are the feelings and pleasures evoked by my reading still sharp and clear, but also the circumstance and place where I was when I read the books. I can still feel my arm numb with cold through holding a heavy book for hours outside the bedcovers in an unheated bedroom, the music being played by one of my brothers in the bedroom next door and the unique smell of the library book paper that frequently accompanied the reading – the synaesthesia of a total book experience. I was literally lost in an imaginative world of the events and lives of characters.

The influence of books in spiritual and moral development

This impact of literature on the imagination was generalized further to assume a potentially damaging effect on the moral development of susceptible adolescents. The influence of our reading was taken so seriously in the 1950s and 1960s that at the convent school I attended there was a list of banned novels which it was a contravention of school rules to read. The novels by D.H. Lawrence were predictably high on the list. The reason for the inclusion of some of those listed remains a complete mystery to me half a century later! Needless to say, the act of 'banning' certain books probably did more for their promotion than any of the suggestions I will make later in this chapter!

However, if the pernicious effect of literature remains unclear, the positive influence is less in doubt. The issue for the teacher today is how to select quality books for use in the setting or classroom, and which books have the potential to 'move children on', to promote understanding and spiritual and moral growth as well as to enthral. Tucker (1993) quotes from Walter de la Mare: 'Only the rarest kind of best in anything can be good enough for the young' (1941: 11). As a psychologist Tucker argues that an important developmental task for the child is to be able to escape 'from egocentricity in favour of a world view that can take into account attitudes and knowledge other than one's own' (1993: 118).

'Good' and 'light' books

Books can undoubtedly be instrumental in enabling the individual to take on another's point of view and this is one of the essential criteria that should be applied. It is this feature, Tucker suggests, that separates a 'good' book from a 'light' one. He says good books

> succeed in going beyond mere story telling towards sharing a particularly interesting or relevant individual vision of the world with the reader. By the end of the story, readers may well feel that they have somehow advanced in their own understanding, not just of the book but of some of the rest of life as well. (1993: 118)

Whitehead agrees when she says 'Perhaps small children are eventually stronger for knowing that John Brown comes to accept the Midnight Cat (Wagner, 1977) and older children develop more insight into complex relationships after reading *The Way to Sattin Shore* (Pearce, 1983) and *Flour Babies* (Fine, 1992)' (2004: 134).

While he admits that this definition of 'good' is simplistic, Tucker considers nevertheless, that it is a helpful distinction for the teacher to make. The criterion of a 'good' book is one that addresses serious topics in a readable and enjoyable way. It is not that the book is 'heavy' or overtly didactic or moralizing but that it has layers of meaning beyond the basic storyline. The book in the opposite category, the 'light' book in Tucker's terms, is one that does not attempt to challenge nor to address the uncomfortable and is more likely to offer stereotypes, social prejudices and clear-cut distinctions of good and evil in its safe, predictable, albeit often addictive, stories. While we might wish to improve on the terms Tucker uses, perhaps to 'weighty' (meaning worth while) and 'light', the distinction is helpful to teachers. Both types of books contribute to the diet of readers of all ages but the latter may not have sufficient potential to reward use with children in school, particularly if read aloud and shared with the whole class. Books used in any educational setting need to offer substance, challenge and the potential for critical discussion. To

Tucker's classification of 'good' and 'light' (and the distinction is not absolute) I would add books in the literary canon (these are what we might term the 'classics'). Such literature would represent the ultimate on the continuum of the categorization. These books stand the test of time, they have within them the power to transport, to enchant and to alter an individual for ever. A classic lives on in the memory and fuels the imagination. Pat Hutchins's (1968) *Rosie's Walk* and Alice Holm's (1965) *I am David* are examples of books which have within them enduring qualities and universal truths and which enable readers to make sense of the world and their place within it.

I am David is the story of a young boy of 10 or, perhaps, 11 years of age who has lived all his life in an internment camp somewhere in central Europe. In the prison camp he has been educated by a cultured man, taught to speak several languages and endowed with a philosophy of life that transcends the miserable, brutalizing existence of the camp. David escapes with the help of a prison guard and begins his archetypal journey from the country in which he has been imprisoned, through Italy, to Denmark in search of a woman whose address and photograph he has been given. On the journey he has many encounters and adventures.

This extraordinary book raises the eternal questions that surround human existence, issues of right and wrong, freedom and imprisonment, birth and death, hope and despair, joy and suffering, endurance, faith and, ultimately, loss and gain. This type of literary experience offers opportunity to learn more about the world, a kind of 'felt history'. Also, through engaging with *I am David*, children are able to learn more about themselves and others, and to try to make sense of some of the enduring values in life.

Not all classics or 'good' books, of course, are as ambitious in the issues they tackle, nor are they so profound or painful, and neither is *I am David* a book for an early years group. But other classics provide glimpses of some of these awareness raising topics. *Not now Bernard* by David McKee (1980) operates at several levels. At one level, Bernard desperately and unsuccessfully attempts to attract and hold the attention of his detached, cool parents. This book has great humour despite the polite cruelty of the aloof adults. McKee has several 'big' themes in *Not now Bernard*. As a result of reflection and through discussion, children will become aware of, perhaps, the 'monster' in each one of us that needs to be, at the very least, acknowledged. Perhaps its readers will pick up on the way that families operate, the power that adults have over children and the power that children are able to exert over adults. Either or both of these interpretations (or indeed others) are valid.

The complexity deepens further because whatever the type of book, its content can only impact on an individual in a receptive psychological and intellectual state. So with 'good' books, where there are inherently several possible interpretations different readers will appreciate only a particular meaning of a story depending on the experiences and the present degree of receptiveness they bring to it.

Reader response

When reading a text (and what might constitute a text will be explored later) children bring to it highly individual, preconceived notions of the world as it is shaped for them by their own previous experience. This personal state of mind and being affects fundamentally what meaning is extracted from a book. Expanding on the causes of the variations of reader response, Evans suggests: 'All children have different societal, and cultural backgrounds and all, at the end of the twentieth century are now 'caught' by many hybridised worlds: the world of television, the world of advertising, computers … the ever changing social rules and values required by today's youth culture' (1998: xiii). These pre-dispositions affect the meaning the reader is able to attribute to a text. Evans continues, 'Factors such as race, gender and social class all have a part to play in forming our previous experiences and therefore influencing the way in which we are able to make sense out of texts' (1998: iv).

Conversely, it is those books which have the most potential to influence the individual that present the widest range of possibilities for interpretation. The more multi-faceted, the greater the number of layers of meaning, the more the 'good' book draws on previous experience and understanding of the world, the wider the range of possible understandings there are. As Anthony Browne says 'I deliberately make my books so that they are open to different interpretations, most of which I never hear about (probably just as well). Once a book is finished I have to let it go, like a child. What happens next is out of my control' (1998: 195, cited in Evans, 1998: xvi).

Browne's statement draws on the ideas of Rosenblatt (1938) presented in her seminal work on reader response which goes so far as to say about the relationship between text and reader that no text exists until it is read or 'interpreted' by an individual . The black marks on the page are brought alive by a reader with an idiosyncratic set of ideas, prior knowledge and socio-cultural heritage. Figure 9.1 helps to demonstrate this interrelationship.

As was hinted earlier, young readers can be supported to be more penetrating and perceptive of the layers of insight offered in a text. This does *not* mean a cold dissection of every story shared with a group of 4-year-olds. But the way a practitioner or teacher sensitively exploits the relationship between reader and text in a way that is personally meaningful, the more memorable the experience becomes. Children need to be given, first, the opportunity to merely savour a 'good' book and even a classic, and then, after personal time to think and respond, have aspects brought to their consciousness through discussion.

Types of books

Picture books

The elevation of the picture book into a category of literature of its own has occurred over the last two decades and has been described by Beard (1990) as

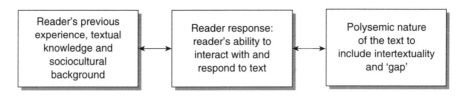

Figure 9.1   *The relationship between the reader and the text (Rosenblatt, 1938, cited in Evans, 1998: xv)*

the 'Third Golden Age' of children's literature. The importance of the picture book as a significant genre in its own right has been recognized by critics, and much has been written on the topic, which is well summarized by Egoff (1981): 'The picture book, which appears to be the cosiest and most gentle of genres, actually produces the greatest social and aesthetic tensions in the field of children's literature' (cited by Evans, 1998: xiii).

The reason for this due recognition of the stature of the picture book is that the picture book is an art form in its own right, bridging the worlds of art and design and literature. Much of the exploration of the issues concerning the interdependence of words and images, these often beautiful, intriguing and hugely complex books, I will have to leave to dedicated volumes such as those of Styles and Watson (1996) and Evans (1998). However, a précis of some fundamental issues is needed to inform my argument about the value of picture books as a key resource in the early years setting and classroom.

The picture book as a polysemic text

In a postmodern world, the conditions of rapid change namely flux, fluidity, uncertainty and simultaneity must be recognized as the norm. Young children need to develop a range of skills and capacities through which they gain access to contemporary culture and are able to make informed choices and imaginative connections. Advances in medicine, technology and communication systems have huge impacts on how individuals and societies think and act. Above all, this current state of affairs challenges twentieth-century models of education, the purpose of schools, the nature of learning and the role of the teacher. Those of us born midway through the twentieth century have to make imaginative leaps and initiate mindshifts in order to empathize with the day-to-day experiences of young children and help us to speculate on their future needs. These pre-schoolers, in the words of the poet, Kahil Gibran, 'dwell in the house of tomorrow'.

These changes and challenges have altered, and will go on altering, the way in which texts are defined, viewed and made sense of. Increasingly, ideas about the nature of texts include the visual, dance, drama, music, media, and information and communications technology, in addition to more traditional written texts. A sign system (semiotic) perspective broadens 'a text' to cover any 'chunk of meaning' (Short, 1986) which, perhaps surprisingly, includes mathematics, movement and mime. A recent cartoon exemplified this bewildering feature of life today with a picture of a teacher giving a puzzled child a book with the exhortation 'Go on! take it. You will enjoy it – it's a bit like a CD-ROM!'

Inevitably this broadening of the categories of what constitutes a text, widens also the meaning of what it is to 'read'. Kress and van Leeuwen (1996) and Kress (1997) explore the inclusive term of visual literacies to embrace the notion of the 'reading' of illustrations, diagrams, computer logos and graphics and maps as well as paintings and sculptures, and other outcomes of fine art practice. This broader definition of reading is touched upon in Chapter 3. Picture books demand such 'reading' as they are far more complex than a book with pictures depicting a story. The design and size of the book, the setting of the print, its format, the visual images on the pages, and the interdependence of the illustration with the written text are all integral to the whole. They make up the key way that the story is told. The 'reading' of these 'signs' is crucial to the meaning-making of the 'text' as a whole.

The children's author Anthony Browne states:

> Making a picture book, for me, is not like writing a story then painting some pictures ... No, it is more like planning a film, where each page is a scene that includes both words and images inextricably linked. What excites me ... is working out the rhythm of the story and seeing how much is told by the pictures, how much by the words, and how much by the gap between the two. (Cited in Evans, 1998: 198)

The elegant simplicity of many of the examples of good picture books belies the complexity behind their conception and the thoughtful interpretations made possible by a well-informed adult with small groups of children, if the book's richness and depth is to be realized.

The concept of the narrative picture book is the telling of a story, often layering it with deeper meaning through the technique of **intertextuality**. Intertextuality capitalizes on reference to traditional tales and other well-known stories with which it is assumed the child is familiar and able to draw on. The prime examples of the use of intertext are the 'Jolly Postman' books by Allan and Janet Ahlberg (1988 and 1995). These enchanting and supremely skilful books intrigue and amuse children of all ages from nursery to the end of primary school, and are capable of being appreciated at different levels. They are, however, rendered completely incomprehensible to children for whom English is an additional language or who are newly arrived in the United

Kingdom and for whom English traditional tales and nursery rhymes are not part of their cultural heritage.

Key Term

Intertextuality: implicit references within text to other texts, without recognition of which the reader will not gain as much meaning as she might otherwise. For example, when Claudius, in *Hamlet*, says, 'O my offence is rank, it smells to heaven', the reader who does not recognize the reference to the Bible story of Cain and Abel will miss much of the potential significance. Or at another level, the child who is not familiar with the traditional fairy tales will find Catherine Storr's *Clever Polly and the Stupid Wolf* or Roald Dahl's *Revolting Rhymes* less entertaining than the children who have the ability to make connections between the two versions as they read.

Polysemic: a term belonging to deconstructive critical discourse, and that can only be defined outside that discourse in a very general way. It means having multiple levels of meaning, in ways that do not allow any final, fixed meaning to be pinned down. In a poem such as Blake's 'The Sick Rose', is it about horticulture, or love or jealousy or ...?

Other examples of intertextuality are the books, with longer text, of Robert Munsch and Babette Cole who overturn the telling of fairy tales with a tongue-in-cheek look at the sexist image they frequently portray. *The Paper Bag Princess*, *Prince Cinders* and *Princess SmartyPants* respectively, all gently parody the much loved tales, and in so doing raise awareness of gender and equality issues for a young audience. Justifiably, picture books are described as complex, with as great an aesthetic appeal as intellectual by reason of their **polysemic** nature and openness to multiple interpretation.

Books without words and longer texts

Wordless books present the emerging reader with opportunities and challenges. A book with no printed text has a universal popularity as, clearly, it can be used with all early years and KS 1 pupils and at all stages of learning English as an additional language. Visual images have the immense advantage that they convey meaning in a way that needs no linguistic interpretation. These books are designed by using multiple and very detailed pictures each depicting a time frame of a single action in the unfolding of the sequence of the story. The size of the frames controls the space, pace and the dramatic intensity of the action. Raymond Briggs immediately comes to mind, as perhaps, the most renowned illustrator/author of this type of picture book. Many thousands of young pupils have developed their story telling skills, and reinforced left-to-right directional sense and, in addition, simply delighted in 'reading' the myriad of sensitive drawings in his classic *The Snowman* (1978) and the *Father Christmas* books, although the latter are a hybrid between wordless books and comic/cartoon series as they contain the occasional thought or speech bubble.

This type of book, it has been argued, is pleasurable only for those children with an already well-developed narrative ability, as many are left feeling inse-cure and longing for words to complete the visual story-telling (Graham, 1998). It would appear that the transformation from visual to verbal is more difficult than is often assumed for many pupils. It would appear also that wordless books present a too painstaking challenge and are, perhaps, rather unappealing to make, as many talented picture book author/illustrators have no titles of wordless books against their names.

Books with greater complexities and length of written text also have their place in the early years classroom, and certainly, by Year 2. They will need to be read to a group in serial style or probably will require adult support in a shared reading situation.

Picture books – an access to print

The intricately crafted picture book is a powerful tool for learning. It provides children with the opportunity to become aware of visual, tactile and spatial qualities that are fundamental to understanding in art and design. In other words, children in nursery, reception and Years 1 and 2 classes are enticed into higher levels of visual literacy. This genre of children's literature, also, through the appealing format and supportive illustrations helps novice read-ers make sense of text and print. Through repeated and delightful encounters with picture books, both alongside an experienced reader and independently, children in the emergent stage of literacy development are enabled to progress to the beginning of conventional reading (see Chapters 3 and 4).

The different ways picture books support early reading

Before children are ready to read print, picture books are a prime source for developing awareness of the nature and purpose of reading in both the broader and more traditional senses. The visual images not only give the books an attraction, accessibility and interest for those at the very earliest stages of literacy acquisition but also they provide a cueing system for those in the transitional stage as children are motivated and supported to move towards beginning conventional reading (see Chapter 5). Children for whom English is an additional language are assisted by the visual element which is integral to the text and as such enables access to the content. In a project, using an ethnographic research methodology, Parkes (1998) studied very young pre-schoolers working with picture books. The study sheds further light on the processes involved before accurate decoding can occur and conventional reading take place (again see Chapter 5). Parkes found that each time the text was read and reread the child interacted with the text in different and increasingly sophisticated ways. She says:

> As children became more familiar with the books and as their experiential and linguistic facility increased, so too did their interactions. They noticed similarities within and across books; made text to life and life to text connections; and borrowed some of the language of books to use for their own purposes. In short, the books became a lived-in and lived-through experience. A further finding was recognition of the active role children assumed as meaning makers. (Parkes, 1998: 45)

Wells (1987) also noted that children of this age who had an opportunity to become immersed in children's literature played more imaginatively and for longer periods of time, thus mirroring the anecdotal experience cited earlier of novels fuelling the understanding and imagination of the older reader.

The last sentence of the Parkes quotation echoes an assertion often repeated in earlier chapters in this volume about the impressive capacity of the child to make meaning. With a picture book the emergent reader, after hearing the text from an experienced literacy user, is able to 'read' the signs (that is, illustrations, format, placing of the print) on the page to reconstruct for herself a narrative that is personally significant and that makes sense. The intricate detail of the illustrations are 'read' and interpreted to construct the child's story. Layered texts such as John Burningham's (1977) *Come away from the Water, Shirley!*, with its double-page spread of illustrations depicting Shirley's imaginative fantasies alongside the everyday stuff of living, are recorgnized for what they are, and are woven into the child's retelling and often offer remarkable insights. As they revisit a favourite text, children make multiple interpretations through continuing to appreciate further features, one detail assuming prominence at one time and then another acquiring quite different emphasis at a further telling. About this finding Parkes writes:

> The text and illustration form an open potential, part of a semiotic data pool, through which the child constantly generates new hypotheses and discovers new meanings. As young children return to previously read books in collaborative and independent reading situations they are able to draw on and make use of the sign systems which are meaningful to them. (1998: 50)

This experience provides the emergent reader with the precursor to the later development of the top-down processing needed for the decoding of print (see the Introduction and Chapters 5 and 6). A skilled adult sharing a picture book with a small group of children, or using the enlarged text version with a larger group of young pupils, helps to develop and then reinforce the prerequisite understandings of concepts about print (see Chapters 3 and 4).

Later in the reception and Year 1 classes, picture books will be used to form the basis of systematic direct teaching of print and sound awareness, and perhaps also wider cross-curricular or topic work will emanate from the engagement of the class with an often requested shared story (see Chapter 6) capitalized upon with several learning purposes in mind.

Early years educators will be aware that in order for their pupils to become avid, competent readers, they themselves, have to be enthusiastic and informed about children's literature. Books for the whole school and those for each class have to be selected carefully according to the rigorous application of appropriate criteria.

The choice of books for the school

The considerations to be addressed when compiling book collections are:

- to maintain a balanced, attractive range of freshly changing high-quality children's literature
- to meet the learning needs, abilities and interests of the pupils
- to ensure that all the books are appealing and in good condition
- to have any portrayal of a culture, race or gender represented fairly and without bias
- to aim to purchase stock regularly so that the library and classroom collections remain fresh, up-to-date, topical and tempting.

Book areas will reflect these considerations, they will also be well thought out, comfortable and meticulously cared for. The maintainance of a book area needs to be one of the priorities in all early years settings and classrooms, and should be seen as an essential component of the learning environment. Books will be frequently changed in order to reflect current interests or a theme and to encourage the spending of time in the area to browse. It is the book area that sends one of the most potent messages regarding the extent to which books are valued by those adults who work in the setting or classroom. Elley (1992) relates the size and quality of the class library to the level of children's reading achievement.

Encounters with books in nursery and school should be carefully planned and designed to entrance the children, to motivate them to read the book and to deepen their understanding of the story and, through associations or more widely, perhaps, an aspect of life itself.

Reading stories to children

Storytime is the prime example of just such an experience. Through reading stories the adult has a unique and regularly frequent opportunity to promote enthusiasm for books and demonstrate his/her own appreciation for literature. In consequence, storytime requires careful thought and planning. The timing needs to be considered. Usually stories are read at the end of sessions but variations can be useful to generate interest, so to start a session with a story or to revisit the previous day's book can be refreshing and reaffirming.

Introducing the book

The value of preparing the ground before reading the book is now well known (Clay, 1991) and the benefit of the teacher preparing the pupils with a rich introduction is acknowledged. This 'tuning in' will include looking at and discussing the cover, title and introducing the author; exploring what the children anticipate the content might be about, the 'big' ideas and the characters and setting. Further time can be spent appreciating and 'reading' the illustrations, considering the illustrator's style and approach to the construction of the format, if the book in question is a picture book. Teachers will make links with books previously enjoyed, and explain words in the text that might not be understood. Adults working with very young pupils will appreciate the importance of everyone being still, quiet and listening attentively before the story begins. Are the children settled comfortably, have they sufficient space and are they able to see the illustrations?

These behaviours have their benefits across other learning opportunities. A central aspect of an arts experience is the need to attend to experience for its own sake and sustain and intensify such attention over a period of time.

The reading of the story

The reading of a story requires thought and practice. Commercial story tapes, CDs and CD-ROMs are excellent models for the inexperienced to become aware of the effect of intonation, pace and dramatic pauses. With rehearsal the use of different voices, facial expressions and gesture can all contribute to enhancing the experience to make it truly spell binding. As Whitehead says:

> [T]he voice of the reader mediates and revitalizes the written text for the child listener. All the subtlety and variety of a familiar voice is brought to the task of re-creating meanings and intentions of the author behind the text. Story and poetry readings are informal demonstrations of the functions of vocal tone, pitch, rhythm, facial expressions, gestures and body language in human communication. And the good reader, like the good teller, must employ all these skills to bring language off the page. (2004: 136)

Discussion of the story

The follow-up discussion and questioning is an important aspect of storytime and as such needs to be carefully planned. Here I am addressing the wider issues connected with the book as a holding form for literature, rather than as a physical resource to support a lesson to teach an aspect of reading development; this is addressed in Chapter 6. Whenever the story is shared sufficient time should be allowed for discussion, allowing the story to 'rinse through' the listeners, and to savour the illustrations and certain aspects of the narrative. The receptive state of the learner is an active ingredient in the learning process.

Ways the book can be enjoyed after the story reading

After storytime the book should be made available to be looked at or reread in the book area, if the story reading has been audio-taped that, too, can be accessible to enhance the later revisiting of the book. Occasionally stories can be followed up with the children writing and illustrating their own alternative versions of the story (or part of it, perhaps, exploring a different ending) in specially preprepared blank books of different sizes.

All encounters with children's literature should aim to encourage the pupil's response to the text through expression of thoughts, ideas and feelings about the story, to develop a critical awareness that deepens understanding and enjoyment of books. The ethos of the setting or classroom should allow also personal expression of disappointment or dislike of a story. And, finally, pupils will be inspired by teachers who are enthusiastic and knowledgeable about books; this will encourage children to become authors themselves, to compile anthologies and book reviews of their favourite poems and stories.

Non-fiction books: reading to learn

The term 'non-fiction', as it is used here, to describe all books that are not story books, is an over simplification in the extreme. Several authors have argued that the terms 'information' or 'reference' books are unsatisfactory also, based, as they are, on a definition of content. None of these terms does justice to the complexity of the range of meanings and linguistic forms of this important category of books (Littlefair, 1993). However, for the purpose of convenience in this section of this chapter regarding the use of information texts in the early years classroom, I shall adopt the generic term 'non-fiction' to accommodate the books under discussion.

Rationale for the use of non-fiction texts

This chapter now addresses the crucial contribution that expository texts make to children's language and cognitive development, and how important it is that all practitioners recognize the need to deepen and enhance children's responses to non-fiction texts. 'Even very young children will grow into informational sorts of reading, using active problem-solving and interaction with their educators. Through these experiences and processes, they will come to realise that reading for information is just as exciting as reading stories' (Arnold, 1996: 206-7).

There are many crucial reasons for including expository texts in the provision for early years settings and classrooms. First, there is a developing body of research evidence to support the view that familiarity with non-fiction texts has a valuable role in developing pupils' concepts and relevant accompanying language and vocabulary. They have the potential to deepen children's understanding of the world (for example, Pappas and Brown, 1987). Recent work by Nicholls (2004) has shown that when reception children were given experience of sharing both fiction and non-fiction books (along with the accompanying conversation) in a one-to-one situation with an adult, for 20 minutes twice a week for periods of six weeks' duration, their spoken language developed. Those children who were given an opportunity to work with expository texts made significantly more progress than those working with narrative texts. The nature of the learning that occurred through the interaction with the text was discussed in Chapter 7 and has important implications for early years teachers.

Secondly, learning to read and write necessitates appreciating the functional variation (or registers) of written language. Sole exposure to the characteristic features of the discourse of narrative will fail to offer children the opportunities to become aware of the different features and structures of written language across non-fiction genres.

As Pappas says, 'a story book, as a type of verbal art, means for different reasons and in different ways from the ways an information book means. These differences of meanings (of storybooks and information books) are expressed by different written registers, by different textual properties and by different "book language"' (1991: 204). Riley and Reedy argue that by exposing children to a variety of written texts 'the child is learning how to reason, to argue and to justify; in these ways her thinking becomes more advanced and qualitatively different' (2000: 6).

Thirdly, school and university learning is largely dependent upon the development of appropriate study skills and the ability to use reference books and other sources of written information. We have discussed earlier in this chapter that Donaldson believes non-fiction books have an important role in encouraging abstract thought, that is, thinking in an impersonal and disembedded way.

Fourthly, the bulk of adult experience of interacting with text is through non-fiction material. Many adults rarely read novels but will rely heavily on information books and the Internet in order to function at work and at home.

Fifthly, the reason for including expository texts centres around reading and the motivation to do so. There is disturbing evidence that indicates that boys lag behind girls in English (particularly reading and writing) from as early as the end of Key Stage 1 and all through Key Stages 2 and 3 until the level of Key Stage 4. The School Curriculum and Assessment Authority (SCAA, 1995) suggested that perhaps with greater emphasis and more informed support in the primary school boys could be motivated, stimulated and challenged into wider reading; this will (to obvious benefit) include greater use of non-fiction books. We cannot afford to be complacent about this issue in the early years of education also.

It is self-evident that teachers need to be equally knowledgeable and actively enthusiastic about the promotion and use of lively, attractive non-fiction texts as they are about narrative texts, so that all children are able to learn to read successfully and effectively in order to obtain information. Learning to read and reading to learn are both key responsibilities of the early years setting and the primary school.

What evidence is there that there is a problem?

That primary-aged children are unable to use non-fiction texts appropriately is not a new concern. In 1991 Her Majesty's Inspectorate (HMI) reported that it would seem that teachers are much more secure in their understanding of how to develop children's reading and writing in fiction than they are of how to use non-fiction. The National Literacy Strategy (DfEE, 1998) redressed the balance considerably. However, the difficulty that children demonstrate with their comprehension of, and inability to use, non-fiction texts appropriately is demonstrated through their writing. The Exeter Study (EXEL) focused on this area of pupils' literacy and Wray and Lewis (1997) identify the all too common 'copying out' phenomenon as one very obvious indication of diffi-culty. This is despite exhortation from the Schools' Examination and Assessment Council Report (SEAC, 1991: 19) which states that 'Pupils should be given opportunities to "reshape" information, into a form different from its source and always for a communicative purpose'. This clearly presents young children with a challenge. In order to achieve the task of 'reshaping' information, pupils have to enter, as discussed earlier, the realm of familiarity with Donaldson's (1989) 'language of systematic thought'.

How can pupils be best supported?

Research evidence from Australia (Littlefair, 1991) has suggested that only greater attention to the children's awareness of genre in both their reading and writing will enable teachers to help their pupils to cope with the literacy demands of school and beyond.

Comprehension goes beyond decoding the words. In order to access the content, children have to be aware of the way that different types of mean-ing are commonly expressed in our culture. The most common expression of meaning that children meet in school and at home is narrative. Even before learning to read children listen to narrative in conversations, in stories that are read to them and the drama they watch on television. Children become familiar with the structure of a story, the setting, the introduction of the char-acters, the unfolding action, possibly a crisis and then a resolution, which is, most commonly, a happy ending! The language used, with which they are most familiar, is specific to the narrative genre.

When young readers meet non-fiction texts they come across quite different forms of meaning-making, this is reflected in the different structures and form of this genre. Halliday (1978) suggests that children need to understand the varieties of language that are used for different purposes and different audiences. Writers select the appropriate 'genre' for their purpose when writing, and previous experience of reading different types of texts informs the ability to write using a variety of genre. Littlefair suggests that 'We know through experience how to organise a letter to a bank manager, a shopping list or an explanation of how to cook a special dish. As soon as we have a purpose for communication we usually know how to organise it' (1993: 128). This tacit knowledge of the relationship between the purpose and its appropriate form needs support in order to be developed and extended into more complex writing. In this way, genre and purpose are interdependent and the types of texts fulfil a variety of purposes.

The types of non-fiction text

Narrative non-fiction

These 'interest' books and information books are organized chronologically within a time sequence. Examples of this type of book are *My Friend Whale* (James, 1992) which handles facts about whales in an accessible way that mirrors the narrative genre. This type of non-fiction book lends itself particularly to the early years classroom. The advantage of this is that this type of non-fiction book can be more easily read aloud or used in group reading sessions (see Chapter 6). The language adopted is usually more accessible and rhythmic than non-narrative, non-fiction books. The disadvantage of these books is that they cannot, very conveniently, be used to research and to retrieve facts, although this can be achieved with thorough indexing.

Key Term

Index: a list of names and subjects in a book which indicates where in the text these terms can be found.

Other examples of non-fiction information stories are diaries and biographies which are less likely to be used with the very youngest pupils except, perhaps, for the quality and aesthetic appeal of the illustrations. For example *The Country Diary of an Edwardian Lady* (Holden, 1977) might be made available as part of a science display of plants, flowers and leaves after a class walk in the countryside or park.

The type of writing that is organized procedurally are notices and books of instructions such as guidebooks, sets of instructions, manuals, stage directions and forms. The most common form of procedural writing that young pupils encounter in nursery and reception are recipes used in cookery sessions and, perhaps, the rules and instructions for games. At home, of course, it is a different matter as this is where the most common form of non-fiction text is to be found. Children will observe adults reading instructions before taking medication or using a new piece of sports equipment, gadgets in the kitchen or garden, or seeking help from a manual when experiencing trouble with a car, video player, mobile phone or computer.

Non-fiction non-narrative

This category of non-fiction book covers the vast majority of what are termed 'reference books' and covers all the following:

- plans, maps, diagrams and computer printouts
- dictionaries, word books, computer data, road signs and logos
- lists of contents, indexes, library classification and library catalogues
- thesauruses, encyclopaedias, subject reference books and databases.

Alphabet books are an enchanting and intriguing type of non-fiction book used extensively in the early years in this category, containing bright, colourful pages with appealing illustrations which incorporate the letters of the alphabet within a theme. Sometimes storybook characters introduce each letter and illustrators show originality, creating visual jokes, puzzles and encouraging interactive engagement with the text through 'pop-up' technology. The many sizes, shapes, designs and themes of these books can make for a bewildering array for the beginning teacher. Mallet suggests some principles which can help in the choice of alphabet books for use in the early years classroom, the most successful books have:

- an organising idea or theme to give coherence; for example, by taking a topic like animals, railways or by using a storybook character
- an imaginative choice of headwords so that some unusual ones like 'iguana', 'octopus', 'quill', 'yolk', and 'zip' are included
- an 'alive' feel so that there is a sense of life and movement and invitations to interact with the text
- originality in format and style to catch young imaginations
- clear letters in both upper and lower case to make for easy demonstration and familiarisation
- a lively written text which is simple without being banal, whether it rhymes or not
- distinctive illustrations to intrigue, challenge or amuse. (2003: 33)

Examples of books for 3-year-olds and above which fulfil the above criteria are *Animalia* by Graeme Base (1993), *John Burningham's ABC* by John Burningham (1999), *Alphie's Alphabet* by Shirley Hughes (1998), *Kipper's A–Z* by Mick Inkpen (2002) and *What's Inside? The Alphabet Book* by Satoshi Kitamura

(2000). Given what is now known about the importance of recognition of the names and sounds of letters of the alphabet (see Chapters 3 and 4), the time and effort spent on selecting collections of quality alphabet books to have permanently available for browsing, will be rewarded. Acquiring this key skill in such a pleasurable way has to be to the benefit of both teacher and children.

Information books comprise the following categories

Expositionary texts describe, explain and, on occasions, present arguments, frequently contain considerable amounts of text and the style of the written language often places great demands on young readers. The books in this category of text are:

- interest and information books – non-chronological
- newspapers, magazines and advertisements.

The difficulties that information books present to primary children

Many young readers, although able to read narrative comfortably, will probably require further support in order to read and comprehend non-narrative texts. This issue is of great relevance to the teachers of pupils in Years 1 and 2. The literary means by which authors express their intentions is highly sophisticated, and that is before the subject matter and its comprehensibility is considered. As Donaldson says of children:

> they need now to enlarge their understanding of the many ways in which words can be handled with skill on the printed page – handled to achieve economy, or elegance, or emphasis or surprise, or cohesion between sentences, or logical clarity in a sustained argument, to name only a few of the aims that concern an author. (1989: 29)

The key to understanding the challenges these texts present is a knowledge of register and genre which provide the linguistic tools with which to evaluate books for primary children. Writers, it has been suggested, choose a genre appropriate for the purpose in hand. The genre form relates to the cultural form of expressing meaning, and can be considered the framework for a written or spoken communication. Writers express the details of the communication in a register of language which is inevitably constrained by the immediate situation and its conventions.

Features of registers in expositionary texts

The language of this important non-narrative genre is complex and presents the greatest challenge to young readers. It is the language of exploration, description, of persuasion and argument. In explanations and descriptions the texts are arranged quite differently from narrative. They may be based on a series of facts that offer an explanation, they are non-chronological and the reader is not borne along by the dynamics of a story. There might be a notion of problem and solution, comparison and contrast, of cause and effect.

Learning and Teaching Suggestions

By 1600, however, low-lying land like this in the Netherlands has been drained to grow crops ... They dug huge drainage channels and built windmills to pump water from the land into these channels taking it to the sea. The newly-reclaimed land was used to graze livestock and later ploughed to grow crops. (Sauvain, 1995: 21)

What could you do as the teacher to enable children to make sense of this as they read it?

The grammar used by writers of expository text is complex. The devices used to link parts of the text may be difficult to follow, the use of the passive voice adds to this opacity. Longer sentences, with complex introductions are frequently seen in these books, making great demands on the reader's short-term memory.

The incomprehensibility is the result of both the nature of the content and the language used to describe it. There are often a larger number of content words, which may be technical words in subject-specific texts. The density of the meaning is the result also of the ideas and concepts being discussed.

Learning and Teaching Suggestions

Unlike deciduous trees, conifers do not shed their needles annually. Their needles last two to three years. When they fall from the tree they take a long time to decompose, and the humus they produce is quite acidic. (Felts, 1996)

Which technical terms would you discuss with children before using the book in class and how would you tackle the task?

This accessible and attractive 'pop-up' book (*Trees*, by Felts, 1996), produced with the younger reader in mind, requires the adult to work and explain terminology to the child.

Implications for practice

Role of the adult

Publishers are becoming more sensitive to the difficulties experienced by primary-aged children reading non-fiction texts and much has been achieved in the last few years, particularly following the introduction of the National Literacy Strategy, to improve the readability of information books generally. The teacher can be a powerful support enabling young readers to engage with non-fiction literature.

'Reading to learn what is known must include the habit of freshly wondering; knowledge must be re-constructed by the learner' (Meek, 1991: 170). Children can be encouraged to 'freshly wonder'. This active process of creating meaning from text needs to be understood by teacher and child. Through spoken language the adult is able to demonstrate to the pupil the cognitive strategies that have to occur in order to make sense of the text. In discussion, the links between what is known and what the text is conveying can be achieved. Once again this refers to what Donaldson describes as 'embedding the thinking', the difficulty arises from the fact that the majority of the thinking required by non-narrative texts is 'disembedded' and is not centred in an immediate or personal context; the phenomena addressed are not in the child's first-hand experience.

The adult is able to help the children first by organizing the prior experience probing, for example, by asking 'What do we already know about lighthouses?' New learning is made real and meaningful through an activity or a visit, in other words, the learning is made concrete by the first-hand experience and this is often capitalized upon by primary teachers, before they turn to the secondary sources of books. The teaching sequence is then followed up or enriched with an appropriate story or poem in order to deepen learning.

Helping children to use information texts

Browne (1998) is very clear that children need to be encouraged to read non-narrative books early and with a clear idea of their function. She suggests that children in the nursery and reception class need to understand that books are a resource for learning and are valuable when wanting to pursue an interest, explore an idea or discover the answer to a question, and an information book may be able to help them.

She continues that the best way to do this is by the adult modelling reading a list of contents, looking and reading quickly through, pointing out text guides such as sideheadings, using the index, and giving an overview of the information presented. Adults demonstrate in this way that one book can be rejected in favour of another and that selective reading is valuable use of time. 'Children become critical readers as they begin to realise that some books do a better job than others' (McKenzie and Warlow, 1977: 48).

Neate (1992) suggests that KS 1 children need to be shown how to find a book they require for a particular purpose by:

- using the cover
- title
- list of contents

- index
- headings and sub-headings
- scanning the book to locate the appropriate section
- skimming through the pages which contain the relevant information.

Supporting the search for and use of information

Indeed, the teacher, previously, will have employed his/her critical faculties to assess the suitability of the non-fiction book through the evaluation of the quality of these features and their potential to help the child into the meaning of the text.

Wray (Wray and Lewis, 1997) suggests from his classroom-based research Exeter Extended Learning (EXEL) project, which attempted to scaffold children in their use of non-narrative texts, that pupils' ability to use non-fiction books appropriately and effectively in order to extend their own learning could be powerfully developed. Wray explains this scaffolding strategy as the use of KWL (Know/Want/Learn) grids.

Know/Want/Learn grids

WHAT DO I KNOW? (now)
WHAT DO I WANT TO FIND OUT? (from the text)
WHAT DID I LEARN? (from reading and working with the text)

This strategy is paralleled by the EXEL team's suggestion for the use of complementary writing frames which aim to provide support in structuring a piece of non-narrative text.

Writing frame

ALTHOUGH I ALREADY KNEW THAT ...
I HAVE LEARNT SOME NEW FACTS. I HAVE LEARNT THAT ...
I ALSO LEARNT THAT ...
ANOTHER FACT THAT I LEARNT ...
HOWEVER THE MOST INTERESTING THING I LEARNT WAS ...

Beard (2000) proposes not such a formulaic approach, but does suggest that comprehension skills need to be systematically taught along with effective modes of information retrieval. The approaches are aimed more at the later years of primary education, but Key Stage 1 teachers might use the approach with very able readers in Year 2. Beard suggests that children have to be taught the way that texts work and how to skim read in order to locate the key sentence of a paragraph in order to access the meaning. The development of argument also can be both followed and used as a model for pupils' own writing.

The criteria for choice of books across the curriculum (adapted from Mallett, 1992)

There will be overlap, obviously, between the criteria for the choice of narrative and non-narrative books:

- attractive format, print and layout
- illustrations that integrate well with text
- clear, lively writing
- new words introduced gradually
- words likely to be unfamiliar embedded in context
- efficient, easy to use retrieval devices, namely, glossary, contents page and index
- books with a chronological sequence, for example, life-cycle or life stories especially for younger readers
- clear topic presentation at beginning of book
- good overall organization (global structure)
- good linkage at sentence level (local cohesion)
- freedom from stereotyping, misrepresenting either gender or ethnic minorities
- factually reliable given current state of knowledge
- not presenting as neutral, information and issues which can be seen from different viewpoints
- books that are lively, thought provoking and that encourage voluntary reading.

Ways of getting children hooked on books

Learning and Teaching Suggestions

Encouraging children to read is an essential part of the teaching of reading. In order that they can promote books, teachers need the knowledge, energy, time, thought and the resources, and they need all these in abundance. Teachers, also have the delightful task of staying abreast of the latest publications so that they can purchase and advise children on their developing reading preferences. The learning and progress of the pupil's reading development literally depends upon it.

- Ensure a variety of fiction and non-fiction books in the library and classroom including poetry, joke books, teacher- and child-made books and recipe books.
- Display books in an interesting, attractive, clearly organized and accessible way.
- Have only books that are in good condition.
- Regularly change books.
- Maintain comfortable, attractive, inviting reading areas in every classroom.
- Have a good supply of taped stories, commercially and school produced, plus spare blank tapes for recording storytimes and child-taped stories.

- Books need to span a wide range of interest and reading level.
- Invite adults, visitors and older pupils to share books as frequently as possible with the children.
- Encourage the sharing of both adults' and pupils' reflections and opinions about books.
- Make class books whenever a topic or other work makes it appropriate.
- Guide choice by offering suggestions of books that will match children's interests.
- Have a home–school reading policy which includes, as well as commercial reading schemes, good quality books of literature.
- Organize an annual book week.
- Set up a school book club.
- Hold a second-hand book sale once a year – sell only books that are in good condition, advertise well and start collecting early.
- Reinforce the pleasure of using the school library by holding storytimes in it.
- Take children to the public library.
- Introduce new books at circle time or assembly.
- Make displays of new books.
- In Year 2 begin a book and then encourage children to complete the reading.
- Offer inspection copies of books for children to evaluate.
- Make displays of each chapter of the class book as it is read.
- Organize additional story-telling and story-reading sessions for specific groups of children such as bilingual learners, advanced or slower readers.
- Be alert to a book programme on television or radio and, perhaps, match a book to its focus.
- Have a 'Book of the week' display. After reading it children can add to the display with a review, with a picture or their response.
- Play games based on books, for example, 'I am thinking about a book that has a very naughty baby in it. The baby makes a huge mess and shakes talcum powder all over the bathroom – does anyone know which book I am thinking about?'
- Use extracts of books on the computer.
- Capitalize on computer programs that are based on books.
- Begin and maintain a chart of 'Books we have enjoyed'.
- Have a puppet theatre available for children to dramatize stories and recollect the language of books.
- Have a collection of story boxes to support the retelling of favourite books.
- Seek the advice of the children before purchasing books – 'Which is the best book you have read?'
- Put the children's book reviews inside the back covers of books to encourage others to read, respond and, maybe, disagree.
- Explicitly enjoy books yourself in the way that you talk about books and reading.

Summary

This chapter has focused on the huge potential of books in the classroom as a motivation for reading, a learning resource and a delight. Books can be used to promote both a love of reading and to teach reading. Non-fiction texts are potentially a source of interest and information, but there is evidence that they can be poorly used in primary schools. The reading skills that children require to capitalize on the opportunities these texts offer, have to be supported by the well-informed and enthusiastic teacher.

Further reading

Mallett, M. (1992) *Making Facts Matter: Reading Non-Fiction 5–11*. London: Paul Chapman Publishing.

Mallett, M. (2003) *Early Years Non-Fiction: A Guide to Helping Young Researchers Use Information Texts*. London and New York: RoutledgeFalmer.

Tucker, N. (1981) *The Child and the Book*. Cambridge: Cambridge University Press.

Wray, D. and Lewis, M. (1997) *Extending Literacy: Children Reading and Writing Non-fiction*. London and New York: Routledge.

Chapter **10**

Supporting Children for whom English is an Additional Language

If the language environment is natural, consistent and stimulating, children will pick up whatever languages are around.

(Crystal, 1986: 221)

Bilingual learners need both the curriculum that motivates and has relevance for them *and* the systematic language development and feedback that enables them to achieve within it.

(Gravelle, 1996: 8)

Introduction

This chapter has as its starting point the belief that all settings and classrooms are enriched by children for whom English is an additional language (EAL). As early years practitioners and teachers plan the implementation of a language and literacy programme for the mother-tongue English-speaking children they will, in many geographical areas, need to consider the significant number of children for whom English is an additional language. Given the close links between oracy and literacy, it will be essential to discuss in this chapter the ways that learning to use language effectively can be supported in the classroom, in order to address, in a comprehensive way the teaching of reading and writing to young EAL pupils in order to maximize their success. Practitioners and teachers also, need to be aware of the wider context and educational policies within which schools operate. This chapter is aimed, mainly, at enabling teachers to support those children who are still in the early stages of spoken English development.

> ## Key Terms
>
> **Mother tongue**: the term used to describe the first language of an individual, literally the language learned from one's mother
>
> **Bilingual and multilingual**: these terms literally mean 'with two languages' (or having regular access to two languages) and 'with many languages' respectively. While the terms usually infer that the individual has a considerable level of competence in the languages, the term 'emerging bilingual' is used for those in the early stages of learning English.

Bilingualism

The faces of bilingualism are many. Bialystock (2001: 2) suggests that it is rare for any monolingual adult to be 'uncontaminated' by even small fragments of another language, but on a continuum between such a minimal level of awareness to fluency in two or more languages the gap is huge. So, at what level of linguistic competence in two languages do we describe an individual as **bilingual**? Also many people have a grasp of 'school' French, Spanish or Italian which is dragged out and used on holidays abroad but fails to qualify a person as being termed a bilingual. Others live in homes where the language, spoken and read, is different from that of the local community, and so, most probably, is their ethnic, cultural and national background. In these situations the child is reared to speak (and perhaps read) the home language as well as the language of the dominant culture, possibly augmented by 'Saturday' or 'Sunday' classes. In some communities, bilingualism is simply expected. In these cases the child is placed in a situation of learning a first language at home and the additional language at school, and can operate competently orally and bi-literately in both.

Children who learn the languages in these ways acquire a different relationship with each, they 'interact in different types of social situations with each, encounter different opportunities for formal study, and may also develop different kinds of attitudes to each language. For these reasons, the various configurations that lead to bilingualism leave children with different levels of competence in each of the languages' (Bialystok, 2001: 3). The language may be used for different purposes, the effect is long lasting, and most bilingual adults will count and pray in the language in which they first learned these behaviours.

The context in Britain

In an age when travel is commonplace and communication systems ever more rapid, society has become correspondingly and increasingly more mobile as people seek employment, often in more flourishing economies. Also some populations of persecuted groups flee from conflict in their countries of origin. The situation at the beginning of the twenty-first century in Britain, as in the rest of Europe, is that a substantial minority of the population is bilingual and **multilingual**. Although the figure nationally is around 7.9 per cent, in some areas of the country, London and Bradford for instance, it is a great deal higher. There are schools in Britain in which 90 per cent of the pupils have English as an additional language.

Many multilingual and bilingual citizens in Britain speak English as an additional language, at varying levels of proficiency, and some may be bi-literate. This linguistic and cultural diversity is reflected in our early years settings and primary schools and accurately and well describes that there are many young pupils who 'move between languages' (Gravelle, 1996: 27).

This situation of a nation with a population that is bilingual and multilingual is certainly not unique to Britain. Gregory states:

> a large majority of countries in the world are multilingual. Between four and five thousand languages are spoken in fewer than two hundred states; in Nigeria over five hundred languages are spoken natively, while India claims over sixteen hundred mother tongues. In some countries, literacies in several languages and scripts will stand side-by-side in different types of schools. (1996: 3)

Different countries will have different attitudes towards, and policies to support, the education of their bilingual pupils. These reflect a variety of situations and contexts. A central issue is that of balance between and the status of the different languages spoken. Those countries which have in operation two official languages, such as in parts of Canada, which have English and French, are more likely to have well organized and considered **immersion language programmes** for their emergent bilingual children. In these counties there is a clear expectation that children will learn to read and write in both the official languages. This is not the general situation in Britain where policies (and historically there have been several) result in very varied provision.

Key Term

Immersion language programmes: a programme that has the clear expectation that the children will be able to speak, read and write in both languages and have full access to the whole curriculum.

British early years professionals are likely to encounter EAL children at some point in their careers and, when they do, they will need to approach the teaching of literacy from a position of knowledge and understanding.

Practitioners and primary teachers are aware that schools are required to provide opportunities within appropriate programmes in order that the abilities of their EAL pupils are developed in all aspects of English. It is not only their entitlement, but a necessity. English is the main medium of learning throughout a setting or school; and without fluency in English, individuals have difficulty securing social and political rights. But what might be an appropriate programme?

The National Association for Language Development in the Curriculum (NALDIC) responded to the Interim Rose Review (December 2005) in the following way:

> At whatever age children begin to learn English in school, they need to learn quickly how to convey knowledge and understanding in English and to engage with new learning through English. Developing their speaking and listening skills in English is the key to their success. This is clearly acknowledged with the development of materials such as the Sure Start/DfES/PNS publication 'Communicating Matters'. (DfES, 2006: 24)

Policies and changing attitudes to bilingualism in Britain

The Bullock Report (HMSO, 1975) marked a change in attitude to the previous official position. There was a move away from thinking in terms of separation and compensation to the inclusion of EAL pupils into a society that itself is acknowledged to be multicultural and multilingual. The following often quoted and eloquent paragraph depicts this view clearly.

> No child should be expected to cast off the language and culture of the home as he crosses the school threshold, nor to live and act as though school and home represent two totally separate and different cultures which have to be kept firmly apart. The curriculum should reflect many elements of that part of his life which the child lives outside school. (HMSO, 1975: para. 20.5: 286)

The type of educational programme that emerged following such changed thinking advocates the maintenance of the first language as well as recognition of and respect for the culture and the home life. The aspirational and predominant features (adapted from Skutnabb-Kangas, 1984) of this type of programme are that:

- the first language is given status by the curriculum being taught through its medium whenever possible
- no separation should be made of the EAL group for teaching and consequent stigmatization for inadequate knowledge of English

- parents are encouraged to be active and involved with these programmes
- English teaching takes place within the classroom
- teacher expectations are high, reflecting a positive stance of the programme, as is the EAL pupils' self-esteem and self-confidence
- the programme leads to a positive bilingual, bicultural identity.

Pupils who have English as an additional language

As has been discussed, many children in our settings and schools speak English, and at least one other language and, possibly, in addition, the dialect form of the first language. Arabic, Bengali, Cantonese, French, Greek, Gujerati, Hindi, Italian, Panjabi, Spanish, Sylheti, Turkish, Twi, Urdu, Welsh and Yoruba are only some of the first languages of the children in British schools. Some schools will have a number of pupils who share the same home language, other schools will have a range of children who have so many different languages as their mother tongue that there is no shared experience. Patently, the task for the early years setting and school in the latter case is very much more complex in terms of resources and teaching practice.

There are differences between EAL children themselves in several ways. First, some may be British born and have experience of English spoken at home but are exposed to varying levels of competence. Secondly, some children may have recently arrived in England and within this group also there will be disparate levels of receptiveness and motivation to speak and learn English. The contrast between the traumatic experience of a refugee and the child of European parents working in Britain will affect greatly the two pupils' predisposition to learn English.

Supporting spoken language development in English

The National Curriculum Orders for English (DfEE, 1999) state unequivocally the expectation that all pupils in England should operate within the four modes of spoken and written language, namely, speaking and listening, reading and writing in the English language. Emphasis is placed not only on fluency in English but also pupils are required to have access to the use of Standard English when the situation demands it. Pupils who have English as an additional language have exemption from the National Curriculum tasks and tests only for their first six months after entry to this country. Practitioners and primary teachers then have the responsibility to ensure that all their pupils are supported in such a way that they are able to fulfil these requirements.

The situation is different in Wales, where Welsh is the official language alongside English, and in this case, children who have Welsh as their first language are not expected to follow the Key Stage 1 Programme of Study for English, nor be involved in its assessment arrangements.

The principles that underpin any teaching approach which is designed to enable pupils to acquire fluency in English as an additional language will have much in common with the discussion in Chapter 1 which considers the language development in English first language speakers. Bialystock (2001) suggests that we should not expect the sequence of acquisition in the second language to replicate exactly the sequence for monolingual children. However, the principles which support successful development of communication and language in the first years of life remain constant for the acquisition of an additional language.

The main principles in the development of oracy

- Children learn to speak because communication fulfils a personal purpose.
- Communication begins with the positive relationship between the communicators. This may be initially through eye contact alone and later with eye contact and possibly other body language in support of the verbal interaction.
- Learning to speak an additional language in the Foundation Stage or primary school develops through stages that mirror the path of first language learning.
- Children progress most typically through the following stages:

  - a silent, receptive stage, that is, understanding but not able to produce language
  - one-word stage
  - two-word stage
  - the over-generalization of rules, for examples, peoples
  - the development of vocabulary and the more sophisticated use of connectives.

For children who are already literate in their first language, the processes will be different. Vocabulary and perhaps the understanding of the grammatical structures will be acquired through learning to read in the second language as well as through learning to speak.

- Great depth of meaning can be communicated in the one- and two-word stages of language development through the use of body language and intonation.
- The context-bound, concrete experience-based and highly personal features of communication need to be appreciated and capitalized upon by the more experienced language user.
- The role of the interested adult signalling enjoyment and providing elaborated models of the expanded form of the utterance is crucial.
- Written language, in the form of stories, rhymes and poetry, promotes spoken language through offering rich, linguistic models for the child.

However, there are important, additional distinctive features in the acquisition of an additional language that need to be recognized. Children are already aware implicitly of the way that languages are structured and work, and the first language is the foundation upon which the additional language is grafted. In addition, it is important that the child should be recognized as a competent language user already. This underlines the importance of first-language maintenance and support whenever possible. Learning a second or additional language enhances cognitive development and linguistic awareness, which is especially valuable when the child is learning to read and write.

Attitudinal aspects of the learning of English contribute significantly to the effectiveness of the provision. The children who feel that their first language, their parents and their culture are respected and drawn upon in the early years setting and school will feel more secure, confident and motivated to speak, read and write English, and also to learn through English.

The Australian Ministry of Education lists specific knowledge, understandings and technical and refined skills that need to be acquired before a second language can be mastered. These are:

- a new set of sounds and sound groupings, which may or may not be like those of the first language
- new intonation patterns and their meanings and new patterns of stress and pause
- a new script or alphabet (possibly)
- a new set of sound–symbol relationships
- new vocabulary
- new ways of putting words together (a new grammar) and organizing information and communication
- new non-verbal signals, and new meanings for old non-verbal signals
- new social signals and new ways of getting things done through language
- new rules about appropriateness of language for specific situations and roles
- new sets of culturally specific knowledge, values and behaviour
- a new culturally specific view of the world
- an ability to relate to people and to express feelings and emotions in the new language (Ministry of Education, 1987, cited in Clarke, 1992).

For young emerging bilinguals the challenge to acquire fluency in the language of the dominant culture is one of high risk and is linked intrinsically with their own cultural identity and with their self-esteem. Awareness of these sensitivities needs to be uppermost in the consciousness of the practitioner and teacher as she/he plans her/his learning environment and programme of work.

What constitutes good practice?

Given the principles discussed above, how might they be translated into effective practice? It is only possible for the early years practitioner or teacher to offer an enabling learning environment, with enriching and purposeful language opportunities for the EAL pupils, if the setting or class is operating with a considered policy, upholding the Race Relations Amendment Act 2000, and creates a positive ethos for the whole of its school community.

School admission procedures

On admission the following details can usefully be recorded: the languages spoken by the child and in the child's home; the level of fluency in both the first language and English; whether the child is literate in a language other than English; and if the child has other experiences out of school, such as formal language learning, for example, learning Hebrew at the synagogue or Arabic at the temple. It is important to know the level of fluency of the parents and whether an interpreter will need to be present at parent–teacher discussions. In addition, the school may wish to record the religion of the child to acknowledge particular observances such as if there are any special dietary requirements.

Involving parents in the education of bilingual children

If schools are to engage parents in the education of their children, it requires commitment on the part of the professionals. To involve the parents of children for whom English is an additional language, takes genuine understanding and empathy. Practitioners and teachers need insight into the cultural expectations of the community they serve, for many immigrants the expectation that they should be involved with the education of their children is literally beyond their experience. While having a keen interest in their child's academic success, frequently it is not in the experience of those from other cultures, particularly those from Asian and African countries, to participate actively in their child's education and school. Occasionally, there is a gulf between the expectations of parents and those of professionals, about many common place ideas and attitudes. In her study of Bangaldeshi children entering a reception class, Brooker (2002) found that the parents told their children to be 'good and quiet at school and to do what they were told', but conversely the teachers expected the pupils to be enquiring, autonomous learners and actively participating in the learning opportunities provided.

On the practical side, parents will be whole-hearted about involving themselves in their children's education only if documentation from the school informing them about its activities is available in the relevant home languages. With this as a starting point, parents will feel welcomed and valued, and in their turn, they will take part in the translation of stories, rhymes, notices and labels. Often adults in the wider community are able to promote the broader cultural life of their children through sharing with all pupils traditional dances or songs, cooking special dishes, celebrating religious festivals, as well as the usual primary school practices of telling stories and supporting art and design, sports and literacy activities. Early years education begins with the whole child and integrates all learning with life both in and out of school.

Good relationships with parents are the key to this, and all the pupils, not just those who have English as an additional language, will benefit from celebrating the rich, cultural diversity in the setting or school.

The plurality of the school

Making overt the multicultural nature of the setting or school is the responsibility of all the staff and requires attention to detail and sensitivity towards individuals from other cultures. Resources should appropriately reflect the languages and ethnicity of the children in a particular school in many interesting and lively ways. Printed material in the form of displays, notices and signs needs to reflect the languages spoken, also all the visual images used should portray the many cultural influences of the school community. Alphabet and number charts not only demonstrate powerfully the symbolism of arbitrary sign systems that represent letters and numbers in different ways, but also will emphasize the inclusive nature of the school environment. Books, games, jigsaw puzzles and all equipment should depict positive images of ethnic minority people. Various cultural artefacts from the relevant countries of origin of the pupils, can transform (and transport!) the atmosphere of the home corner and role-play areas. Art materials, for example, wax and pencil crayons, that are offered need to make as realistic as possible a representation of the variations of skin tone. Dolls also should typically represent different races. If measures of this kind are taken, important, positive messages will be sent so that the language and culture of the majority of the population is not seen as repressively dominant within the micro-society of the setting and school.

Bilingual learners along with all pupils need a secure and accepting environment in which to practise and perfect their spoken language.

Stages of learning an additional language

It goes almost without saying that a teacher will only be able to provide appropriate learning activities which will enable children to develop their English, if she/he is clear about the stage of spoken language development of each of the children in her class. Hester's (1990) stages are helpful here (Figure 10.1).

When teaching children at different stages of learning English as an additional language, it should be recognized that fluency in basic interpersonal communication skills occurs usually after about two years of immersion in the second language. But, it has been suggested that the ability to learn concepts not already established, for example, mathematical or scientific concepts, takes much longer (Cummins, 1979). This Cummins calls **cognitive, academic language proficiency** which may take five years or so of immersion in the new language, and interestingly it remains about this length of time, whatever the age of the child when learning the additional language began.

The following scale describes aspects of bilingual children's development through English which teachers might find helpful. It is important to remember that children may move into English in very individual ways, and that the experience for an older child will be different from that of a young child. The scales emphasise the social aspects of learning, as well as the linguistic. Obviously attitudes in the school to children and the languages they speak will influence their confidence in using both their first and second languages.

Stage 1: *new to English*
Makes contact with another child in the class. Joins in activities with other children, but may not speak. Uses non-verbal gestures to indicate meaning – particularly needs, likes and dislikes. Watches carefully what other children are doing, and often imitates them. Listens carefully and often 'echoes' words and phrases of other children and adults. Needs opportunities for listening to the sounds, rhythms and tunes of English through songs, rhymes, stories and conversations. If young may join in repeating refrain of a story. Beginning to label objects in the classroom, and personal things. Beginning to put words together into holistic phrases (e.g. no come here, where find it, no eating that). May be involved In classroom learning activities in the first language with children who speak the same first language. May choose to use first language only in most contexts. May be willing to write in the first language (if s/he can), and if invited to. May be reticent with unknown adults. May be very aware of negative attitudes by peer group to the first language. Many choose to move into English through story and reading, rather than speaking.

Stage 2: *becoming familiar with English*
Growing confidence in using the English s/he is acquiring. Growing ability to move between the languages, and to hold conversations in English with peer groups. Simple holistic phrases may be combined or expanded to communicate new ideas. Beginning to sort out small details (e.g. 'he' and 'she' distinction) but more interested in communicating meaning than in 'correctness'. Increasing control of the English tense system in particular contexts, such as story-telling, reporting events and activities that s/he has been involved in, and from book language. Understands more English than s/he can use. Growing vocabulary for naming objects and events, and beginning to describe in more detail (e.g. colour, size, quantity) and use simple adverbs. Increasingly confident in taking part in activities with other children through English. Beginning to write simple stories, often modelled on those s/he has heard read aloud. Beginning to write simple accounts of activities s/he has been involved in, but may need support from adults and other child, her/his first language if s/he needs to. Continuing to rely on support of her/his friends.

Stage 3: *becoming confident as a user of English*
Shows great confidence in using English in most social situations. This confidence may mask the need for support in taking on other registers (e.g. in science investigation, in historical research). Growing command of the grammatical system of English – including complex verbal meanings (relationships of time, expressing tentativeness and subtle intention with might, could, etc.) and more complex sentence structure. Developing an understanding of metaphor and pun. Pronunciation may be very native-speaker like, especially that of young children. Widening vocabulary from reading a story, poems and information books and from being involved in maths and science investigations, and other curriculum areas. May choose to explore complex ideas (e.g. in drama/role-play) in the first language with children who share the same first language.

Stage 4: *a very fluent user of English in most social and learning contexts*
A very experienced user of English, and exceptionally fluent in many contexts. May continue to need support in understanding subtle nuances of metaphor, and in Anglo-centric cultural content in poems and literature. Confident in exchanges and collaboration with English-speaking peers. Writing confidently in English with a growing competence over different genres. Continuing and new development in English drawn from own reading and books read aloud. New developments often revealed in own writing. Will move with ease between English and the first language depending on the contexts s/he finds her- himself in, what s/he judges appropriate, and the encouragement of the school.

(Hester, 1990: 41)

Figure 10.1 Stages of learning of English as an additional language

Home languages will be viewed positively if children who share the same first language are grouped together for some tasks and if the more experienced speakers are used as interpreters.

All the practitioner- or teacher-led speaking and listening activities such as 'circle time' have the potential to be especially valuable for the EAL learners in the group if skilfully exploited. Awareness of the ways that they can be used to develop confidence gives a feeling of inclusion and allows useful practice of a speech structure which some of the class members are finding difficult.

Learning and Teaching Suggestions

The class is discussing how to make a dolls' house. Every child is invited to make a contribution to the topic and is encouraged to use the sentence constructions 'My dolls' house will be made of … I will use … This is because … '.

In what other ways is the teacher able to utilize individual approaches and group teaching methods to support the developing spoken language of all the pupils?

Early years professionals will often introduce tasks to EAL pupils with concrete examples to aid better understanding of what is to be done. An introduction to an art and design project is best undertaken alongside the materials in the art area, so that, with demonstration of how materials are to be handled, the activity approached can be reinforced.

Reporting back in a plenary session needs to be similarly embedded in the context and accompanied by the painting, model or print with a clear and simple explanation of how it was made. Bilingual learners will gradually be able to report back on their own work if given appropriate support (either by a classmate or an adult) when giving the report and with possibly a prior rehearsal of what and how it is to be said. Games of the turn-taking and the sentence completion types can also be useful for learning vocabulary and the practising of particular structures, for example, 'I went to the shop to buy a brand new … alligator/a big box/a calendar/a dinosaur/an elephant …'. The list could be usefully scribed by the adult with the letters of the alphabet written and emphasized in another colour.

Children teaching children

Practical experiences are important for all early years pupils, but for emerging bilinguals they are essential. Children learning an additional language need strong contextual and visual support for any educational task they engage with. In addition, working alongside fluent English speakers provides opportunities to interact with valuable spoken language role models. Games and structured play provision offer stress-free, and sufficiently open-ended, learning opportunities for children to apply their developing skills.

The role-play area offers particularly rich learning provision for the children and a vehicle for observation for the practitioner or teacher.

Case Study 10.1

Simon (5 years) and David (4 years) are playing in the home corner. Simon says to Abdul (5 years):

Abdul, you play with us, you play with us.
(To children outside) You can't come in,
Abdul's playing here. You can't come in, Abdul's playing here.
Abdul do you want a dress?
Would you like a dress?
Do you want a dress?
Do you want a dress?
Do you want a nice dress, Abdul?
Here is a dress, Abdul.
This is gorgeous, Abdul.
Good boy Abdul.
That is gorgeous, Abdul.

Simon holds up a voluminous flowing skirt. He says:

Put your feet in, Abdul.
Put your feet in, Abdul.
This is gorgeous, Abdul.
Put your feet in, Abdul.

Simon tries to push Abdul into the skirt.

Abdul: No
Simon: Abdul, you are a good boy.
         Abdul, you're a good boy.
         Abdul is a good boy in the home corner.

Learning and Teaching Suggestions

What in particular does Simon intuitively do to enable Abdul to understand him?

Can you list four different ways of capturing attention and reinforcing meaning?

How does it differ from an exchange that Abdul might have with an adult?

While one might not applaud the coercion of this bilingual child newly arrived in a reception class, it cannot be denied that this conversational exchange is facilitative for Abdul's spoken English!

Children learn successfully through interaction with and by learning alongside their peers. Sociable and compatible pupils from the same class demonstrate that they are able to support intuitively the language development of their friends. Both the patient repetition and the contextually embedded nature of the situation play a powerful part in the reasons that make the learning effective. Collaborative language games (both of the board and playing-card types), promote vocabulary practice, as do problem-solving tasks in design and technology, science and construction activities.

Learning language through stories

The provision of a facilitative language environment allows the learners to make meaning of the language they hear around them. Every early years practitioner or teacher will want to make the spoken language input comprehensible through providing extra-linguistic clues to support the meaning and to make it clearer. These clues might include pictures, gestures, mime, practical activities or artefacts. Professionals will be quick also to exploit the use of high-quality stories in the setting or classroom, in order to develop the oracy of all the children, both monolingual and those for whom English is an additional language. Hester (1983) has made helpful suggestions about how this might be achieved, on which the following list is based:

- using a story board to retell a favourite well-known story
- making, and then labelling models arising from the story
- collecting artefacts and items that can be used in the retelling (or reworking through imaginative play) of a story, for example, dolls' house chairs, bowls, beds of different sizes and a doll in order to retell 'The Three Little Bears'. These are known now as 'story boxes' and have been discussed in Chapter 2. The mini-collections are housed in labelled boxes for ease of storage and access
- retelling and sequencing a story through a set of pictures drawn either by the child him- or herself or by adult artists

- playing bingo games based on the words used in a simple book
- making a concept 'map' of a story
- making simple two-dimensional soft flannel puppets and using a 'fuzzy felt board' to retell the story
- making a dual text version of the story with the help of a parent or more experienced speaker of the first language
- writing a new ending or different beginning for the story
- following up an aspect of the story – researching into elephants, the countries they come from, drawing them, making a frieze, inventing some drama after reading *Tusk, Tusk* (McKee, 1978).

Learning to read and write in English

It has been discussed that the learning of literacy has its foundation in rich and meaningful opportunity to use spoken language. It will be recalled also that the literacy process is one that is multi-faceted and interrelated (see Chapter 6). For EAL children learning to read in English this generally holds true but some of the aspects of the process will be more useful and accessible than others.

An EAL child's processing of text

Chapters 5 and 6 discussed the differing roles of the comprehension and decoding processing that operate when reading text to inform the individual about the written words. Writers such as Adams and Clay propose that the comprehension processing of the text relies on the context when reading. This includes both the global context or meaning of the overall story and the semantic and syntactic context of the internal sense and grammar of the sentence which enable the reader to predict what a word is likely to be. These predictions are then confirmed (or not!) by the decoding processing which involves a grasp of the grapheme–phoneme correspondences (GPC) of the word; that is, children's awareness of the alphabetic code. If pupils are reading in their mother tongue, and if they have had appropriate teaching, then these two processing strategies are likely to be used equally. In fact, Adams and Clay would argue that they both need to be drawn upon, in parallel and simultaneously, and that fluent, fast, reading depends upon this capability.

The EAL child, however, owing to a relatively weaker knowledge of the language structures of English, has less familiarity with its patterns, vocabulary, sentence structure and grammar, and so finds this prediction of text more difficult. It is likely that the bilingual novice reader will find the decoding of text to be more useful and hence rely heavily on this strategy.

The child will almost certainly have an appreciation of the one-to-oneness of spoken units of sound to print. This will depend in part on whether children are functional in another script and whether this prior knowledge is from an alphabetic or logographic script. Also, Sassoon (1995) points out that those pupils familiar with much more complex scripts (such as Chinese or Japanese which place huge demands on the visual memory) will find the orthography of the English language relatively straightforward and so will be advantaged. However, there is a risk that if all the focus is on the decoding aspect of reading, the comprehension and the essential accessing of the meaning of text will be lost.

Learning and Teaching Suggestions

Gregory demonstrates the above beautifully with her transcript of the young bilingual child at the early literacy stage (National Curriculum Pre-level 1) of acting like a reader with one of the Mr Men books, *Mr Bump* (Hargreaves): 1998.

Kalchuma: (turning the pages and 'reading' each word very definitely) Bump.

>   Mr Bump is go to gone bump.
>   Mr Bump is go to gone.
>   Mr Bump is to all down.
>   He went there to bump.
>   Mr Bump to ... what's in there missing?
>   Mr Bump go stick ... his stick, there stick. (means a sticking plaster)
>   (continues using similar English constructions 'go to go/go sitting/go he go to his steps' etc. throughout a number of books). (1996: 57)

Which kinds of books are particularly supportive of the young bilingual child's early attempts at reading?

Which books will encourage an appreciation of the language patterns and structures of English?

Children who have English as an additional language will be aware of the code aspect of written language. This might be, possibly, because they have experience of another written language, even if they are unlikely to be bi-literate, or because they are older and more experienced about print, when they operate in the early stages of reading in English in school. This is demonstrated well by Kalchuma's use of strategies. It is clear that she has an idea of the one-to-oneness of a word representing a unit of sound, she has a developing print awareness and a small sight vocabulary which is shown by the way that she uses letter shapes to inform her 'reading', and 'Mr Bump' is recognized and said, as is 'go' and the beginning 'st' of sticking plaster. Much harder for this child is prediction through remembering accurately the pattern and rhythm of the written language, although clearly this book has been read and reread often. This is the aspect that a mother-tongue reader is likely to find the easiest, as shown in the story of a 5-year-old saying to her teacher with reference to a well-known and much loved book, 'Look miss, I can read so good now I can even do it with me eyes closed!'

An 'inside-out' approach to teaching reading

This approach to teaching children to read, in a language that is not the mother tongue, is described by Gregory (1996) in detail, and is essentially 'starting from the known'. As she says: 'The child's cultural knowledge is used rather as a spring board for comparing differences and similarities between languages and cultural practices, for showing children that stepping into a new world provides access to exciting experiences but need not mean abandoning the language and culture of home' (Gregory, 1996: 101).

It is in this important way that Gregory sees the teacher as a mediator. Language learning through activities such as cooking and socio-dramatic play are effective for linking the familiar to the new. Making foods such as breads or soups that have equivalents in different countries, and learning the words for them in the relevant languages can then be followed by stories and rhymes about food. This type of work capitalizes on what is familiar, and compares it with and relates it to the new experiences.

Children who are at this stage of learning to read, while still learning to speak English fluently, need to become familiar with a bank of words and phrases in English, which Gregory calls 'chunks of language'. The fact that the words and groups of words will be specific to each situation and to a particular book is not important, as over time, and given many opportunities, the words and phrases will mesh together and so provide a deep understanding of the patterns and rhythms of English. The use of verse and rhymes both orally and in reading is of great value to the child at this stage as the rhyme is a mnemonic for remembering the exact way the words are placed together. 'Chunks' are needed if syntactic prediction cueing systems (that is, 'what sort of word is likely to fit here?') are to kick in and so become a useful reading strategy.

Learning 'chunks of language' occurs most naturally in activities that are embedded in a practical context. Frequently, adults learn a second language in the contexts of visiting restaurants and through different kinds of travel abroad and so memorize accurately whole conversations in order to reserve tables when hungry and to buy tickets for trains when needing to return home. In the same way, children will learn through the doing of activities in order to get them done, reading and writing goes alongside this and with one language mode supporting the use of the other. As we have seen earlier with the monolingual child, the class-made book of an activity embeds, for example, the visit to the post office in a permanent record to be shared and enjoyed. Sentences and parts of sentences are used, rehearsed, sounded out and written down, and then read back. Gregory extends this approach for teaching bilingual children to read through enabling the prior learning of 'chunks' of language and practice of the structures of language soon to be encountered in a story, perhaps through the use of puppets or drama activities before reading the book. This is an elaboration of Clay's rich book introduction described in Chapter 9. Gregory uses this technique to go one step beyond raising an expectation of what language structures might be to the actual rehearsal of structures and words. This enhances the child's ability to utilize prediction as a cueing strategy even if, initially, it is through partially memorized text.

Words and phrases may be learned through the support of written language in the manner of *Breakthrough to Literacy* with look-alike materials where key words are written on strips of card, which then are read, made into sentences, rearranged and read again, and learned. Rereading on subsequent days makes the spoken and written language links internalized through practice and familiarity.

An 'outside-in' approach to teaching reading

Gregory (1976) writes about the 'outside-in' approach as being complementary to the previous one and as a means of 'introducing the unknown' and this she bases on the work of Meek (1981). This way into reading capitalizes on the magic of stories to internalize literary conventions, vocabulary and experiences beyond the child's world. Through this process children learn the 'grammar' of stories. As Harold Rosen suggests, stories are 'the commonest possession of humankind – part of the deep structure of the grammar of the world' (1984: 14).

Stories that are both memorable and contain layers of meaning (discussed fully in Chapter 9) have the richest potential for language learning. Gregory demonstrates how the traditional tale of 'The Little Red Hen' has the potential to provide opportunity for the child to come to at least four different types of understanding. Semantic knowledge or understanding about the world and its practices is gained, such as in the case of this specific tale – flour is made from grain and bread is made from flour, and so on. There is opportunity to acquire syntactic knowledge or 'chunks of language' with the repeated phrases of 'Who will help me?', 'No I won't'. Lexical knowledge can be developed through the words that form meaning (lexical) sets such as cut/corn, plant/seeds, bake/cake, mill/grind and, finally, orthographic/ grapho-phonic knowledge learning opportunities such as b........ake/ c.......ake /r.....ake.

The way that stories are read and discussed for the full potential of the book to be capitalized upon is important for EAL learners. This is explored in more depth in Chapter 9. The Primary National Strategy: Framework for teaching literacy (DfES, 2006) endorses, with the approach Shared Reading, this way of working with texts (see Chapter 6). Shared Reading allows groups of children to have opportunities to hear and learn spoken language, and to practise reading together with mutual support. Hard-pressed early years professionals will maximize the learning through group approaches in order to develop the spoken and written language of the EAL children alongside their monolingual peers. A sound understanding of both the theoretical issues and the learning needs of each child in her/his class will mean that it is more likely that the teacher is able to offer the appropriate provision for her/his bilingual pupils.

The Rose Report gives an example of a successful approach to supporting bilingual pupils:

For example, one school visited by HMI for the review had a predominantly Asian British population, with over 30% of the pupils eligible for free school meals. Nearly 70% of the pupils did not have English as their first language. The development of speaking and listening skills, and vocabulary building, were strong features of the work. The school introduced a commercial phonics scheme. Underpinning much of the programme's success was its approach to assessment and intervention. … The school's data show a big increase in the proportion of children learning to read at Key Stage 1, with far fewer 'working towards' or achieving only Level 1 in reading. Such data add weight to the view that systematic, high quality teaching, detailed assessment and early intervention are as important for learners of English as an additional language as for all children. (DfES, 2006: 25)

Summary

This chapter has introduced briefly the teaching of language and literacy to EAL pupils, so that practitioners and teachers can be aware of the main issues. Professionals will know that the best practice for early years children is effective for EAL pupils also, and that bilingual pupils' spoken English can be supported successfully within the classroom alongside a planned programme to teach literacy to children who are still in the process of acquiring English fluency.

Further reading

Brooker, E. (2002) *Starting School: Young Children Learning Cultures*. Buckingham: Open University Press.
Drury, R. (2005) *Young Bilingual Children Learning at Home and School*. Stoke-on-Trent: Trentham Books.
Gregory, E. (1996) *Making Sense of a New World*. London: Paul Chapman Publishing.
Kenner, C. (2004) *Becoming Literate*. Stoke-on-Trent: Trentham Books.
Siraj-Blatchford, I. and Clarke, P. (2000) *Laying the Foundations for Racial Equality*. Stoke-on-Trent: Trentham Books.

Chapter **11**

Supporting Learning, Language and Literacy with ICT

Children are early adopters of new technology. They always have been.

(Kinnes, 2002: 50, cited in Mallett, 2003: 138)

[S]chool learning is at odds with authentic ways of learning to be in the world, and with social practice beyond the school gates.

(Lankshear and Knobel, 2003: 31)

[T]he future is already here, that we are literally staring at it, but within school education we are not really engaging with it.

(Lankshear and Knobel, 2003: 19)

Introduction

This chapter will look at the ways that various forms of information and communications technology (ICT) can support, in imaginative ways, the learning and teaching of language and literacy in early years settings and primary schools. Here it is argued that ICT should be approached critically and creatively in order for it to become an integral part of the learning environment. Only then can its particular contribution to the development of literacy be realized and not viewed merely as a 'sexy' addition to other resources and materials in the professionals' armoury.

Why use ICT in the setting or classroom?

Twenty-five years ago Seymour Papert, the American technology guru envisaged a world where computers would make schools obsolete. He wrote that,

'Computers will gradually return to the individual the power to determine the patterns of education. Education will become more of a private act' (1980: 37). In addition, educationalists were considering a world in which increasingly powerful forms of technology would reduce individual need for a high level of literacy. Neither prophecy could be further from the truth as we experience life today. Schools have not embraced ICT with the enthusiasm that Papert foretold (Buckingham, 2005) and advanced literacy skills are even more essential if society is to capitalize on the potential that new technology presents in almost every facet of life. Browsing a web page or writing with a word-processing package call into operation different kinds of reading and writing skills from those demanded by the older technologies of books and pencils but they are similarly, if not more, cognitively challenging. In other words, the process of literacy becomes adapted to allow participation in all that the digital era offers. Information and communications technology has brought new tools into existence and with their usage the products have also evolved beyond recognition. For example, in the workplace handwritten texts have largely been replaced by professional-looking desktop-published and word-processed documents, e-mails (a hybrid form of discourse between the handwritten memo and a phone conversation) and the ultimate of 'cool' – the phone text message. All these exist in abundance and in evolving applications everywhere, except, by and large, in the classroom. So the relationship it now seems is reciprocal – ICT offers new modes of communication, and so the communication (both the content and the form) itself changes, in the nature of discourse as it broadens and extends its range and purpose. Telephones began to replace letter writing (for a certain strata of society) at the turn of the twentieth century and in so doing altered ways of communicating. Mobile phones changed the conventions of phone conversations further as their convenient portability enhanced recipients' availability, to the 'anytime/anyplace' current state of affairs. Text messages as a coded communication of extreme brevity (with its modified written code system for example, 'how r u? Hope u r gr8 2!') have transformed communication still further.

Theories have developed around the cultural transformations of these constantly evolving modes of communicative practice which is also altering the ways that we relate to others. Notions of 'new literacies' have been suggested which embrace both the skills demanded by the different types of technology and concepts of multi-modality in literacy such as those put forward by Jewitt and Kress. They 'challenge the implicit assumption that speech and writing are always central and sufficient for learning' (Jewitt and Press, 2003: 2) as they take a 'theoretical position that treats all modes as equally significant for meaning, at least potentially so' (2003: 2). Theorists suggest that educators should reconsider the 'deep grammar of schooling' (Lankshear and Knobel, 2003: 3) where traditional technologies are privileged but have been largely replaced by the new technologies and communicative practices in the out-of-school lives of young people. Early years professionals need to take account of the new literacies and view them as ways of being and acting in the world. In addition, not only are the new technologies very relevant to the needs of young people, the digital world is one in which they are inordinately competent and confident. Often this fact passes unrecognized, unacknowledged and unadmired by teachers. But this too must change. Kerin argues that the 'new digital world is a place that educators must begin to engage with and explore more thoroughly and seriously' (2005: 176) so that they are able fully to appreciate its educational potential.

In this chapter, we consider how children can be assisted by ICT to use spoken language fluently and to become literate. We also discuss how pupils' competence with the new technologies enables them to use their literacy skills to read and to learn, and to express themselves in innovative and trans-forming ways.

ICT, computers and oracy

Television, video films, DVDs, audio cassette recorded rhymes, poetry and sto-ries, CD-ROMs and the use of websites as well as computer programmes can be a rich source of something immediate and captivating to talk about in early years classrooms. For example, a computer program that has a problem-solving element to it invites peer or adult collaboration in order to puzzle together and debate options and scenarios. 'Albert's House', 'Zoombini's Logical Journey' are well-known useful examples of software programs which pro-mote valuable talk. The CD-ROMs of the 'Peter Rabbit Adventures' can pro-vide a stimulus for small group discussions. Effective speaking and listening can arise from website searches and through the use of CD-ROMs to seek addi-tional information for the class topic or area of individual interest. 'Smart Learning' has produced interactive literacy programs which combine Shared Reading sessions with animated and interactive speaking and listening activ-ities connected to the story.

Listening to story audiotapes is the cherished way to develop a love of sto-ries, to foster concentration and active listening skills. A story enjoyed in a group situation can be audiotaped or digitally recorded on a computer to allow individual children to relive the pleasure of revisiting the story through audio cassettes, CDs or on screen, in another place and at another time.

Further suggested resources

Jump Ahead Pre-school (2–5 years)
Infant Video Toolkit (5–7 years)
Smart Learning Interactive Literacy (see www.smart-learning.co.uk).

Television and video film

Television in schools is used in two ways. Valuable use can be made of pre-recorded programmes designed with specific age groups in mind and usually targeted at skills acquisition such as 'Adventures in Letterland' or 'Words and Pictures'. Practitioners and teachers often incorporate the programme in their planning, have opportunity to stop and replay the programme where appropriate and follow up on the content, after the viewing, with their own teaching. Television, video and DVD also can be capitalized upon to supplement teaching on a particular topic, as can use of the Internet. Teachers will prerecord a wildlife programme from mainstream television for their own use in school: using a programme on brown and polar bears in the wild, for example, to weave into a project on the Teddy Bears' Picnic. As with all teaching resources, maximum benefit is gained from television programmes if the adult considers how and exactly when to use the programme or video clip in the lifespan of the project, and the type and level of mediation that will be offered. These, of course, are the same principles that influence the choice and enhance the effect of any technology, for example, books which accompany a project or theme.

Research undertaken by Brown (1999) indicates that reading books and watching television can be mutually reinforcing and that children gain immensely from experience with the different but complementary forms of texts. Both television and books will evoke personal responses, especially if teachers allow these to be critically discussed and enjoyed alongside the specific learning intentions for a given session.

A worked example: a Year 2 classroom project on the Second World War

Pupils in a Year 2 class were studying the Second World War (the Programmes of the Study for History National Curriculum, 1999). The class teacher had developed a cross-curricular approach to the project but was focusing intensively on the social historical content and the opportunities for language and literacy. The starting point for the project was the television programme *The 1940s House: Women at War*, first televised in 2002 but available from www. channel4.com/history/microsites/0–9/1940house/.

The programme reconstructs a family – grandmother, mother and two young boys – living through the Blitz in London and reveals the privations of wartime Britain, including the limited food available, the importance of the blackout and houses, and even the restrictions on the depth of bathwater allowed in order to minimize fuel consumption. Clearly the fear and horror of the war as it affected the population was implicit, but in this television programme the point is made powerfully, how relentlessly hard and uncomfortable life was for the whole population. The challenges of joining the military are dealt with along with the different difficulties for the women left at home coping with households of young children and elderly parents. The domestic struggle of feeding and keeping families warm on meagre rations with little respite and very few pleasures is depicted. Each member of the Year 2 class began a wartime journal, describing how their father had been 'called up' to take part in the fighting, even to go abroad, and how some domestic challenges impacted upon them as children as they took on new roles of responsibility in the household. The children wrote colourfully as they recorded how they dug up lawns in small London gardens to plant potatoes and carrots, how it was they who were in charge of weighing and controlling the weekly allowance of coal, and checking the windows every night to ensure that the law was upheld and not a chink of light was visible from outside.

Deepening experience with drama

Drama was the vehicle adopted to give the children a concrete experience of an air raid. The drama was also videoed using a Digital Movie Creator 2 camera for possible later use in reflection and discussion. The class drama began with the shrieking of an air raid siren and the children running to shelter in the local underground station. All the neighbourhood are there, their friends and their relatives. The children act out how they huddle all night underground, with no beds, only blankets and a cushion, imagining the bombs as they fall above … thinking are they falling in our street? On our house? What will we find when we return home in the morning? Is our little cat safe? Snowy hates loud noises. Mum has brought a flask of cocoa which comforts the family as they wait. The morning comes at last and the 'All clear' siren sounds … stumbling out into the cold morning light … yawning and shivering. Oh no … is the house still there? … yes … it is standing and what a welcome sight … what a relief! Mum soon has the kitchen fire lit before we all go to bed for a few hours before getting up for school.

The teacher lets this experience 'rinse' through the class and then later that day she heightens the reality of the blitz through a genuine social historical record. She plays an audiotape of the account of an elderly woman who lived in Acton, in west London throughout the 1939–45 war. The old lady describes how as a 20-year-old she did her war work in a munitions factory, and she recounts her personal and horrifying experience of being trapped in a collapsed building when it was bombed during an air raid. The oral narrative, of how the mounds of rubble fallen across her body trapped and pinned her to the floor, is simply told, unembellished and touching. In time the air-raid wardens find Violet and dig her out. The woman's account ends with her lying on a door as a makeshift stretcher while a red London bus takes her to hospital. As it drives away Violet hears one warden say to the other, 'I think she's lost her legs poor girl … they are crushed to pieces'.

The next day the children write their own 'personal' accounts of an air raid, with alternative paths, some return home safe and sound but others choose to have something dramatic happen to them, or again some are involved in a rescue – the choice is theirs and the level of engagement after the simulation is high.

Some of the recounts are word-processed straight onto the computer and others are supported by the teacher in Guided Writing using an interactive whiteboard. Both modes of production are published for reading by other members in the class, and some are chosen for the wall display on the war and to accompany the paintings by the children.

The history project continues through the next few weeks and accompanying it is the reading of *The Lion and the Unicorn* by Shirley Hughes as the class book at storytime. The tale is of a small boy evacuated away from the danger of London to the safety of the country who experiences aching homesickness and religious prejudice.

A visit to the Imperial War Museum takes place towards the end of the project to extend the learning further through direct experience of various artefacts and interactive displays.

Further suggested resources

The National Archives have resource items such as online movie clips and people talking about their war experiences which might be used also in Year 2 classrooms, for example, interactive displays at the Science Museum.

See the Digital Blue Movie Creator on www.taglearning.com.

Computers and literacy

Computer programs cover a range of 'learning to read' packages and reading to learn opportunities. Through CD-ROMs and 'talking books' (possibly accessed online from the Children's Literature Web Guide) children can engage with the experience of a well-loved story or poem. These will include animation and sound effects, games and activities, and complement traditional story experiences well for small group situations and for individuals. Often key words are highlighted to support sight word learning for later recognition, such as the Oxford Reading Tree Scheme. Reading on a computer screen facilitates competence across a range of literacies. The multimedia CD-ROM (or online story) offers the perfect synergy of visual and conventional literacy as children interpret semiotic systems in addition to the alphabet code system in order to access the information and meaning. Children aged 5, 6 and 7 years learn to read both scrolled and linear text, and they develop reading skills which enable them to scan and select a particular piece of text to be read. They do not necessarily read from left to right, or in top to bottom order, they can cope with the simultaneity of images, text boxes and sound effects, and they are able to operate and make sense of interactive diagrams.

Mallett (2003: 140) offers criteria based on the British Interactive Media Association (BIMA) guidelines to assess the quality of a non-fiction CD-ROM which are consistent with those one might use to assess an expository book, namely:

Does the chosen CD-ROM

- meet the needs of the age group for which it is intended?
- engage, educate and entertain?
- make imaginative use of the technology?
- provide a suitable medium for the subject?
- enable the user to navigate easily?
- provide quality search systems and bookmarks?
- offer quality content – taking account of accuracy, comprehension, creativity and interest?
- offer quality images and audio experiences?

Technology-assisted learning to read and write

Software packages designed to teach reading skills such as phonological awareness, or letter recognition, and sound–symbol relationships are valuable resources to support a particular stage of reading development. As with all skill-based learning opportunities, practitioners and teachers will want to be sure that the item used is appropriate for the individual learner at any particular time.

Suggested resources

Learning Ladder Preschool (3–5 years)
ABC Learning Adventures 3–5 years (book and CD-ROM)
Spark Learning (www.bbcshop.com)
Spark Island learning at www.sparkisland.com/
Fast Phonics First from primary.marketing@harcourteducation.co.uk or visit www.fastphonicsfirst.co.uk for a preview
Letterland Living ABC available from www.r.e.m.co.uk
The soon to be released Letterland Starter Pack with full guidance from a teacher's manual entitled *Early Years Handbook*.

The Rose Report (DfES, 2006) notes an improvement in schools and settings regarding the use of ICT particularly in the use of electronic whiteboards. Rose writes:

The opportunities afforded by this interactive technology were exploited to good effect, and the benefits were apparent for both teaching and learning. At best, electronic whiteboards extended teachers' repertoire of skills, helped them to plan and teach sequences of work that captured children's interests, intensified their concentration and sustained attention. (DfES, 2006: 25)

Computers, reading and learning

The computer has unleashed a vast range of texts in a variety of forms beyond paper and traditional books into children's lives both at home and at school. Programs with essentially a game format which are designed to develop computer skills alongside specific learning such as consolidation of number bonds in mathematics, will also have print to be read. Some of these programs are no more than technology-assisted and superficially seductive workbooks to support the development of skills, and are low on features that provoke thought or challenge. Ease of navigation is an important criterion with this type of software as with CD-ROMs for children in the Foundation Stage. 'Talking books' is a term used to describe computer-based storybooks that allow pupils to hear parts of the story and individual words read aloud. These e-books are favoured by teachers over isolated skills programs as they embed the learning intention in a meaningful context. 'Talking books' develop facility in the 'comprehension' processing of texts with what is essentially a screen-presented narrative with sound effects, different voices for the various characters and animation to entrance the reader.

Research has demonstrated that software designed to support sub-word segmentation skills does promote reading attainment in reading and phonological awareness (for example, Barron et al., 1998). But there has been relatively little research looking at whether children who are in the early stages of learning to read might also benefit from computer-based reading support. To this end, Chera (2000) designed a multimedia, interactive 'talking book' which enabled children to seek help at different levels if they had difficulties reading a text. The software enables children to make choices to hear the whole page read aloud, to hear single individual words read complete, or to hear them 'sounded out' (for example, D-ad). Additional activities allow children to play games with onsets and rimes, such as making a string of words with the same rime, for example, m-an, p-an, St-an, r-an, f-an, t-an, and so on. A study investigated the differential effects of half of the sample of 5- and 6-year-olds using the 'talking book' and the other half working with an adult for the same period of time (15 minutes daily) for six days, reading the 'Bangers and Mash' series. There were no significant differences between the two groups of children in their attainment regarding phonological awareness, but the 'talking books' group demonstrated gains in rhyme detection ability and changes were identified in the children's reading strategies.

LeapFrog educational toys

This company with a well-known brand image in the commercial market is entering the educational world with its technology-assisted learning tools. The 'LeapPad Learning System' through the use of touchpad technology, enables books to become interactive to support the child's learning needs in an individualized way. The LeapPad capitalizes on the concept of the book itself, rather than through a screen, to bring the technology-assisted learning to support the child's early reading experience. The child-held pen points at words and individual letters to either hear them read aloud or to have them sounded out phonetically. The LeapFrog brochures claim that the LeapPad:

- brings books to life with touch-interactive technology
- helps pupils learn letter names and sounds, practise decoding words, and builds reading fluency
- provides immediate and corrective feedback and unlimited repetition and practice opportunities.

These learning tools might be viewed as a bridge between formal and informal learning as children often are comfortable and familiar with the LeapPad from the home. Early trials suggest that LeapPads can be beneficial when used as a resource in early years classrooms as they are highly motivating when used both by individuals and in groups.

Non-fiction versions of talking books are also highly engaging ways of learning about life cycle, biological processes and the working of machines; these require the development of similar reading skills as discussed earlier for use with expository texts such as the consideration of the questions to be asked of the text and locating information. An additional benefit to learning is gained by collating information, reporting back to a group and writing a summary of the findings.

Suggested resources

Collins enlarged texts, *Spotlight on Fact*, on themes such as 'Toys and Games' and 'The Seaside' accompanied by a CD-ROM, writing frames and notes for teachers, see www.collinseducation.com.

Computers and supporting writing development

Writing assisted by computer word-processing packages is making its presence felt in early years settings and classrooms, being used to produce highly polished products (texts) rather than to provide a unique contribution to the process of generating, shaping and modifying texts. These are mainly for display purposes and for producing 'final draft' copies of the contributions to the class or group book. The lack of availability of computers or laptops in classrooms (the computer suite is still the most favoured organizational decision for many primary schools) is as much the reason for this as children's levels of mastery of the keyboard. Given the ease of the reorganization of text and correction of misplaced letters and words with a word processor, this can, at one level, seem a missed opportunity. Perhaps this will change in a short space of time as affordable computers designed especially with the needs of young children in mind begin to become available for home and school purchase.

Some academics (for example, Stainthorp, 2004b) recommend the teaching of typing skills from reception age, alongside handwriting skills when anticipating the increasing use of technology to write in the future. Certainly this would be a great improvement on the 'hunt and peck' approach to keyboards of many people of my generation. The use of word processors by very young children, alongside learning to write with pencils and paper, has many strengths and advantages. Interestingly, one of the early and thought-provoking software writing programs, 'Developing Tray', is still available from www.devtray.co.uk.

Talking word processors are the ultimate for ease of composition. Generic software tools such as 'Clicker 5' or 'Textease' with either embedded or topic-specific and adaptable word banks can be valuable, as can facilities which allow the children to hear a word read aloud or read their own text back to them. Children are supported into appreciating the nature of the alphabetic code system, just as with handwriting, but with a greater level of reinforcement, through first identifying the sound to be represented, then finding the appropriate letter on the keyboard (perhaps using an overlay) and then having a perfect representation of the letter appear on the screen. Any alterations can be managed painlessly. There is some evidence that conventional spelling is more easily memorized and reinforced by typing and presentation on the screen (Bowell et al., 1994).

Guided Writing is most effective with a small group of children clustered around the computer as they can see the text clearly as it is developing. The format and presentation can be adapted also for different purposes around a range of options to make a professional-looking product and several copies to take home too. In Key Stage 1 children also have the opportunity, with adult support, to develop their own talking books with animation and sound effects – literacy learning is enhanced as is the awareness of design principles, and visual literacy as images and text work together to achieve the intended outcome. Some search engines (for example, www.altavista.com) allow searches for sound files.

Writing branching stories with multimedia authoring software such as Hyperstudio or 2Create from 2Simple, or using simple draw programs such as MyWorld, allow children to write texts with multiple developments or story paths. These provide opportunity for discussion and debate about the decision-making processes and individual notions of appropriateness.

Suggested resources

Scally's World of Verbs, a CD–ROM with a handbook, storybook and an Intellikeys keyboard for literacy activities. Options exist, for example, Watch and Say and Watch and Write, to develop early skills.

Learning and the Internet

The Internet is a powerful resource for practitioners and teachers in the early years, but Buckingham argues convincingly that at some level critical engagement with the content needs to take place. He says 'The internet is now essentially an unregulated commercial medium, a medium for selling; and while this does not necessarily undermine its educational value, it does mean that it can no longer be seen merely as a neutral conduit for information' (Buckingham, 2005: 7). While searching websites is probably beyond the capabilities of most pupils of 3–7 years without adult support for individuals and small groups, websites offer reviews of books and software, share ideas for good practice as well as provide reference material and information. Downloading worksheets is not to be recommended except after close scrutiny, as they are rarely appropriate for a specific group of young children. Visiting the web pages through the Children's Literature Web Guide of a children's author is an intriguing addition to the pleasure of sharing of the current class story.

Virtual experiences are possible too – teachers can visit websites such as Google Earth where children can explore planets, appreciate what our planet looks like from space, see aerial views of countries, mountains and river beds, and so on. In investigations in geography and history, where much is beyond the day-to-day experience of pupils, technology offers much enjoyment and educational benefit from these opportunities.

Summary

The Rose Report is cautious about the impact of ICT on the learning of literacy and writes:

> The range of ICT initiatives and programmes available to settings and schools has grown apace in recent years. Discussions with providers suggest that reading especially phonic work, is an area for further growth. Users will need to be sure not only that they have the expertise to exploit these resources but also that the ICT resources themselves are fit for purpose and money. (DfES, 2006: 25)

Perhaps the issue is more a philosophical one. This chapter has discussed how the use of a range of ICT can deepen and extend learning in the early years setting and classroom through motivating and engaging children; not only in the way digital media can assist children as they learn to become literate but also how they develop ways of learning about the world. Challenges exist for professionals, which are somewhat in tension. The first is that educational settings need to take into account the out-of-school lives of children and to maximize the potential of the peer culture and their pupils' enthusiasm for the digital media. The second is to ensure that the technology used in settings and schools is appropriate and worthy of adoption. This necessitates that all educationalists truly engage with what is on offer. As Buckingham suggests:

> The school could and should be playing a much more positive role in providing both critical perspectives on technology and creative opportunities to use it. Media literacy – including digital media literacy itself – should be seen as a core curriculum entitlement for all children, and an indispensable requirement for modern life. Ultimately, this means that we need to stop thinking merely in terms of technology, and start thinking afresh about learning, communication and culture. (2005: 27).

Further reading

Buckingham, D. (2005) *Schooling the Digital Generation: Popular Culture, New Media and the Future of Education.* Professorial lecture at the Institute of Education, University of London, October. ISBN. 085473726 X.

Mallet, M. (2003) *Early Years Non-Fiction: A Guide to Helping Young Researchers Use Information Texts.* London: RoutledgeFalmer. (Chapter 10.)

Chapter **12**

Children who Find Learning to Read and Write Difficult

Reading affects everything that you do.

(Matthew, cited in Stanovich, 1986)

Introduction

Both professionally and personally I have known children who entered the reception class reading fluently, or once there, appeared with minimal support to learn to read as if by magic. Appropriate, differentiated teaching is essential for these children who learn to read successfully and easily so that they maintain their headstart and continue to progress in keeping with their ability. But a book devoted to the learning and teaching of oracy and literacy would be seriously flawed without a section that addresses the relatively small, but significant, group of children who find learning to read and write difficult.

Children develop and learn at very different rates and a wide range can be found in what might be described as meeting the criteria for 'normal' development. While this is so, in every class, in every school there will be a varying (between 10 and 20 per cent on average but rising to 40 per cent in areas of very high deprivation) percentage of pupils who do not progress in literacy in line with their peers. Marie Clay, the originator of the Reading Recovery programme which now operates in most of the English-speaking world, predicts that, however effective the teaching programme in primary schools, there are a minority of pupils who will remain in need of diagnosis and some type of additional support if they are to learn to read and write.

Why do some children appear not to benefit from class teaching programmes?

Clay (1992) suggests that there will always be a 'tail' of underachievement in any classroom setting. Some of these children will not have had the opportunity before school to experience literacy as a meaningful, purposeful and, most importantly, enjoyable activity. In addition, pupils may struggle with learning to read and write for the following reasons:

> Children differ from one another in intelligence, language, cultural, organic or psychological competencies that interact with learning ...
>
> Some children do not achieve well in our classrooms because they cannot get to grips with the setting and the culture of the classroom, or with our teaching or the tasks we set them.
>
> The first year of school is a time of many sicknesses and absences, and the individual lives of children are full of dramas and crises.
>
> Once we begin to teach children we create differences between them in rates of progress. (Clay, 1992: 71)

Given the previous chapters of this book reveal the complexity of the reading and writing processes, it is small wonder then that some individuals will have problems with their mastery. Educational psychologists have drawn up frameworks that explain the interrelated nature of learning problems, of which difficulty in learning with literacy often causes the most distress and concern.

The Rose Report quotes the Special Educational Needs Code of Practice:

> It should be recognized that some difficulties in learning may be caused or exacerbated by the school's learning environment or adult/child relationships. This means looking carefully at such matters as classroom organization, teaching style and differentiation in order to decide how these can be developed so that the child is enabled to learn effectively. (DfES, 2006: 43)

Blagg (1981) considers that the factors that affect the child's ability to learn, namely, the physical, cognitive, social and emotional factors, and those that affect attitude and learning style, present a problem that needs to be viewed within a broad conceptual framework. Blagg suggests that this framework should encompass the dimensions of the situation from a *within the family*, *within the child* and *within the school* perspective.

This kind of interrelated framework reminds the early years practitioner and teacher that the cause of a difficulty is rarely unitary and, if not addressed from a multi-faceted point of view, the various separate factors multiply in their effect on the child's functioning. The underlying cause of the learning difficulty can be seen to be exacerbated or ameliorated by the child's home and school situation in the following examples.

Learning and Teaching Suggestions: Three Case Studies

Winston

Six-year-old Winston is the youngest child of five children, all of whom attend the local primary school. He is absent regularly from class and when he does attend he is often late for school owing to the pressure experienced by his mother of getting all the children out in the mornings. Winston is a friendly rather vague little boy. He has integrated rather superficially into school. He is happy enough to be there but without any real engagement or positive contribution to discussions or the life of the class. He appears to be happiest when working with construction materials particularly 'big bricks' or playing in the home corner on his own. After 14 months at school Winston has made little progress with reading and writing. His parents are beginning to be concerned.

Analysis of Winston's 'problem'

Winston knows books are for pleasure and information, he has acquired some of the concepts about print, recognizes a few letters of the alphabet but is unsure of the sounds that they make and is still at the scribble-writing stage of mark-making.

Within the child – owing to poor attendance and his frequent late arrivals this child feels slightly on the outside of the school culture, in addition to which he frequently misses the explanation to 'tune' him in to the tasks and teaching at the start of the day.

Within the family – Winston is the youngest child in a slightly chaotic, disorganized, noisy family situation. He has had little individual attention from an adult before school. His speech development was delayed, but not at the level of clinical concern, which is most likely due to the lack of one-to-one conversations of the quality and type that promote language development (see Chapter 1). Following on from this, Winston's pre-school experiences of print, books and stories have been limited and he came into reception class with only vague notions of texts and print and the way that they work. His home life also has given him few opportunities to develop the ability to learn how to learn, to concentrate and to focus on sedentary tasks.

Within the school – the teacher is newly qualified and only just coping with the organization of the learning for the 30 other pupils in her class. She is caring but has not fully come to grips with being able to differentiate work for her class, so reluctantly leaves Winston to the teaching assistant who works with him on his reading and writing. The relative inexperience of the class teacher means that she has not fully assessed Winston and so has been unable to analyse exactly what he knows and does not know about literacy. Therefore, she is not aware of what he needs to learn before further progress can be made. This assessment needs to occur before any additional teaching approaches and resources can be considered.

What do you consider to be the main priority for Winston to enable him to be placed on a learning path?

[handwritten margin note: Difficult to read and write]

Bernice

Bernice is 5 years old, a happy but rather disobedient little girl. She appears to ignore instructions, frequently failing to complete the tasks set for her. The class teacher, who is very experienced, is concerned that after two terms in the reception class Bernice is making no connections between print and sound when either reading or writing.

Analysis of Bernice's difficulty

She enjoys stories and looking at books and has acquired most of the concepts about print. She can identify and label the letters of the alphabet by name. Her reading is accomplished through memorizing the text and a small sight vocabulary; she makes no attempt to word-build. Her independent writing is still at the scribble-writing stage or with the random use of letters.

Within the child – during her three terms at the nursery, it was recorded that Bernice was frequently absent with upper-respiratory infections. Through one-to-one conversations with the child, the reception teacher has had opportunity to identify a possible hearing difficulty. A referral to the school medical service resulted in a diagnosis of **glue ear**. This condition can cause varying degrees of hearing loss. The deafness, although often inter-mittent in nature, blunts auditory discrimination. This, in turn, affects reading progress particularly in the early stages. Typically the child is often unable to distinguish aurally between ma**n**, ma**d** and ma**t**.

Key Term

Glue ear: a medical condition in which repeated ear infections have resulted in a build-up of a thick, glue-like liquid in the inner ear.

Within the family – Bernice comes from a relaxed family the members of which believe in children being supported with their education, but not put under pressure. They share the books with her from the home–school reading scheme but are not concerned with how well she is progressing.

Within the school – Bernice's class occupies a large room, adjacent to the parallel recep-tion class with a shared resources area for painting, model-making and construction. On occasions there are 50 or 60 children working in the area as a whole. The noise levels are high.

What do you consider to be the main issue in this situation?

What should the class teacher do before and after the medical condition has been remedied?

The Rose Report makes a valid point when it says: 'An obvious, sometimes overlooked, first response to concerns about early reading difficulties must be to make sure that the child has been reliably assessed for medical conditions such as sight and hearing problems that can be easily corrected. Thereafter consideration should be given to providing targeted intervention' (DfES, 2006: 41).

Adam

Adam has been in school for two years, and at 7, he has made only a beginning with reading. He writes very little and when he does it is ill-formed, and his invented spelling shows little letter–sound correspondence. His class teacher is puzzled by this as he is articulate and demonstrates good general knowledge, he loves stories and looking at books and is of average ability at mathematics. Adam's parents are now very anxious as the younger brother in the reception class is progressing more rapidly than Adam on the school reading scheme.

Analysis of Adam's 'problem'

Within the child – Adam came to school with high expectations, he was motivated to read, coming from a family in which books and literacy are given high status. Once at school Adam had difficulties making letter–sound connections (GPC) in both reading and writing. He has acquired a small sight vocabulary of 20 or so words, which he can recognize when reading, but can only spell about five of them. He has problems distinguishing between some letters of the alphabet (for example, d/b, g/p and m/n/h/) and in remembering the sequence of the letters in words, even, on occasions, in his own second name. Both his visual memory and aural memory are poor. He is able to predict words from the global and local context well.

Within the family – initially the parents worked hard with Adam to develop his reading. They read books with him several times a week to practise. The unfavourable comparison with his younger brother, now has made Adam's parents increasingly worried. The relationship between the two boys is fast becoming an issue; Adam is beginning to be naughty both at home and at school.

Within the school – for two years Adam has been taught within the standard school literacy provision. The previous teacher identified a learning difficulty but after some extra reading help, when some progress was made, she had considered that Adam would soon 'catch up'. The current class teacher, now, believes that the time has come for Adam to be formally assessed by the educational psychologist.

What do you think is the most worrying aspect of Adam's problem?

What makes the problems experienced by Adam different from those of Bernice?

Would the same teaching approach in class be useful to them both?

These case studies indicate clearly how learning difficulties are often multi-factorial and the more dimensions to a problem there are, the greater the disabling effect of each one. In other words, the separate influence of each factor is multiplied several times, as the impact accumulates one on the other. Conversely, a difficulty such as a hearing loss or **dyslexia** can be compensated for by an enabling, supportive home and school situation.

Key Term

Dyslexia: this literally means difficulty with reading. It is a complex syndrome in which children often present, on a continuum of severity, both visual and aural perceptual and sequencing difficulties that appear not to have been caused by inappropriate teaching, general low intelligence or be the result of poor motivation to learn to read and write.

Factors in children experiencing difficulties with literacy

Children who are making a slow start with learning to read and write may be experiencing one or several of the following difficulties.

Physical factors

These factors affect children's ability to benefit from the school provision. The state of a child's general health affects enthusiasm, concentration and receptiveness to learning opportunities. The adequacy of hearing, eyesight, speech and motor skills will affect literacy development in obvious and direct ways. Following the diagnosis of a physical impairment adaptation of the learning environment will be required in terms of specialized equipment, and, in the case of hearing loss, a reduction of extraneous background noise might need to be considered.

In Bernice's case, her deafness, once diagnosed, is relatively easy to remedy through medical intervention. Drainage tubes (often called grommits) can be placed into the inner ear to keep it free of liquid, and this should restore hearing ability.

Social and emotional factors

These factors have great potential to either boost or damage a child's personal coping mechanisms. A challenge to certain personality characteristics such as sensitivity, confidence, maturity, sociability, stress tolerance and so on, in either the parents or the child, will affect the quality of their relationship and the bond between them. This in turn influences the child's perception of self-worth, and feeling of being supported and valued. Children with poor self-esteem have notoriously low reserves of perseverance and risk-taking ability, which reduces their success in any learning situation but in the huge challenge that learning to read presents it can be even more disabling.

Cognitive factors

These factors cover the range of abilities such as receptive and expressive language skills; verbal and non-verbal reasoning ability; visual and auditory perceptual skills; and visual and auditory long- and short-term memory functions. The literacy-specific skills of phonological and orthographic processing are included as a subset within these. This is expanded upon later in this chapter.

Encompassed in this category of learning difficulty is a specific learning difficulty or **dyslexia**. Adam, in our case study, may be an example of this type of specific learning difficulty.

These factors have a great potential to influence the child's capacity to learn to read. The positive attitudes of parents towards education, literacy and their expectations of, and for, the child are key features in achievement of success at school.

Through these parental attitudes the child's own confidence, interest and expectations in turn are moulded, and rebound on the outcomes for the child for either good or ill. The qualities of persistence and concentration are fostered through positive role models and satisfying, enriching literacy opportunities both at home and at school, which reinforce a sense of the worthwhile nature of the task.

Literacy difficulties: early diagnosis and intervention

The Rose Report discusses the 'three waves' of intervention currently suggested in the UK, in paragraph 133 of the Review:

> The Primary National Strategy distinguishes three 'waves' of teaching and intervention which adequately cover the range of provision that best supports children with significant difficulties. It is important to recognize that these 'waves' signify types of provision and not categories of children. High quality phonic work, as defined by the review, should be a key feature of the provision in each of these 'waves':
>
> - Wave 1 – the effective, inclusion of children in daily 'quality first teaching'
> - Wave 2 – additional interventions to enable children to work at age-related expectations or above

- Wave 3 – additional, highly personalized interventions, for example, specifically targeted approaches for children identified as requiring SEN support (on School Action, School Action Plus, or with a statement of special educational needs). (DfES, 2006: 41–2)

The Code of Practice for children with special educational needs (DfES, 2001) firmly places the initial responsibility for helping children with literacy difficulties in the hands of the school. It is necessary for the class teacher to be both aware of children who are not making the progress that might be expected of them through first, information collected at school entry or, secondly, through the continuous assessment of pupils. This enhances the class teacher's ability to be proactive in implementing an appropriate programme of differentiated teaching.

The conscious and public recognition of slower than 'normal' progress is problematic for most early years teachers. Not only is it in the mind-set of these individuals to be both unwilling to label pupils as having a problem, but also teachers wish to give very young children a chance to adjust to the school system and to mature as learners. One might have easily argued this way about Winston and Adam in our case studies.

Early detection and action is important on many counts

- It is essential that confusions about written text are quickly resolved. Early inappropriate literacy behaviour can become entrenched, which is much harder to rectify later.
- An early successful start to literacy sets the child on the path to academic achievement; learning to read becomes reading to learn and access to the whole curriculum is curtailed by an inability to read.
- A sense of competence and self-worth is easily bruised and affects the whole of the child's functioning.
- Early intervention often makes a complete recovery possible and renders unnecessary expensive remedial support later in school life.

Detection of difficulty

Even an inexperienced teacher will become concerned about a reception class child if no progress has been made between the first assessment, on admission, and the next, which occurs after a few weeks in school (see Chapters 3 and 4). Most children will have developed from the baseline assessment in terms of confidence and conceptual understandings about print and with texts. Teachers will recognize the progress that has been made in some or all of the following measures.

Early literacy behaviours

- The ability to talk about stories and their illustrations.
- The awareness of the concepts about print.
- Knowledge of letter names and sounds.
- The ability to hear and separate sounds in words.
- The ability to write their own name and a few words.
- The ability to concentrate for longer periods will be evident.

All these skills and concepts will develop once the receptive child is in a formal school literacy programme. If a difficulty is noticed, however minor or potentially transient, the class teacher will need to discuss the child with the special educational needs co-ordinator (SENCO). Monitoring the child may be sufficient for a short passage of time or the next step may be taken immediately.

   More extensive and specific assessment will be undertaken, if and when it is considered appropriate, perhaps on the lines of Clay's (2002) *Observational Survey of Early Literacy Achievement* in order to establish the nature and extent of the literacy difficulty. The next stage, which is at the first level of the special needs Code of Conduct, would be to record the concern following the requirements of the school or local authority policy, and so inform the parents officially who should then be invited to come to school to discuss the situation. What needs to happen next? Views and individual situations vary.

Different views of remedial teaching and their theoretical bases

Earlier in this volume (see the Introduction and Chapter 6) and elsewhere (Riley, 1996) I have argued that in order for early years teachers to be effective teachers of literacy they need to have a clear idea of the cognitive processes involved. It needs to be stated also that when children begin to experience difficulties with learning to read and write, the class teacher needs to have not only an understanding of the literacy process but also an idea of what is going amiss with the processing. In addition, she/he needs to be well informed about the approaches that experimental psychology tells us are effective in order to enable the child to make progress.

   If we consider the separate processes that take place within the activity of reading, it makes sense that these separate processes need support. The question is which of these processes is most likely to be poorly developed when the child fails to learn to read. Teachers who adopt traditional remedial methods reply to the question very clearly and loudly that the fault lies with the decoding skills and that these have not been learned thoroughly. Commonly, in junior schools and secondary remedial departments the methods of teaching adopted are overwhelmingly phonic instruction approaches such as 'Alpha and Omega' covering the 1001 ways to teach letter–sound relationships, Phono-Graphix TM or THRASS. These approaches result in varying degrees of success for probably a number of reasons. The children being older, have struggled for longer, have lost heart and often have fallen behind their peers with their work in other curriculum subjects. A programme of phonics and more phonics does not appear to be the complete answer.

Reading Recovery for children at Wave 3

Other systems of support adopt a more holistic approach to intervention. Reading Recovery is a school-based early intervention system for young children beginning to fall behind their peers and has been designed for all the reasons cited earlier. Reading Recovery works on a 'prevention being better than cure' principle and it is highly effective (Hurry, 1995). Hobsbaum (1997) maintains that 80 per cent of the children who enter the programme, as the lowest achievers of their age group, are able to work in their classes as capable readers and writers in approximately 20 weeks, and that only one child in five in this group of delayed readers will need further support. It is undeniably expensive, at the point of delivery, for two reasons: first, the teachers have to be trained to operate the programme; secondly, children in the Reading Recovery programme need daily one-to-one tuition in half-hour sessions for a period of between 12 and 20 weeks. It is argued, however, that this cost is minimal compared with statementing an older child and/or instigating remedial teaching over many years. Certainly it is possible to justify Reading Recovery on humanitarian grounds alone.

Clay describes the programme as one that 'was developed from an interactionist view of reading (reading continuous text), based on information theory which emphasises how knowledge, strategies and processes at each level of language organisation expand and become interrelated' (Clay, 1992: 70). What the child knows about letters, sounds, syntax, meanings, stories and various kinds of texts is applied to reading and writing tasks simultaneously in both integrated and separate ways. Reading Recovery teachers enable children to build these bodies of knowledge and develop links and interrelationships across both reading and writing. A key concept in the change over time in a successful reader and writer is the strategies which the active, constructive learner comes to apply to problem-solving tasks. Reading Recovery assumes that, whatever the origins of their low achievements, less successful readers have to learn to work in the way that successful readers work.

The Reading Recovery lesson

Each lesson aims to promote this type of problem solving through engaging the child in several literacy tasks in the daily half-hour session. Children in the Reading Recovery programme have opportunities to:

- discuss and work through understandings of stories and other texts
- revise and consolidate known sight vocabulary in a variety of tasks
- develop and integrate the four text processing strategies (see Figure 5.1 in Chapter 5)

- develop reading strategies with texts and apply them reciprocally when writing
- operate within the alphabetic system through writing and then reading
- segment the sounds within spoken words when both reading and writing
- develop appropriate strategies when reading continuous text to use comprehension processing of prediction drawing on context, syntax and background knowledge and then cross-checking through use of decoding skills and self-correcting strategies.

This standard format for the lesson also provides the Reading Recovery teacher with rich data for analysing the child's performance in order to monitor progress. There is, therefore, provision for a direct assessment, planning and teaching cycle which allows for the programme to be tailored to individual learning within the suggested tasks.

Reading Recovery is currently available in 28 local education authorities in the UK with over 1000 trained Reading Recovery teachers, but this leaves a considerable shortfall if all the children (approximately 10–20 per cent of the school population) at risk of reading failure are to be reached.

The Fischer Family Trust (FFT) programme

Other programmes of support at the Wave 3 level of intervention involve the training and capacity-building of teaching assistants. The aims of the programme are to enable children to participate more fully in the literacy hour and develop sufficient skills and knowledge to benefit from a Wave 2 intervention. For those who continue to experience difficulties, the daily lesson records provide an evidence base for future action, for example individual education plans (IEPs), School Action Plus, and so on.

The FFT programme trains teaching assistants (TAs) to undertake Reading Recovery-type sessions with a carefully selected population of pupils who need a boost to their literacy learning. The programme gives a structure for the alternating daily reading and writing sessions. However, detailed daily lesson plans are not provided, as each child will have a different starting point as identified through the diagnostic assessments. Critical to the success of the intervention is the partnership between the class teacher and the TA. Both should attend the training together and the class teacher should mentor the TA. The early signs from the pilot are promising, the programme proves especially effective when TAs are able to work regularly with the children (preferably daily) and where a Reading Recovery teacher can offer additional support.

What should schools do at the first stage of intervention (Wave 2)?

Given the demands of the classroom, what is it within the Reading Recovery programme that a hard-pressed class teacher can usefully adopt and which of the various ingredients of the Clay session structure are likely to be the most effective and economical of time in terms of results for the child? In other words, what should the class teacher concentrate on and using which approach can she be confident of success? Which aspect of reading should be focused upon? The comprehension or word recognition skills? A combination of both? Should it be either one or the other depending on the outcome of the individual child's assessment? Where does more instruction in phonics come in?

Given that we know that children with well-developed phonological skills are very much more likely to be successful at learning to read (see Chapter 3) than those who do not have those skills, it is likely that a programme that concentrates on learning letter–sound relationships will be valuable. But will it be sufficient? I have already suggested that the time-honoured remedial programmes that focus on this approach to the exclusion of all else have not had impressive results.

Research evidence for the effectiveness of different class-based programmes

A study by Hatcher et al. (1994) sheds some light on this issue. The researchers designed a study with 128 Year 2 children experiencing literacy difficulties who were randomly selected to undergo any one of three intervention programmes or to be in a non-intervention control group. The three programmes covered different theoretical standpoints. The children received additional support in programmes that provided extra help through concentrating on:

- reading alone
- phonological training alone
- reading and phonological training.

The control group received the normal school programme.

The group who were given extra support with both phonological training and reading made the most progress. Hatcher et al. consider that this is the result of a phenomenon that they call their phonological linkage hypothesis. This is explained very simply by recognizing that phonological training is only really useful if it is immediately linked to reading. In other words, children who are experiencing difficulty probably cannot make the connections for themselves between being able to discriminate the sounds in spoken language and their connection with print on the page when reading and writing, as many children are able to do. These delayed readers are not able to operate within the alphabetic code, so they need to be shown explicitly how it works.

Information about how this can be achieved in schools and classrooms is provided by Enters and Brooks (2005) in their booklet for the Basic Skills Agency, *Boosting Reading in Primary Schools*. This offers information to headteachers and their special educational needs (SEN) staff about various schemes which aim to develop the child's meaning-gaining strategies, and abilities in phonics and fluency. Fluency is used here to describe the print-processing skills of word recognition, through specifically designed programmes of teaching activities, games and tasks. This organizing framework of the booklet overlays well onto the Adams model of processing arriving at meaning through the use of context, syntax and semantics, the child having first grasped the concepts about print. Also the word recognition skills are addressed through the support of the mutually reinforcing skills of phonological and orthographic awareness.

Implications for practice

Developing provision and support for the child experiencing difficulties

The children may still be at the National Curriculum pre-Level 1 stage of literacy development described in Chapters 3 and 4. The assessment of their understanding of concepts about print (see Clay, 2002) is the starting point for an assessment of their ability to identify and label the letters of the alphabet by both names and sounds.

As with the Primary National Strategy: Framework for teaching literacy (DfES, 2006) all teaching of beginning literacy needs to focus on text-level work and with the provision of a book that is within the child's capability at 95 per cent accuracy level. This may be a simple caption book at the earliest stages of reading schemes. At this precarious stage of literacy development it is important that the child reads many short books for the reward of satisfaction and access to the whole story. Books with a sense of narrative are valuable at this early stage of competence to support the child into the meaning and to offer a sense of satisfaction on completion. The purpose of reading needs to be reinforced through emphasis on comprehension and the prediction skills with the use of both global and local context cues (see Chapters 3 and 4). The level of the book used with the child is crucial. Children experiencing difficulties must not lose sight of the enjoyment of reading and any book attempted needs to have exactly the right level of challenge, but she/he should not find more than one word in 15–20 too difficult to read. A text that is harder than that for the child will make it impossible for the child's meaning-making strategies to operate.

The publication *Book Bands* (Reading Recovery National Network, 2003) is useful here as it indicates the different levels of books from published reading schemes. This provides invaluable guidance for teachers so that only very gradual increases in text difficulty are introduced to a struggling pupil. (See Chapter 6 for further discussion about the appropriate match of book to child.)

National Curriculum (pre-Level 1)

Observation of the child reading

This supplementary list (see the teaching suggestions in Chapters 4 and 5) covers some of the understandings indicated by the literacy behaviours that are characteristically displayed by the delayed reader still at this stage of development.

Literacy behaviour displayed by the child:

- voluntarily choosing and enjoying books
- reconstructing the story through both acting like a reader and retelling the narrative in the accurate sequence
- concentrating and focusing on the activity for a reasonable and appropriate time span.

An understanding of the literacy task is demonstrated by:

- knowing that print has a communicative function
- being aware of and making use of environmental print, that is, recognizing name tags/labels /notices/messages
- knowing the conventions of print and being able to distinguish

  - between the correct orientation of a book/the front and back covers
  - that the illustrations and text tell the story in different but complementary ways
  - where you start reading, even when it is not the typical left-hand corner of page
  - knowing where the text flows even if it is not the typical sweep back on line
  - where to start reading on the following page

and being able to match the spoken word with the printed word.

Approaches for the child arrested in National Curriculum pre-Level 1 stage

The appropriate match of book to child enables the teacher to work with the child by, first, undertaking a book introduction before reading and then by encouraging the child to:

- talk about the story
- talk about the illustrations
- guess what might happen in the story

and then

- retell the story using the pictures alone.

Sound awareness (phonological awareness) is developed by:

- playing games orally with rhyming words starting with words that rhyme in the book just read
- playing games with pictures of rhyming pairs (see a commercially produced version in Reason and Boote, 1994: 101 ff.)
- learning and chanting well-known nursery rhymes, playing with the rhyming words by substituting ones that do not rhyme or alternative ones that do.

Print awareness (orthographic awareness) is developed by:

- identifying individual distinctive words in books
- matching words with word cards
- matching letters by sight with letter cards (special note should be made of children who have difficulty distinguishing between letters that have similar shapes, for example, p/b/d ... m/n ... f/t ... g/q ... h/n ... r/n ...w/m ... v/w
- consolidation of letter knowledge through identification with both names and sounds
- playing games to learn the recommended PNS high-frequency words in a reading book
- rearranging word cards into simple sentences.

Additional teaching note

Handwriting practice develops not only the correct formation of letter shapes but also reinforces letter–sound association. Also note that it is at this stage that print and sound awareness become more strongly linked and mutually reinforcing as the children begin to have access to and understand the links between spoken and written language through their own writing.

National Curriculum Level 1 (early stage)

Observation of the child reading

The following list of literacy behaviours that demonstrate understanding and progress are characteristically displayed by the child at this delayed stage of literacy development:

Literacy behaviour is displayed by:

- an ability to read text from the previous day with support
- pointing accurately word by word as s/he or adult reads, that is, with one-to-one correspondence of word to unit of sound.

Understanding of the literacy task is demonstrated by indicating a more advanced awareness of concepts of print:

- an awareness of punctuation
- knowing the difference between capital and lower-case letters
- knowing the terms letter and word.

Also:

- being able to discuss the story plot at literal level
- beginning to appreciate that long words when spoken will require a correspondingly long symbol when written, that is, noticing that it must be **bicycle** not **bike**
- being able to read accurately words containing the same letters but in different or reverse order, for example, *was/saw*.

Print-processing skills of the child are demonstrated by:

- accurate knowledge of the alphabet
- recognizing a few high-frequency words out of context
- having acquired a small sight vocabulary linked to her/his interests/ the reading scheme/and knowledge of all the reception year Primary National Strategy: Framework for teaching literacy (DfES, 2006) high-frequency words.

Approaches for the child in National Curriculum Level 1 (early stage)

Children at this stage are moving from the emergent literacy phase towards the beginning of conventional reading. This means that they are just beginning to get to grips with the alphabetic system. Word-skills teaching can be developed effectively from the context, practice and consolidation of the child's reading book from the previous day and self-chosen words used when writing. Work continues to aim to build prediction skills using the meaning to inform problem-solving. Ask questions such as, 'What do you think is going to happen?' Different types of texts with different formats and patterns of language should be used in order to familiarize the child with several literary models.

Sound awareness (phonological awareness) can be additionally supported by:

- an ability to read and write single letter sounds
- choosing appropriate words from the text and by asking children to supply words that rhyme, for example, mill----------- hill, fill, pill, kill, till, chill. Write them for the children asking them to spell the word for you as she/he begins to recognize the pattern and understand the task
- generating other rhyming games from the book read by the child...... choosing a sentence and inventing a rhyming couplet for it, for example, The boy can see his Mum. *His Mum will pat his tum!* The more nonsensical the more fun the child will have
- encouraging the child to play 'I Spy' which is the ability to separate onset and rime
- practising reading vowel–consonant words, for example, it, at, on, in
- practising reading consonant–vowel–consonant words, for example, man, sun, rat, pot, pit, and so on
- helping child to hear the syllables in words beginning with children's names, for example, say 'Can you listen carefully? I am going to say some people's names in bits ... can you clap once for each bit of the word ... Ben-jam-in, Jen-ny, Da-vid', and so on.

Print awareness (orthographic awareness, now word recognition) is supported by helping children to:

- make the child's own version of a book on the same theme as a favourite book, perhaps personalized, using the child's name as the main character
- choose words that extend their sight vocabulary from the book, and take words from the PNS high-frequency words. Children should learn to both read and write them.

National Curriculum Level 1 (later stage)

Observation of the child reading

This is a list of literacy behaviours demonstrating understanding and progress characteristically displayed by the child at this delayed stage of literacy development.

Progress in literacy is displayed by:

- greater fluency due to increasing sight vocabulary and improving word building strategies
- starting to show awareness of mismatch by self-correcting, plus evidence of scanning ahead
- spelling becoming more conventional when writing using invented spelling with her/his own text.

Understanding of the literacy task is demonstrated by:

- being able to use all the four cueing systems – *context* (including picture cue), *syntax*, the *look of the word*, that is, length/distinctive features, and *phonic analysis* (see Figure 5.1). The use of the strategies may be erratic with over-reliance on first one then another cue depending on individual strengths, but nevertheless the awareness of the different strategies for decoding print is developing
- beginning to consider the plot and character of the story in greater detail.

Print-processing skills of the child are demonstrated by:

- having an increasing sight word vocabulary of high-frequency words.

Approaches for the child in National Curriculum Level 1 (later stage)

Use the activities as appropriate for the earlier stages. The child will have moved from the logographic phase through to the alphabetic phase of print processing and will have both strategies at her/his disposal for reading and writing.

Progress in literacy is demonstrated by:

- increasing awareness of mismatch and self-corrects
- reading ahead to problem-solve when not able to read a word
- ability to see 'little words' in 'big words'

- occasionally being able to analyse whole letter strings and not just decode letter by letter (that is, moving towards the phase of orthographic print processing)
- an increasingly expressive reading voice.

Use a range of books with a child, ensuring that these have varying vocabulary, language structures and patterns, and that they focus on enjoyment and humour. Following reading, encourage discussion about the book, its meaning and any subtleties should continue to reinforce the purpose of and satisfaction in reading. Give praise where positive strategies occurred; in other words, make explicit what the child knows and can do when reading a text.

Sound awareness (phonological awareness) is supported by:

- making explicit the grapheme–phoneme association (GPC) when reading and writing
- encouraging reading and writing of words with consonant blends, for example, truck, slim, grass
- encouraging reading and writing of words with consonant digraphs, for example, shop, chip, thrush
- using knowledge of at least initial sounds to act as a cue in order to make a choice between two or three words when reading connected text
- using analogy to help write new words from known ones, for example, t-**ook** from l-**ook**.

Print awareness (orthographic awareness/word recognition) is developed by:

- practising sight vocabulary with games, context sentence cards (both commercial and teacher-made), with and without pictures
- using correct spellings of a few common words in the course of her/his own writing. These will be words within children's sight vocabulary. When constructing own text their attention can be drawn to the standard spelling (of one or two words only) with word lists in the classroom or personal word banks when appropriate and in context
- continuing to learn high-frequency words in Primary National Strategy: Framework for teaching literacy (DfES, 2006)

Children who are still causing concern after this type of additional support and differentiated teaching within the early years classroom will require further attention following discussions with the SENCO and the local authority SEN team. A within-school intervention may be recommended before the need of an assessment from an outside agency such as the School Psychological Service. After this decisions will be made regarding further appropriate action to be taken and, by using such evidence, more informed judgements can be made about the most appropriate course of action in each individual case.

Summary

This chapter has discussed that learning difficulties are often multi-factorial and that the effect of each additional factor multiplies in impact increasingly adversely on the child's functioning. Early diagnosis is important as literacy difficulties become entrenched early, slowing the child's learning and affecting self-esteem. There are many kinds of intervention for children with literacy difficulties and three of these are addressed along with the theoretical rationales. The last part of the chapter makes suggestions for an individual programme for the children who have begun to slip behind their classmates, based on in-depth assessment of individual readers' literacy development and the implementation of customized support for effective literacy learning. The Rose Report, citing a US report on the prevention of reading difficulties, says: 'The way that a school meets the needs of all children has a direct bearing on the nature of the additional help required by children with special educational needs, and on the point the additional help is required' (DfES, 2006: 44).

Further reading

Clay, M. M. (2002) *An Observational Survey of Early Literacy Achievement.* 2nd edn. Auckland: Heinemann.

Enters, I. and Brooks, G. (2005) *Boosting Reading in Primary Schools.* London: DfES, for The Basic Skills Agency.

Reason, R. and Boote, R. (1994) *Helping Children with Reading and Spelling.* London: Routledge.

Bibliography

Adams, M.J. (1993) 'Beginning to read: an overview', in R. Beard (ed.), *Teaching Literacy and Balancing Perspectives*. London: Hodder and Stoughton.

Adams, M.J. (1996) *Beginning to Read: Thinking and Learning about Print*. 2nd edn. Cambridge, MA: MIT Press.

Arnold, H. (1996) 'Penguins never meet polar bears', in D. Whitebread (ed.), *Teaching and Learning in the Early Years*. London: Routledge.

Aubrey, C. (1993) 'An investigation of the mathematical competencies which young children bring to school', *British Educational Research Journal*, 19(1): 19–27.

Auden, W.H. (1963) *The Dyer's Hand*. London: Faber and Faber.

Baker, P. and Raban, B. (1991) 'Reading before and after the early days of schooling', *Reading*, April: 6–13.

Barron, R.W., Lovett, M.W. and McCabe, R. (1998) 'Using computers to remediate reading and spelling disabilities: the critical role of the print to sound unit', *Behaviour Research Methods Instruments and Computers*, 30: 610–16.

Beard, R. (1990) *Developing Reading 3–13*. 2nd edn. London: Hodder and Stoughton.

Beard, R. (ed.) (1993) *Teaching Literacy Balancing Perspectives*. London: Hodder and Stoughton.

Beard, R. (1999) *National Literacy Strategy: Review of Research and Other Related Evidence*. London: DfEE and Standards and Effectiveness Unit.

Beard, R. (2000) *Developing Writing 3–13*. London: Hodder and Stoughton.

Bereiter, C. and Scardamalia, M. (1993) 'Composing and writing', in R. Beard (ed.), *Teaching Literacy Balancing Perspectives*. London: Hodder and Stoughton.

Berniger, V.W. (1999) 'Co-ordinating transcription and text generation in working memory during composing: automatic and constructive processes', *Learning Disability Quarterly*, 18: 293–309.

Berniger, V.W., Yates, C., Cartwright, A., Rutberg, J., Remy, J. and Abbott, R. (1992) 'Lower-level developmental skills in beginning writing', *Reading and Writing: Interdisciplinary Journal*, 4, 257–80.

Bialystok, E. (1991) 'Letters, sounds and symbols: changes in children's understanding of written language', *Applied Psycholinguistics*, 12: 75–89.

Bialystok, E. (2001) *Bilingualism in Development : Language, Literacy and Cognition*. Cambridge: Cambridge University Press.

Bielby, N. (1994) *Making Sense of Reading: The New Phonics and its Practical Implications*. Leamington Spa: Scholastic.

Bielby, N. (1998) *How to Teach Reading: A Balanced Approach*. Leamington Spa: Scholastic.

Bielby, N. (1999) *Teaching Reading at Key Stage 2*. Cheltenham: Stanley Thornes.

Blagg, N. (1981) 'The diagnosis of learning difficulties', in Somerset Education Authority, *Ways and Means 2: Children with Learning difficulties*. Hong Kong: Globe Education.

Blatchford, P. (1991) 'Children writing at 7 years: associations with handwriting on school entry and pre-school factors', *British Journal of Educational Psychology*, 61: 73–84.

Blatchford, P. and Plewis, I. (1990) 'Pre-school reading related skills and later reading achievement: further evidence', *British Educational Research Journal*, 16(4): 425–28.

Blatchford, P., Burke, J., Farquhar, C., Plewis, I. and Tizard, B. (1987) 'Associations between pre-school reading related skills and later reading achievement', *British Educational Research Journal*, 13(1): 15–23.

Bond, G.L. and Dykstra, R. (1967) 'The co-operative research program in first grade reading instruction', *Reading Research Quarterly*, 2: 5–141.

Bowell, B., France, S. and Redfern, S. (1994) *Portable Computers in Action*. Coventry: National Centre for Educational Technology.

Bradley, L. and Bryant, P.E. (1983) 'Categorising sounds and learning to read: a causal connection', *Nature*. 310: 419–21.

Brooker, E. (2002) *Starting School: Young Children Learning Cultures*. Buckingham: Open University Press.

Brown, N. (1999) *Young Children's Literacy Development and the Role of Televisual Texts*. London: Falmer Press.

Browne, A. (1996) *Developing Language and Literacy 3–8*. London: Paul Chapman Publishing.

Browne, A. (1998) *A Practical Guide to Teaching Reading in the Early Years*. London: Paul Chapman Publishing.

Browning, E. Barrett (1978) 'Aurora Leigh: Fifth Book', 11. 139–222, in C. Cosman, J. Keefe, and K. Weaver (eds), *The Penguin Book of Women Poets*. London: Penguin.

Bruce, J. (1964) 'The analysis of word sounds', *British Journal of Educational Psychology*, 34: 154–70.

Bruner, J.S. (1983) *Child's Talk: Learning to Use Language*. Oxford: Oxford University Press.

Bryant, P.E. and Bradley, L. (1980) 'Why children sometimes write words which they do not read', in U. Frith (ed.), *Cognitive Processes in Spelling*. New York: Academic Press.

Bryant, P.E. and Bradley, L. (1985) *Children's Reading Problems*. Oxford: Blackwell.

Bryant, P.E., Bradley, L., Maclean, M. and Crossland, J. (1989) 'Nursery rhymes, phonological skills and reading', *Journal of Child Language*, 16: 407–28.

Buckingham, D. (2005) *Schooling the Digital Generation: Popular Culture, New Media and the Future of Education*. Professorial lecture at the Institute of Education, University of London, October. ISBN 085473726 X.

Cazden, C.B. (1988) *Interactions between Maori Children and Pakeha Teachers*. Auckland: Auckland Reading Association.

Chall, J.S. (1967) *Learning to Read: The Great Debate*. New York: McGraw-Hill.

Chapman, M.L. (2004) 'Phonemic awareness: clarifying what we know'. Retrieved 1 June 2004 from www.reading recovery.com/pdfs/LTLvol7no1 2/Chapman.pdf.

Chera, P.D.K. (2000) 'Multimeda CAL and early reading: iterative design, development, and evaluation'. Unpublished thesis, University of Bristol.

Chomsky, N. (1957) *Syntactic Structures*. The Hague: Mouton.

Clark, M.M. (1976) *Young Fluent Readers*. Oxford: Heinemann Educational.

Clarke, P. (1992) *English as a Second Language in Early Childhood*. Richmond, Victoria: Multicultural Resource Centre.

Clay, M.M. (1966) *Emergert Reading Behaviour*. Unpublished doctoral thesis. University of Auckland, NZ.

Clay, M.M. (1972b). *The Early Detection of Reading Difficulties: A Diagnostic Survey with Recovery Procedures*. Portsmouth, NH: Heinemann.

Clay, M.M. (1979) *Reading: The Patterning of Complex Behaviour*. Oxford: Heinemann Educational.

Clay, M.M. (1987) 'Implementing reading recovery: systematic adaptations to an education innovation', *New Zealand Journal of Education Studies*. 22(1): 35–58.

Clay, M.M. (1991) *Becoming Literate: The Construction of Inner Control*. Oxford: Heinemann.

Clay, M.M. (1992) 'A second chance to learn literacy', in T. Cline (ed.), *The Assessment of Special Educational Needs*. London and New York: Routledge.

Clay, M.M. (1993) *An Observational Survey of Early Literacy Achievement*. Portsmouth, NH: Heinemann.

Clay, M.M. (1998) *Different Paths to Literacy*. Oxford: Heinemann.

Clay, M.M. (2002) *An Observational Survey of Early Literacy Achievement.* 2nd edn. Auckland, NZ: Heinemann.

Clay, M.M. and Cazden, C.B. (1990) 'A Vygotskian interpretation of reading recovery', in L.C. Moll (ed.), *Vygotsky and Education.* Cambridge: Cambridge University Press.

Cipielewski, J. and Stanovich, K.E. (1992) 'Predicting growth in reading ability from children's exposure to print', *Journal of Experimental Child Psychology.* 54: 74–89.

Cox Committee (led into DES) (1988) *English in the National Curriculum.* London: HMSO.

Crevola, C.A. and Hill, P.W. (1998) 'Evaluation of a whole-school approach to prevention and intervention in early literacy', *Journal of Education for Students Placed at Risk* 3(2): 133–57.

Crystal, D. (1986) *Listen to your child: A parent's guide to Children's Language.* London: Penguin Books.

Crystal, D. (1987) *The Cambridge Encyclopaedia of Language.* Cambridge: Cambridge University Press.

Cummins, J. (1979) 'Linguistic independence and the educational development of bilingual children', *Review of Educational Research,* 49: 222–51.

De la Mare, W. (1941) *Bells and Grass.* London: Faber and Faber.

Department for Education and Employment (DfEE) (1995) *English in the National Curriculum.* London: HMSO.

Department for Education and Employment (DfEE) (1997) Circular 10/97 and (1998) Circular 4/98 *Teaching: High Status, High Standards.* London: DfEE.

Department for Education and Employment (DfEE) (1998) *The National Literacy Strategy Framework for Teaching.* London: DfEE.

Department for Education and Employment (DfEE) (2001) *Developing Early Writing.* London: Standards and Effectiveness Unit/NLS.

Department for Education and Employment/Qualifications and Curriculum Authority. (DfEE/QCA) (1999) *The National Curriculum: handbook for primary teachers in England.* QCA/99/454. London: QCA.

Department for Education and Employment/Qualifications and Curriculum Authority. (DfEE/QCA) (2000) *Curriculum Guidance for the Foundation Stage.* London: QCA.

Department for Education and Skills (DfES) (2001) *The Special Educational Needs Code of Practice.* DfES 581/2001. London: DfES.

Department for Education and Skills (DfES) (2006) *Independent Review of the Teaching of Reading. Final Report.* March. (Rose Report). London: DfES.

Department for Education and Skills (DfES/Sure Start) (2006) Primary National Strategy: Draft Framework for teaching literacy. DfES.

Department of Education and Science (DES) (1988) *English in the National Curriculum.* London: HMSO.

Department of Education and Science (DES) (1988) *English 5–16.* London: HMSO.

Department of Education and Science (DES) (1991) *Education Observed: The Implementation of the Curricular Requirements of the ERA in 1989–90.* London: HMSO.

Donaldson, M. (1978) *Children's Minds.* Glasgow: Fontana.

Donaldson, M. (1989) *Sense and Sensibility: Some thoughts on the teaching of literacy* (Occasional Paper No. 3). Reading: Reading and Language Information Centre, University of Reading. Reprinted in R. Beard, (ed.) (1993) *Teaching Literacy Balancing Perspectives.* London: Hodder and Stoughton.

Donaldson, M. (1993) See above.

Donaldson, M. and Reid, J. (1985) 'Language skills and reading: a developmental perspective', in M.M. Clark (ed.), *New Directions in the Study of Reading.* London and Philadelphia, PA: Falmer Press. pp. 12–25.

Donaldson, M., Grieve, R. and Pratt, C. (eds) (1983) *Early Childhood Development and Education: Readings in Psychology.* Oxford: Blackwell.

Dowker, A. (1989) 'Rhymes and alliteration in poems elicited from young children', *Journal of Child Language,* 16: 181–202.

Downing, J. (1979) *Reading and Reasoning.* Edinburgh: W.C. Books.

Dyson, A.H. (1989) *Multiple Worlds of Child Writers: Friends Learning to Write*. New York: Teachers College Press.

Eggleton, J.M. and Windsor, J. (1995) *Linking the Language Strands*. Auckland, NZ: Wings Publication.

Egoff, S. (1981) *Thursday's Child*. Chicago, IL: American Library Association.

Ehri, L.C. (1983) 'Summary of Dorothy C. Ohnmacht's study: the effects of letter knowledge on achievement in reading in the first grade', in L.M. Gentile, M.L. Kamil and J.S. Blanchard (eds), *Reading Research Revisited*. Columbus, OH: Charles E. Merrill. pp. 141–2.

Ehri, L.C. (1992) 'Reconceptualising the development of sight word reading and its relationship to recoding', in P. Gough L.C. Ehri and R. Treiman (eds), *Reading Acquisition*. Hillsdale, NJ: Lawrence Erlbaum Associates.

Ehri, L.C. (1995) 'Phases of development in learning to read words by sight', *Journal of Research in Reading*, 18(2): 116–26.

Ehri, L.C. and Wilce, L.S. (1985) 'Movement into reading: Is the first stage of printed word learning visual or phonetic?', *Reading Research Quarterly*, 20: 163–79.

Elley, W.B. (1992) *How in the World Do Students Read?* Hamburg: International Reading Association.

Engel, S. (1995) *The Stories Children Tell: Making Sense of the Narratives of Childhood*. New York: W.H. Freeman.

Enters, I. and Brooks, G. (2005) *Boosting Reading in Primary Schools*. London: DfES, for the Basic Skills Agency.

Evans, J. (ed.) (1998) *What's in the Picture? Responding to Illustrations in Picture Books*. London: Paul Chapman Publishing.

Fanthorpe, U.E. (1992) *Heck-Verse, Half-Past Two*. Calstock, Cornwall: Peterloo Poets.

Fenson, L., Dale, P.S., Reznik, J.S., Bates, E., Thal, D.J. and Pethnick, S.J. (1994) 'Variability in early communicative development', *Monographs of the Society for Research in Child Development*, 59(5, no. 242).

Ferreiro, E. (1985) 'The relationship between oral and written language: the children's viewpoints', in M.M. Clarke (ed.), *New Directions in the Study of Reading*. London and Philadelphia, PA: Falmer Press.

Ferreiro, E. and Teberosky, A. (1982). *Literacy Before Schooling*. Oxford: Heinemann.

Fisher, R. (1992) *Early Literacy and the Teacher*. London: Hodder and Stoughton.

Flower, L.S. (1981) 'A cognitive process of writing', *College Composition and Communication*, 32: 365–86.

Flower, L.S. and Hayes, J.R. (1980a) 'Writing as problem-solving', *Visible Language*, 14(4): 388–99.

Flower, L.S. and Hayes, J.R. (1980b) 'The dynamics of composing; making plans and juggling constraints', in L.W. Gregg and E.R. Steinberg (eds), *Cognitive Processes in Writing*. Hillsdale, NJ: Lawrence Erlbaum Associates.

Foggin, J. (1991) *Real Writing*. London: Hodder and Stoughton.

Fox, C. (1993) *At the Very Edge of the Forest: The Influence of Literature on Storytelling by Children*. London: Cassell.

Frith, U. (1980) 'Unexpected spelling problems', in U. Frith (ed.), *Cognitive Processes in Spelling*. New York: Academic Press. pp. 495–516.

Frith, U. (1985) 'Beneath the surface of developmental dyslexia', in K.E. Patterson, M. Coltheart and J. Marshall (eds), *Surface Dyslexia*. London: LEA.

Frith, U. and Snowling, M. (1983) 'Reading for meaning and reading for sound in autistic and dyslexic children', *British Journal of Developmental Psychology*, 1: 329–42.

Fry, S. (2005) *The Ode Less Travelled: Unlocking the poet within*. London: Hutchison.

Funnell, E. and Stuart, M. (eds) (1995) *Learning to Read: Psychology in the Classsroom*. Oxford: Blackwell.

Gee, J.P. (1992) *The Social Mind: Language, Ideology and Social Practice*. New York: Bergin and Garvey.

Gentry, J.R. (1981) 'Learning to spell developmentally', *Reading Teacher*, 34(4): 378–81.

Gibran, K. (1926) *The Prophet*. Oxford: Heinemann.

Gibson, E.J. and Levin, H. (1975) *The Psychology of Reading*. Cambridge, MA: MIT Press.

Goodman, K.S. (1972) 'Reading: the key is in children's language', *The Reading Teacher*, March: 505–8.

Goodman, K.S. (1973) 'Psycholinguistic universals in the reading process', in F. Smith (ed.), *Psycholinguistics and Reading*. New York: Holt Rinehart and Winston.

Goodman, K.S. (1976) 'Reading: a psycholinguistic guessing game', in H. Singer and R.B. Ruddell (eds), *Theoretical Models and Processes of Reading*. Newark, DE: International Reading Association. pp. 497–508.

Goodman, K.S. and Goodman, Y.M. (1979) 'Learning to read is natural', in L.B. Resnick and P.A. Weaver (eds), *Theory and Practice of Early Reading*, vol 1. Hillsdale, NJ: Lawrence Erlbaum Associates. pp. 137–54.

Goodman, Y. (1991) 'The Development of initial literacy', in R. Carter (ed.), *Knowledge about Language and the Curriculum: The Link Reader*. London: Hodder and Stoughton.

Goodman, Y.M. (1980) 'The roots of literacy', in M.P. Douglass (ed.), *Reading: A Humanising Experience*. Claremont, CA: Claremont Graduate School.

Gopnik, A. and Meltzoff, A.N. (1986) 'Relations between semantic and cognitive development in the one-word stage: the specificity hypothesis', *Child Development*, 57: 1040–53.

Goswami, U. and Bryant, P. (1990). *Phonological Skills and Learning to Read*. Hove: Lawrence Erlbaum Associates.

Gough, P.B. and Tunmer, W.E. (1986) 'Decoding, reading and reading disability', *Remedial and Special Education*, 7: 6–10.

Graham, J.(1998) 'Turning the visual into the verbal, children reading wordless books', in J. Evans, (ed.), *What's in the Picture? Responding to Illustrations in Picture Books*. London: Paul Chapman Publishing.

Gravelle, M. (1996) *Supporting Bilingual Learners in Schools*. Stoke-on-Trent: Trentham Books.

Gravelle, M. (2000) *Planning for Bilingual Learners. An Inclusive Curriculum*. Stoke-on-Trent: Trentham Books.

Graves, D. (1983) *Writing: Teachers and Children at Work*. Exeter, NH: Heinemann Education Books.

Gregory, E. (1996) *Making Sense of a New World: Learning to Read in a Second Language*. London: Paul Chapman Publishing.

Guthrie, J.T. and Wigfield, A. (2000) 'Engagement and motivation in reading', in M.L Kamil, P.B. Mosenthal, H. Pearson and R. Barr (eds), *Handbook of Reading Research*, vol. 8 Mahwah, NJ: Lawrence Erlbaum Associates.

Hall, E.T. (1959) *The Silent Language*. Garden City, NY: Doubleday.

Hall, N. (1987). *The Emergence of Literacy*. London: Hodder and Stoughton.

Hall, N., Larson, J. and Marsh, J. (eds) (2003) *Handbook of Early Childhood Literacy*. London: Sage.

Halliday, M.A.K. (1975) *Learning How to Mean: Explorations in the Development of Language*. London: Edward Arnold.

Halliday, M.A.K. (1978) *Language as a Social Semiotic: The Social Interpretation of Language and Meaning*. London: Edward Arnold.

Hardy, B. (1977) 'Towards a poetics of fiction: an approach through narrative', in M. Meek, A. Warlow and G. Barton (eds), *The Cool Web: The Pattern of Children's Reading*. London: The Bodley Head.

Harris, M. (1992) *Language Experience and Early Language Development: From Input to Uptake*. Hove: Lawrence Erlbaum Associates.

Hatcher, P.J., Hulme, C. and Ellis, A.W. (1994) 'Helping to overcome reading failure by combining the teaching of reading and phonological skills', in E. Funnell, and M. Stuart (eds), *Learning to Read*. Oxford: Blackwell.

Hayes, J.R. and Flower, L.S. (1980) 'Identifying the organization of writing process', in L. Gregg and E. Steinberg (eds), *Cognitive Processes in Writing*. Hillsdale, NJ: Lawrence Erlbaum Associates.

Heath, S.B. (1982) 'What no bedtime story means: narrative skills at home and school', *Language in Society*, 11: 49–76.

Her Majesty's Inspectorate (HMI) (1978) *Primary Education in England: A Survey by H.M. Inspectors of Schools*. London: HMSO.

Her Majesty's Inspectorate (HMI) (1991) *The Teaching and Learning of Reading in Primary Schools*. London: Department of Education and Science.

Her Majesty's Stationery Office (HMSO) (1967) *Children and their Primary Schools* (The Plowden Report). London: HMSO.

Her Majesty's Stationery Office (HMSO) (1975) *A Language for Life* (The Bullock Report). Report of the Committee of Inquiry appointed by the Secretary of State for Education and Science. London: HMSO.

Hester, H. (1983) *Stories in the Multicultural Classroom*. London: Harcourt Brace Jovanovich.

Hester, H. (1990) 'Stages of English Learning', in *Patterns of Learning: The Primary Language Record and the National Curriculum*. London: Centre for Language in Primary Education.

Hobsbaum, A. (1997) 'Reading Recovery – a lifeline for some', in N. McClelland, (ed.), *Building a Literate Nation: The Strategic Agenda for Literacy over the Next Five Years*. Stoke-on-Trent: Trentham Books.

Holbook, D. (1961) *English for Maturity*. Cambridge: Cambridge University Press.

Holdaway, D. (1979) *Foundations of Literacy*. Gosford, NSW: Scholastic Publications.

Holdaway, D. (1982) 'Shared book experience: teaching reading using favourite books, *Theory into Practice*, 21(4): 293–300.

House of Commons Education, Science and Arts Committee (1991) *Standards of Reading in Primary Schools*. Third Report of 1990/91 Session, vol 1. London: HMSO.

Hull, R. (1988) *Behind the Poem*. London: Routledge.

Hunt, P., Joyner, J. and Stephens, J. (1987) *The English Curriculum: Poetry*. London: ILEA.

Hurry, J. (1995) 'What is so special about Reading Recovery?', *The Curriculum Journal*, 7(1): 93–108.

Jewitt, C. and Kress, G. (eds) (2003) *Multimodal Literacy*. New York: Palgrave Macmillan.

Jolly Phonics (see Lloyd et al., 1993).

Kennedy, M.M., Birman, B.F. and Demaline, R.E. (1986) *The Effectiveness of Chapter 1 Services*. Washington, DC: Office of Educational Research and Improvement, US Department of Education.

Kerin, R. (2005) 'The review essay', *Journal of Early Childhood Literacy*, 5(2): 176.

Kinnes, S. (2002) 'Are you raising a technotot?', *Sunday Times Culture*, 8 September, pp. 49–50.

Kintgen, E.R., Kroll, B.M. and Rose, M. (1988) *Perspectives on Literacy*. Carbondale, IL: Southern Illinois University Press.

Kress, G.R. (1997) *Before Writing: Re-thinking the Paths to Literacy*. London: Routledge.

Kress, G. and Van Leeuwen, T. (1996) *Reading Images: the Grammar of Graphic Design*. London: Routledge.

Language in the National Curriculum (LINC) (1992) Language in the National Curriculum: Training Materials. (unpublished).

Lankshear, C. and Knobel, M. (2003) *New Literacies: Changing Knowledge and Classroom Learning*. Buckingham and Philadelpia, PA: Open University Press.

Letterland (1993) *Picture Dictionary*, Letterland Ltd, Barton, Cambridge CB3 7AY.

Liberman, I.Y., Shankweiler, D., Fischer, F.W. and Carter, B. (1974) 'Explicit syllable and phoneme segmentation in young children', *Journal of Experimental Psychology*, 18: 201–12.

Lloyd, S., Wernham, S. and Jolly, C. (1993) 'Jolly Phonics'. Singapore: Jolly Learning Ltd.

Littlefair, A.B. (1991) *Reading All Types of Writing*. Buckingham: Open University Press.

Littlefair, A.B. (1993) 'The "good book": non-narrative aspects', in R. Beard, (ed.), *Teaching Literacy Balancing Perspectives*. London: Hodder and Stoughton.

Longacre, R. (1976) *An Anatomy of Speech Notions*. Lisse, Holland: Peter de Ridder.

Lundberg, I., Frost, J. and Peterson, O. (1988) 'Effects of an extensive program for stimulating phonological awareness in pre-school children', *Reading Research Quarterly*, 23: 263–84.

Mackay, D., Thomson, B. and Shaub, P. (1970) *Breakthrough to Literacy*. Glendale, CA: Bowmar.

Mallet, M. (1992) *Making Facts Matter: Reading Non-Fiction 5–11.* London: Paul Chapman Publishing.

Mallet, M. (2003*) Early Years Non-Fiction: A Guide to Helping Young Researchers use Information Texts.* London and New York: RoutledgeFalmer.

Marsh, G., Friedman, M., Welch, V. and Desberg, P. (1980) 'The development of strategies in spelling', in U. Frith (ed.), *Cognitive Processes in Spelling.* New York: Academic Press.

Marsh, J. (2003) 'One-way traffic? Connections between literacy practices at home and in the Nursery', *British Educational Research Journal,* 29: 369–83.

Marsh, J. and Millard, E. (2000) *Literacy and Popular Culture: Using Children's Literature in the Classroom.* London: Paul Chapman Publishing.

McClelland, N. (ed.) (1997) *Building a Literate Nation: The Strategic Agenda for Literacy over the Next Five Years.* Stoke-on-Trent: Trentham Books.

McGaw, B., Long, M.G., Morgan, G. and Rosier, M.J. (1989) *Literacy and Numeracy in Australian Schools* (ACER Research Monograph No. 34). Hawthorn, Victoria: ACER.

McGee, L., Lomax, R. and Head, M. (1984) 'Young children's functional reading', paper presented at the National Reading Conference, Florida.

McGee, L., Lomax, R. and Head, M. (1988) 'Young children's written language knowledge: what environmental and functional print reading reveals', *Journal of Reading Behaviour,* 20: 99–118.

McKenzie, M. and Warlow, A. (1977) *Reading Matters.* London: Hodder and Stoughton.

Meek, M. (1981) 'Handing down the magic', in P. Salmon, (ed.), *Coming to Know.* London: Routledge and Kegan Paul.

Meek, M. (1982) *Learning To Read.* London: The Bodley Head.

Meek, M. (1988) *How Texts Teach What Readers Learn.* Gloucester: Thimble Press.

Meek, M. (1991) *On Being Literate.* London: The Bodley Head.

Meek, M. (1996) *Information and Book Learning.* Gloucester: Thimble Press.

Millard, E. (1997) *Differently Literate: The Schooling of Boys and Girls.* London: Falmer.

Morais, J., Bertleson, P., Cary, L. and Alegria, J. (1986) 'Literacy training and speech segmentation', *Cognition,* 24: 45–64.

Morais, J., Cary, L., Alegria, J. and Bertelson, P. (1979) 'Does awareness of speech as a sequence of phonemes arise spontaneously', *Cognition,* 7: 323–31.

Mortimore, P., Sammons, P., Stoll, L., Lewis, D.R. and Ecob, R. (1988). *School Matters.* London: Open Books.

Neale, M.D. (1989) *The Neale Analysis of Reading Ability.* Rev British edn. Windsor: NFER/Nelson.

Neate, B. (1992) *Finding Out about Finding Out: A Practical Guide to Children's Information Books.* London: Hodder and Stoughton with UKRA.

Nelson, K. (1973) 'Structure and strategy in learning to talk', in *Monographs of the Society for Research in Child Development,* 38(1–2, serial no. 149).

NFER/DfES (2004) *Progress in International Reading Literacy Study.* Slough: NFER.

Nicholls, E. (2004) 'The contribution of the Shared Reading of expository books to the development of language and literacy', unpublished thesis, University of Oxford, Department of Educational Studies.

Ninio, A. (1980) 'Picture-book reading in mother-infant dyads belonging to two subgroups in Israel', *Child Development,* 51: 587–90.

Ninio, A. and Bruner, J. (1978) 'The achievement and antecedents of labelling'. *Journal of Child Language,* 5: 1–15.

Office for Standards in Education (Ofsted) (1996) *The Teaching of Reading in 45 Inner London Primary Schools.* London: HMSO.

Oldfather, P. and Dahl, K. (1994) 'Towards a social constructivist reconceptualisation of intrinsic motivation for literacy learning', *Journal of Reading Behavior,* 26: 139–58.

Palmer, S. and Bailey, R. (2004) *Foundations of Literacy.* Stafford: Network Educational Press.

Pappas, C.C. (1991) 'Young children's strategies in learning', the 'book language', of information books', *Discourse Processes,* 14: 203–25.

Pappas, C.C. and Brown, E. (1987) 'Learning to read by reading: learning how to extend the functional potential of language', *Research in the Teaching of English*, 21(2): 160–77.

Papert, S. (1980) *Mindstorms: Children, Computers and Powerful Ideas*. New York: Basic Books.

Parkes, B. (1998) 'Nursery children using illustrations in shared readings and re-readings', in J. Evans (ed.), *What's in the Picture? Responding to Illustrations in Picture Books*. London: Paul Chapman Publishing.

Pedersen, E., Faucher, T.A. and Eaton, W.W. (1978) 'A new perspective on the effects of first-grade teachers on children's subsequent adult status', *Harvard Educational Review*, 48(1): 1–31.

Perrera, K. (1993) 'The "good book": linguistic aspects', in R. Beard (ed.), *Teaching Literacy Balancing Perspectives*. London: Hodder and Stoughton.

Piluski, J.J. (1994) 'Preventing reading failure: a review of five effective programmes', *The Reading Teacher*, 48: 31–9.

Pinker, S. (1994) *The Language Instinct: The New Science of Language and Mind*. London: Allen Lane/Penguin.

Pinker, S. (2002) *The Blank Slate: The Modern Denial of Human Nature*. London: Penguin.

Pumfrey, P.D. and Elliott, C.D. (1992) 'A reaction', *British Psychological Society Education Section Review*, 16(1): 15–19.

Purcell-Gates, V. (1996) 'Stories, coupons and the TV guide: relationship between home literacy experiences and emergent literacy knowledge', *Reading Research Quarterly*, 31(4): 406–28.

Qualifications and Curriculum Authority (QCA) (1998) *Can Do Better: Raising Boys' Achievement in English*. London: QCA.

Rayner, K. and Pollatsek, A. (1987) 'Eye movements in reading: a tutorial review', in M. Coltheart (ed.), *Attention and Performance XII: The Psychology of Reading*. London: Lawrence Erlbaum Associates. pp. 327–53.

Read, C., Zhang, Y., Nie, H. and Ding, B. (1986) 'The ability to manipulate speech sounds depends on knowing alphabetic spelling', *Cognition*, 24: 31–44.

Reading Recovery National Network (1998) *Book Bands*. London: Orchard Books.

Reading Recovery National Network (2003) *Book Bands*. 3rd edn. London: Orchard Books.

Reason, R. and Boote, R. (1994) *Helping Children with Reading and Spelling: A Special Needs Manual*. London and New York: Routledge.

Reid, J.F. (1993) 'Reading and spoken language: the nature of the links', in R. Beard, (ed.), *Teaching Literacy Balancing Perspectives*. London: Hodder and Stoughton.

Richgels, D.J. (2002) 'Informational texts in kindergarten', *The Reading Teacher*, 55(6): 586–95.

Riley, J.L. (1994) 'The development of literacy in the first year of school', unpublished PhD thesis, University of London.

Riley, J.L. (1995a) 'The transition phase between emergent literacy and conventional beginning reading: new research findings', *TACTYC* (Journal for Tutors of Advanced Courses for Teachers of Young Children) 16(1): 55–9.

Riley, J.L. (1995b) 'The relationship between adjustment to school and success in reading by the end of the reception year', *Early Child Development and Care*, 114: 25–38.

Riley, J.L. (1996) *The Teaching of Reading: The Development of Literacy in the Early Years of School*. London: Paul Chapman Publishing.

Riley, J.L. and Reedy, D.(2000) *Developing Writing for Different Purposes: Teaching about Genre in the Early Years*. London: Paul Chapman Publishing.

Riley, J.L., Burrell, A. and McCallum, B. (2004) 'Developing the spoken language skills of reception class children in two multi-cultural, inner-city primary schools', *British Educational Research Journal*, 30(5): 657–72.

Rosen, H.(1984) *Stories and Meanings*. Sheffield: National Association for the Teaching of English, 49 Broomgrove Road, Sheffield S10 2NA.

Rosenblatt, L. (1938) *Literature as Exploration*. New York: Appleton-Century.

Sammons, P. (1995) 'Gender, ethnic and socio-economic difference in attainment and progress: a longitudinal analysis of student achievement over nine years', *British Educational Research Journal*, 21(4): 465–87.

Sassoon, R. (1995) *The Acquisition of a Second Writing System.* Oxford: Intellect.

School Curriculum and Assessment Authority (SCAA) (1995) *Boys and English.* London: SCAA

Schools Examination and Assessment Council (SEAC) (1991) Assessment of performance Unit Report on the 1988 APU Survey in *Assessment Matters No. 4: Language and Learning* (1991: 127–37) London: HMSO.

Sealey, A. (1996) *Learning about Language: Issues for Primary Teachers.* Oxford: Oxford University Press.

Senechal, M., Lefevre, J., Thomas, E. and Daley, K.E. (1998) 'Differential effects of home literacy experiences on the development of oral and written language', *Reading Research Quarterly,* 33(1): 96–116.

Shankweiler, D. and Fowler, A.E. (2004) 'Questions people ask about the role of phonological processes in learning to read', *Reading and Writing,* 17(5): 483–575.

Short, K. (1986) 'Literacy as a collaborative experience', unpublished doctoral dissertation, Indiana University.

Siraj-Blatchford, I. (1995) *The Early Years: Laying the Foundation of Racial Equality.* Stoke -on Trent: Trentham Books.

Siraj-Blatchford, I., Sylva, K., Muttock, S., Gilden, R. and Bell, D. (2002) *Researching Effective Pedagogy in the Early Years. Research Report 356.* REPEY technical paper. London: DfES.

Skuttnab-Kangas, T. (1984) 'Multilingualism and the education of minority children', in T. Skutnab-Kangas and J. Cummins (eds), *Minority Education.* Clevedon: Multilingual Matters.

Slavin, R.E., Madden, N.A., Dolan, N.J., Wasik, B.J., Ross, S.M., Smith, L.J. and Dianda, M. (1996) 'Success for all: a summary of research', *Journal for Education for Students Placed at Risk,* 1: 41–76.

Slobin, D. (1979) *Psycholinguistics.* 2nd edn. Glenview, IL: Scott Foresman.

Smith, J. and Elley, W. (1998) *How Children Learn to Write.* London: Paul Chapman Publishing.

Snow, C. (1991) 'The theoretical basis for relationships between language and literacy development', in *Journal of Research in Childhood Education,* 6(1): 5–15.

Snow, C.E. (1983) 'Literacy and language: relationships during the preschool years', in *Harvard Educational Review,* 53(2): 165–89.

Snowling, M.J. (2000) *Dyslexia.* 2nd edn. Oxford: Blackwell.

Stainthorp, R. (2004a) 'W(h)ither phonological awareness? Literate trainee teachers' lack of stable knowledge about the sound structure of words', *Educational Psychology,* 24(6): 753–65.

Stainthorp, R. (2004b) 'What is involved in writing? Understanding the processes that enable children to become fluent writers: a psychological perspective', unpublished paper presented at ESRC Seminar at the Institute of Education, University of London, November.

Stanovich, K.E. (1986) 'Matthew effects in reading: some consequences of individual differences in the acquisition of literacy', *Reading Research Quarterly,* 21: 360–406.

Stanovich, K.E., Cunningham, A.E. and Cramer, B.Q. (1984) 'Assessing phonological awareness in kindergarten children: Issues of task comparabiity', *Journal of Experimental Child Psychology,* 38: 175–90.

Stuart, M. (1995) 'Recognising printed words unlocks the door to reading: how do children find the key?', in E. Funnell, and M. Stuart, (eds), *Learning to Read.* Oxford: Blackwell.

Styles, M. and Watson, V. (eds) (1996) *Talking Pictures.* London: Hodder and Stoughton.

Sulzby, E. (1989) 'Assessment of writing and of children's language while writing', in L. Morrow and J. Smith (eds), *The Role of Assessment in Early Literacy Instruction.* Englewood Cliffs, NJ: Prentice-Hall. pp. 83–109.

Sulzby, E. (1992) 'Research directions: transitions from emergent to conventional writing', *Language Arts,* 69: 291–7.

Sulzby, E. and Teale, W. (1991) 'Emergent literacy', in J. Barr, M. Kamil, P. Mosenthal and D. Pearson (eds), *The Handbook of Reading Research.* vol. 2. London: Longman. 727–57.

Sure Start/DfES/PNS (2005) *Communicating Matters.* London: DfES.

Sylva, K., Melhuish, E.C., Sammons, P., Siraj-Blatchford, I. and Taggart, B. (2004) *The Effective Provision of Pre-School Education (EPPE) Project: Final Report.* London: DfES/Institute of Education, University of London.

Sylva, K., Sammons, P., Melhuish, E., Siraj-Blatchford, I. and Taggart, B. (1999) *Technical Paper 1. An Introduction to the EPPE Project: A Longitudinal Project funded by the DfEE, 1997–2003* (actually still on going in 2006). London: University of London, Institute of Education.

Taylor, D. and Dorsey-Gaines, C. (1988) *Growing up Literate*. Portsmouth, NH: Heinemann.

Teale, W. (1986) 'Home background and young children's literacy development', in W.H. Teale and E. Sulzby (eds), *Emergent Literacy: Writing and Reading*. Norwood, NJ: Ablex.

Thompson, D. (ed.) (1969) *Directions in the Teaching of English*. Cambridge: Cambridge University Press.

Tizard, B. (1993) 'Early influences on literacy', in R. Beard (ed.), *Teaching Literacy Balancing Perspectives*. London: Hodder and Stoughton.

Tizard, B. and Hughes, M. (1984). *Young Children Learning*. London: Fontana.

Tizard, B., Blatchford, P., Burke, J., Farquhar, C. and Plewis, I. (1988) *Young Children at School in the Inner City*. Hove and London: Lawrence Erlbaum Associates.

Treiman, R. (1992) 'The role of intrasyllabic units in learning to read and spell', in P.B. Gough, L.C. Ehri and R. Treiman (eds), *Reading Acquisition*. Hillsdale, NJ: Lawrence Erlbaum Associates. pp. 85–106.

Treiman, R. and Baron, J. (1981) 'Segmental analysis: development and relation to reading ability', in G.C. Mackinnon, and T.C. Waller (eds), *Reading Research: Advances in Theory and Practice,* vol.111. New York: Academic Press.

Trevarthen, C. (1993) 'Playing into reality: conversations with the infant communicator', *Winnicot Studies,* 7: 67–84.

Tucker, N. (1993) 'The "good book": the literary and developmental aspects', in R. Beard (ed.), *Teaching Literacy Balancing Perspectives*. London: Hodder and Stoughton.

Tunmer, W.E., Herriman, M.L. and Nesdale, A.R. (1988) 'Metalinguistic abilities and beginning reading', *Reading Research Quarterly*, 32: 134–58.

Turner, J.C. (1995) 'The influence of classroom contexts on young children's motivation for literacy', *Reading Research Quarterly*. 30: 410–41.

Turner, M. (1990) *Sponsored Reading Failure*. Warlingham, Surrey: IPSET.

Turner, M. (1991) 'Finding out', *Support for Learning*, 6(3): 99–102.

Turner, M. (1992) 'Organised inferiority? Reading and the National Curriculum', *British Psychological Society Educational Section Review*, 16(1): 1–25.

Vygotsky, L.S. (1962) *Thought and Language*. Cambridge, MA: MIT Press.

Vygotsky, L.S. (1978), *Mind in Society: The Development of Higher Psychological Processes*. Cambridge, MA: Harvard University Press.

Vygotsky, L.S. (1986) *Thought and Language*. 3rd edn. Cambridge, MA: MIT Press.

Washtell, A. (1998) 'Routines and resources', in J. Graham and A. Kelly (eds), *Writing under Control: Teaching Writing in the Primary School*. London: David Fulton.

Weinberger, J. (1996) *Literacy Goes to School: The Parents' Role in Young Children's Literacy Learning*. London: Paul Chapman Publishing.

Wells, C.G. (1983) 'Talking with children: the complementary roles of parents and teachers', in M., Donaldson, R. Grieve, and C. Pratt (eds), *Early Childhood Development and Education*. Oxford: Blackwell.

Wells, C.G. (1987) *The Meaning Makers: Children Learning Language and Using Language to Learn*. London: Hodder and Stoughton.

Wells, C.G. (1988) 'The roots of literacy', *Psychology Today,* 22: 20–2.

Wells, C.G. and Raban, B. (1978) 'Children learning to read', unpublished Final SSRC Report (lodged in School of Education Library, University of Bristol, 19 Berkeley Square, Bristol).

Whitehead, M. (1997) *The Development of Language and Literacy*. London. Hodder and Stoughton.

Whitehead, M.R. (2004) *Language and Literacy in the Early Years*. 3rd edn. London: Paul Chapman Publishing/Sage.

Wilkinson, A. (1982) *Language and Education*. Oxford: Oxford University Press.

Wray, D. and Lewis, M. (1997) *Extending Literacy: Children Reading and Writing Non-fiction*. London and New York: Routledge.

Children's literature referred to in the text

Fiction

Ahlberg, A. and Ahlberg, J. (1988) *The Jolly Postman or Other People's Letters*. Oxford: Heinemann.

Ahlberg, A. and Ahlberg, J. (1995) *The Jolly Pocket Postman*. Oxford: Heinemann.

Beck, I. (1998) *Five Little Ducks*. London: Orchard Books.

Briggs, R. (1975) *Father Christmas*. London: Puffin Books.

Briggs, R. (1978) *The Snowman*. London: Hamish Hamilton.

Brown, R. (1996) *Toad*. London: Red Fox.

Burningham, J. (1977) *Come away from the Water, Shirley*. London: Jonathan Cape.

Burningham, J. (1978, 1999) *Would you rather......?* London: Red Fox.

Burningham, J. (1994) *Courtney*. London: Red Fox.

Butterworth, N. (1997) *Thud!* London: HarperCollins.

Bush, J. and Paul, K. (1993) *The Fish Who Could Wish*. Oxford: Oxford University Press.

Cain, S. and Tickle, J. (2000) *The Crunching, Munching Caterpillar*. London: Little Tiger Press.

Cole, B. (1986) *Princess Smartypants*. London: Picture Lion.

Cole, B. (1987) *Prince Cinders*. Hayes: Magi.

Dahl, R. (1970) *Fantastic Mr Fox*. London: Puffin Books.

Dahl, R. (2001) *Revolting Rhymes*. London: Puffin Books.

Donaldson, J. (1999) *The Gruffalo*. Basingstoke: Macmillan

Fine, A. (1992) *Flour Babies*. London: Hamish Hamilton.

Gene, Z. (1992) *Harry the Dirty Dog*. London: Red Fox; also published by The Bodley Head.

Giles, A. and Parker Roes, G. (1999) *Giraffes Can't Dance*. London: Orchard Books.

Holm, A. (1965) *I am David*. London: Methuen.

Hughes, S. (1998) *The Lion and the Unicorn*. London: The Bodley Head.

Hutchins, P. (1968) *Rosie's Walk*. London: The Bodley Head.

Hutchins, P. (1998) *Goodnight, Owl*. London: Random House.

Inkpen, M. (2002) 'Lullabyhullabaloo', in *The Inkpen Treasury*. London: Hodder Children's Books.

James, S. (1992) *My Friend Whale*. London: Walker Books.

Kerr, J. (2005) *Mog and the V.E.T.* London: HarperCollins.

Hargreaves, R. (1998) *Mr Bump* (Mr Men Series) Stern Sloan.

Kerr, J. (2006) *Mog in the Dark*. London: HarperCollins Children's Books.

McKee, D. (1978) *Tusk Tusk*. London: Anderson Press.

McKee, D. (1980) *Not now, Bernard*. London: Anderson Press.

Moore, I. (1990) *Six Dinner Sid*. London: Prentice Hall.

Munsch, R.N. (1980) *The Paper Bag Princess*. London: Scholastic.

Murphy, J. (1995) *Peace at Last*. London: Young Puffin.

Pearce, P. (1983) *The Way to Sattin Shore*. London: Puffin Books.

Rosen, M. (1989, 1993) *We're Going on a Bear Hunt*. London: Walker Books.

Storr, C. (1999) *Clever Polly and the Stupid Wolf*. London: Penguin.

Sutton, E. (1978) *My Cat Likes to Hide in Boxes*. London: Picture Puffin.

Tomlinson, J. (1968) *The Owl that Was Afraid of the Dark*. London: Methuen.

Wadell, M. (1998) *Can't you Sleep, Little Bear?* London: Walker Books.

Ward, H. (2001) *The Cockerel and the Fox*. London: Templar.

Wagner, J. (1977) *John Brown and the Midnight Cat*. London: Puffin Books.

Non-fiction

Base, G. (1993) *Animalia*. New York: Harry N. Abrahams.

Burningham, J. (1999) *John Burningham's ABC*. London: Jonathan Cape

Davis, N. (2002) *Bat Loves the Night*. London: Walker Books.

Felts, S. (1996) *Trees*. London: Tango Books.

Holden, E. (1977) *The Country Diary of an Edwardian Lady*. London: Sphere Books.

Hughes, S. (1998) *Alphie's Alphabet*. London: The Bodley Head.

Inkpen, M. (2002) *Kipper's A–Z*. London: Hodder Children's Books.

Kitamura, S. (2000) *What's Inside? The Alphabet Book*. London: Anderson Press.

Ripley, C., illustrated by Ritchie, S. (1997) *Why do Stars Twinkle? and Other Night Time Questions* Oxford: Oxford University Press.

Sauvain, P. (1995) *The Tudors and Stuarts*. Dorchester: Wayland.

Walpole, B. (2002) *I Wonder Why the Sun Rises and Other Questions about Time and Seasons*. London: Kingfisher.

Collins Rhyming Dictionary, Collins.

DK Dictionary, Dorling Kindersley.

My ABC Dictionary, Collins.

Poems Mentioned:

'November the Fifth' by Leonard Clark.

'My Puppy' by Aileen Fisher

Both in *The young Puffin Book of Verse* compiled by Barbara Ireson (1970) Puffin Books Ltd.

Index

Added to a page number 'f' denotes a figure.